First World War
and Army of Occupation
War Diary
France, Belgium and Germany

21 DIVISION
Divisional Troops
Royal Army Medical Corps
63 Field Ambulance
28 August 1915 - 7 May 1919

WO95/2147/1

The Naval & Military Press Ltd
www.nmarchive.com
Published in association with The National Archives

Published by

The Naval & Military Press Ltd

Unit 10 Ridgewood Industrial Park,

Uckfield, East Sussex,

TN22 5QE England

Tel: +44 (0) 1825 749494

www.naval-military-press.com

www.nmarchive.com

This diary has been reprinted in facsimile from the original. Any imperfections are inevitably reproduced and the quality may fall short of modern type and cartographic standards.

© **Crown Copyright**
Images reproduced by permission of The National Archives, London, England, 2015.

Contents

Document type	Place/Title	Date From	Date To
Heading	WO95/2147/1		
Heading	21st Division 63rd Field Ambulance Aug 1915-1919 May		
Heading	21st Division 63rd Field Ambulance Vol I August & Sept. 15		
War Diary	Witley Surrey	28/08/1915	31/08/1915
War Diary	Witley	01/09/1915	07/09/1915
War Diary	South Augthe	08/09/1915	08/09/1915
War Diary	Havre	09/09/1915	09/09/1915
War Diary	Moulle	11/09/1915	20/09/1915
War Diary	Blaringhen	21/09/1916	21/09/1916
War Diary	Lierette	22/09/1916	22/09/1916
War Diary	Haut Rieux	23/09/1916	24/09/1916
War Diary	Noeux Les Mines	25/09/1915	27/09/1915
War Diary	Halte	28/09/1915	28/09/1915
War Diary	Bethune	29/09/1915	29/09/1915
War Diary	Blessy	30/09/1915	30/09/1915
War Diary	Morbecques	01/10/1915	01/10/1915
War Diary	21st Division 63rd Field Ambulance Vol 2 Oct 15		
War Diary	Morbecques	01/10/1915	01/10/1915
War Diary	Strazeeles	02/10/1915	30/10/1915
Heading	21st Division 63rd F.A. Vol 3 121/7624 Nov 15		
War Diary	Strazeeles	01/11/1915	08/11/1915
War Diary	Armentieres	09/11/1915	30/11/1915
Heading	21st Div 63rd F.A. Vol 4 December 1915		
War Diary	Armentieres	02/12/1915	31/12/1915
Heading	21st Div F/16/12 63rd F.A. Vol 5 Jan 1916		
War Diary	Armentieres	01/01/1916	31/01/1916
Heading	63. F.a. Vol 6 21st Div. Feb 1916		
War Diary	Amentieres	01/02/1916	28/02/1916
Heading	63 F. Amb Vol 7 21st Div March 1916		
War Diary	Armentieres	29/02/1916	22/03/1916
War Diary	Staazeele	23/03/1916	31/03/1916
Heading	No. 63 F.A. April 1916		
War Diary	Poulainville	01/04/1916	06/04/1916
War Diary	Aubigny	07/04/1916	29/04/1916
War Diary	Allonville	30/04/1916	30/04/1916
Heading	21st Div Po 63 F. Amb May 1916		
War Diary	Alliville	01/05/1916	31/05/1916
Heading	B. 63 F.A. June 1916		
Miscellaneous	DAG'S Office GHQ Base		
War Diary	Allonville	01/06/1916	23/06/1916
War Diary	Buire	24/06/1916	30/06/1916
Heading	21st Division 63rd Field Ambulance July 1916		
War Diary	Buire	01/07/1916	04/07/1916
War Diary	St Sauveuazu	05/07/1916	07/07/1916
War Diary	Saisselal	08/07/1916	10/07/1916
War Diary	Becordel	11/07/1916	17/07/1916
War Diary	Buire	18/07/1916	18/07/1916
War Diary	Allonville	19/07/1916	19/07/1916

War Diary	Riencourt	20/07/1916	22/07/1916
War Diary	Ternas	23/07/1916	24/07/1916
War Diary	Givenchy Le Noble	25/07/1916	27/07/1916
War Diary	Habarcq	28/07/1916	31/07/1916
Heading	21st Div. 63rd (W. Lancs). F.A. Aug 1916		
War Diary	Habarcq	01/08/1916	31/08/1916
Heading	21st Division 63rd Field Ambulance. Sept 1916		
War Diary	Habarcq	01/09/1916	02/09/1916
War Diary	Ilelles Haneaa	03/09/1916	09/09/1916
War Diary	On route	10/09/1916	10/09/1916
War Diary	Becordel	11/09/1916	30/09/1916
Heading	21st Div. 63rd Field Ambulance. Oct 1916		
War Diary	Becordel	01/10/1916	04/10/1916
War Diary	Bouchon	05/10/1916	08/10/1916
War Diary	Labeuvriere	09/10/1916	10/10/1916
War Diary	Bethune	11/10/1916	31/10/1916
Heading	21st Div. 63rd Field Ambulance. Nov. 1916		
War Diary	Bethune	06/11/1916	30/11/1916
Heading	21st Division 63rd Field Ambulance Dec 1916		
War Diary	Bethune	01/12/1916	26/12/1916
War Diary	Auchel	27/12/1916	31/12/1916
Heading	21st Div. 63rd Field Ambulance. Jan 1917		
War Diary	Auchel	01/01/1917	27/01/1917
War Diary	Droglandt	28/01/1917	31/01/1917
Heading	21st Div. 63rd Field Ambulance Feb 1917		
War Diary	Droglandt	01/02/1917	12/02/1917
War Diary	Bethune	13/02/1917	28/02/1917
Heading	21st Div. 63rd Field Ambulance. Mar 1917		
Heading	Bethune	01/03/1917	05/03/1917
War Diary	Robecq	06/03/1917	08/03/1917
War Diary	St Hilaire	09/03/1917	10/03/1917
War Diary	Pernes	11/03/1917	11/03/1917
War Diary	Honval	12/03/1917	12/03/1917
War Diary	Brevillers	13/03/1917	22/03/1917
War Diary	Grenas	23/03/1917	27/03/1917
War Diary	La Cauchie	28/03/1917	31/03/1917
Heading	21st Div. 63rd (W.L.) F.A. April 1917		
War Diary	La Cauchie	01/04/1917	04/04/1917
War Diary	Boiry St Rictrude	05/04/1917	14/04/1917
War Diary	Bassex	15/04/1917	23/04/1917
War Diary	Boisleux Gill Mont	24/04/1917	25/04/1917
War Diary	Henin	26/04/1917	30/04/1917
Heading	Summary Of Medical War Diaries For 63rd F.A., 21st Divn. 7th Corps., 3rd Army Western Front April-May 17		
Miscellaneous	63rd B.A. 21st Divn. 7th Corps. O.C. Lt. Col. E.J. Kavanagh. 3rd Army.		
Heading	21st Divn. No. 63 F.a. May 1917		
War Diary	Henin	01/05/1917	10/05/1917
War Diary	Ransart	11/05/1917	30/05/1917
War Diary	Henin	31/05/1917	31/05/1917
Heading	Summary Of Medical War Diaries For 63rd F.A. 21st Divn. 7th Corps., 3rd Army Western Front April-May 17		
Miscellaneous	63rd F.A. 21st Divn. 7th Corps. O.C. Lt. Col. E.J. Kavanagh. 3rd Army.		

Heading	No. 63 F.a. June 1917		
War Diary	Henin	01/06/1917	03/06/1917
War Diary	Boyelles	04/06/1917	19/06/1917
War Diary	Ransart	20/06/1917	29/06/1917
War Diary	Boyelles	30/06/1917	30/06/1917
Heading	No. 63. F.a. July 1917		
War Diary	Boyelles	01/07/1917	31/07/1917
Heading	No. 63 F.a. Aug 1917		
War Diary	Boyelles	01/08/1917	09/08/1917
War Diary	Ervillers	10/08/1917	24/08/1917
War Diary	Barly	25/08/1917	25/08/1917
War Diary	Izel Les Hameau	26/08/1917	31/08/1917
Heading	No 63 F.A. Sept 1917		
War Diary	Izel-Les-Hameau Map Ref Sheet 5fc J2 A8.4	01/09/1917	06/09/1917
War Diary	Izel-Les-Hameau	07/09/1917	16/09/1917
War Diary	Caestre Map Ref Sheet 27 Q 33 C 2.4	17/09/1917	18/09/1917
War Diary	Caestre	19/09/1917	22/09/1917
War Diary	Meteren Map Refernce Sheet 27 X16.D.8.9	23/09/1917	25/09/1917
War Diary	Micmac Camp Ollderdom Map Ref Sheet 28 H 31 C 9.9	26/09/1917	26/09/1917
War Diary	Mic Mac Camp	27/09/1917	29/09/1917
War Diary	Camp At M 6a 8.5 Sheet 28 (1-400000)	29/09/1917	29/09/1917
War Diary	Quickbusch	30/09/1917	30/09/1917
Heading	No 63 F.A. Oct 1917		
War Diary	Dickebusch	01/10/1917	09/10/1917
War Diary	Blaringhem	10/10/1917	20/10/1917
War Diary	Ypres I 9.c.6.2 (Map Ref Sheet 28)	21/10/1917	23/10/1917
War Diary	Ypres	24/10/1917	31/10/1917
Heading	No. 63 F.a. Nov 1917		
War Diary	Ypres I 9 C 6.2 (Map Ref Sheet 28)	01/11/1917	07/11/1917
War Diary	Ypres	08/11/1917	15/11/1917
War Diary	Ouderdom Doninion Camp	16/11/1917	16/11/1917
War Diary	Doulieu	17/11/1917	17/11/1917
War Diary	La Couronne	18/11/1917	18/11/1917
War Diary	Annezin	19/11/1917	19/11/1917
War Diary	Barlin	20/11/1917	20/11/1917
War Diary	Maroeuil Map Ref Sheet 51C L 4 A. 2.9	21/11/1917	21/11/1917
War Diary	Maroeuil	22/11/1917	30/11/1917
Heading	No. 63 F.A. Dec 1917		
War Diary	Tincourt	01/12/1917	02/12/1917
War Diary	Longavesnes Sheet 62C E 25 B.1.3	03/12/1917	05/12/1917
War Diary	Longavesnes	06/12/1917	31/12/1917
Heading	No 63 F.A. Jan 1918		
War Diary	Long Avesnes E 25 b 1.3	01/01/1918	15/01/1918
War Diary	Longavesnes	16/01/1917	31/01/1917
Heading	No. 63 F.a. Feb 1918		
War Diary	Loncasvesnes E 25 b 1.3. sheet 62c	01/02/1918	07/02/1918
War Diary	Longavesnes	08/02/1918	28/02/1918
Heading	No. 63 F.a. Mar 1918		
War Diary	Longavesnes Sheet 62c E 25 B 1.3	01/03/1918	07/03/1918
War Diary	Longavesnes	08/03/1918	21/03/1918
War Diary	Peronne	22/03/1918	22/03/1918
War Diary	Maricourt	23/03/1918	23/03/1918
War Diary	Bray-S-Somme	24/03/1918	24/03/1918
War Diary	Sailly Le Sec	25/03/1918	25/03/1918
War Diary	Contay	26/03/1918	28/03/1918

War Diary	Molliens Au Bois	29/03/1918	30/03/1918
War Diary	Bollrdon	31/03/1918	31/03/1918
Heading	63rd Field Ambulance April 1918		
War Diary	Bourdon	01/04/1918	01/04/1918
War Diary	Kennel	02/04/1918	03/04/1918
War Diary	Yonce St (near Kemmel) Map Ref N 29 A. 3.9 Sheet 28)	04/04/1918	05/04/1918
War Diary	Yonce Street (Near Kemmel)	06/04/1918	06/04/1918
War Diary	Locre	07/04/1918	09/04/1918
War Diary	Laclytte (N 7 C 5 5 Sheet 28)	10/04/1918	11/04/1918
War Diary	Laclytte	12/04/1918	14/04/1918
War Diary	Sheet 27 L 23 C 5.8 Near Poperinge	15/04/1918	18/04/1918
War Diary	L 23 C 5.8 Sheet 27	19/04/1918	30/04/1918
Heading	No. 63 F.a. May 1918		
War Diary	Sheet 27 K 11 C 74	01/05/1918	01/05/1918
War Diary	Lederzeele	02/05/1918	03/05/1918
War Diary	In Trench	04/05/1918	05/05/1918
War Diary	L'Hery	06/05/1918	12/05/1918
War Diary	Jonchery	13/05/1918	27/05/1918
War Diary	Ville En Tardenois	28/05/1918	28/05/1918
War Diary	Festigny	29/05/1918	29/05/1918
War Diary	Boursalt	30/05/1918	30/05/1918
War Diary	Soulieres	31/05/1918	31/05/1918
Heading	No. 63 F.a. June 1918		
War Diary	Conblizy	01/06/1918	16/06/1918
War Diary	Vassimont	17/06/1918	18/06/1918
War Diary	(Enroute)	19/06/1918	19/06/1918
War Diary	Inval-Bourin	20/06/1918	20/06/1918
War Diary	Le Cornet	21/06/1918	21/06/1918
War Diary	Deville	22/06/1918	22/06/1918
War Diary	Crandcourt	23/06/1918	30/06/1918
Heading	63rd F.A. July 1918		
War Diary	Grandcourt	01/07/1918	01/07/1918
War Diary	Beaquesne	02/07/1918	24/07/1918
War Diary	Acheux	25/07/1918	31/07/1918
Heading	63rd F.A. Aug 1918		
War Diary	Acheux	01/08/1918	23/08/1918
War Diary	Hailly-Maillet	24/08/1918	24/08/1918
War Diary	Miraumont	25/08/1918	31/08/1918
Heading	63rd F. Amb. Sept 1918		
War Diary	Mirazmont	01/09/1918	03/09/1918
War Diary	Ginchy	04/09/1918	05/09/1918
War Diary	Sailly Saillesel	06/09/1918	15/09/1918
War Diary	Firicourt	16/09/1918	24/09/1918
War Diary	Fins	25/09/1918	28/09/1918
War Diary	Goureaucourt	29/09/1918	30/09/1918
Heading	No. 63 Fd Ambu Oct 1918		
War Diary	Gouzeaucourt	01/10/1918	05/10/1918
War Diary	Baivtouzeele	06/10/1918	09/10/1918
War Diary	Walincourt	10/09/1918	21/09/1918
War Diary	Neuvilly	22/10/1918	22/10/1918
War Diary	Ovillers	23/10/1918	23/10/1918
War Diary	Vendegies Au Bois	24/10/1918	25/10/1918
War Diary	Neuvilly	26/10/1918	31/10/1918
Heading	63rd F.A. Nov 1918		
War Diary	Neuvilly	01/11/1918	05/11/1918

War Diary	Vendegies Au Bois	06/11/1918	06/11/1918
War Diary	Locquignol	07/11/1918	07/11/1918
War Diary	Latetenoir	08/11/1918	09/11/1918
War Diary	Aymeries	10/11/1918	11/11/1918
War Diary	Balhant	12/11/1918	22/11/1918
War Diary	Bachant U18d Cent	23/10/1918	30/10/1918
Heading	No 63 F.A. Dec 1918		
War Diary	Bachant	01/11/1918	16/11/1918
War Diary	Enclefontaine	17/11/1918	17/11/1918
War Diary	Inchy	18/11/1918	18/11/1918
War Diary	St Pierre A Gouy	10/12/1918	31/12/1918
Heading	No. 63 F.a. Jan 1919		
War Diary	St Pierre a Gouy	01/01/1919	31/01/1919
Heading	No. 63 Field Ambulance Feb 1919		
War Diary	St Pierre a Gouy	01/02/1919	28/02/1919
Heading	63rd F.A. Mar 1919		
War Diary	St Pierre Agouy	01/03/1919	05/03/1919
War Diary	Picquigny	06/03/1918	31/03/1918
Heading	War Diary Of The 63rd Field Ambulance. West Lancs. from April 1st 1919 to April 30th 1919		
War Diary	Picquigny	01/04/1919	03/04/1919
War Diary	Longuet	04/04/1919	30/04/1919
Heading	War Diary Of The 63rd Field Ambulance from 1/5/19 to 7/5/19 Vol 45		
War Diary	Lehavre	01/05/1919	01/05/1919
War Diary	Harfleur	02/05/1919	06/05/1919
War Diary	En Route	07/05/1919	07/05/1919

w095/2147/1

21ST DIVISION

63RD FIELD AMBULANCE

AUG 1915-DEC 1918

1919 MAY

WO/121/7083

21st Division

summarised

63rd Field Ambulance
Vol I

Aug 15 & Sept 15
Dec 15

Aug 1915
Sept 15

August 1915

WAR DIARY

INTELLIGENCE SUMMARY

Army Form C. 2118.

Place	Date	Hour	Summary of Events and Information	Remarks and references to Appendices
Witley Surrey	28	1.30 pm	Saturday. No. 63 Fd Amb&e arrived here from Eastbourne 8 Officers, 172 NCO's & horses. Advance party, 1 Officer 10 other ranks having arrived on 27th inst. Personnel complete except Quartermaster who has been away for Manchest 3 miles to camp near Portsmouth road, took over hutments allotted, weather fine. Usual duties posted. Reported arrival at Divisional HqQ. (21:)	KM
	29		Sunday. 1130 Church Parade, Cleaning up,	KM
	30		Monday. Took over from Ordnance Equipment which had arrived by train. Checked Contents - lists of deficiencies made out. 12 riding horses received. 4 of 7 bought exchanged with Remounts (A'shot) - 15. Progress Report furnished to A.D.M.S. (J.F. Shine)	KM
	31st		Tuesday. Checking continued. Harness [illd?] [stamped?] under M.O. A.S.C. Indents for deficiencies submitted. 1 Officer 2 men & one ambce wagon sent with 62nd Bgd. 40 NCO's & men sent on 4 days speed leave 150 for 3 days. will approved. Progress reported.	KM

Officers. Lt. Col. K. R. Barnett.
Lieut. S. Sharples.
" J. H. Mather
" J. P. Thierens
" W. F. Young
" C. G. Schurr (S.R.)
" K. L. MacKinnon T.C.
" W. E. Campbell (T.C)
" J. D. Adamson (T.C)

Lt. Col. Barnett placed on sick list with Influenza & Stomatitis

Army Form C. 2118

WAR DIARY
INTELLIGENCE SUMMARY.
(Erase heading not required.)

September 1915

Instructions regarding War Diaries and Intelligence Summaries are contained in F. S. Regs., Part II. and the Staff Manual respectively. Title pages will be prepared in manuscript.

Place	Date	Hour	Summary of Events and Information	Remarks and references to Appendices
Witley	1st		Wednesday. Checking equipment continued. Lieuts. Adamson McKinnon Young proceeded on 4 days Special Leave. Progress reported	KBB
"	2nd		Thursday. Ooversearfs drawn, indents for Ordnance Stores, etc. to Complete equipment submitted. 21 H.D. horses + 18 mules taken over from Remount A's Lot, brought here by road. Completing Transport horses. Stationery + Books rec'd from War Office. Blankets &c personnel not required returned to A.O.D. A's Lot. Lieut. Therens proceeded on 3 days leave. Progress reported.	KBB
"	3rd		Friday. Lieut. Campbell, 1 man + 1 Amb. wagon detailed to accompany Divisional March. No QMr. has yet arrived.	KBB
"	4th		Saturday. Documents A.S.C. received to-day. G.S. Wagons + Water Carts with yet received. Other Stores to Complete indented for. All leave for to-day cancelled by Orders. Major R. Sloan's R.A.M.C. reported his arrival yesterday afternoon to take command of unit in my reply. Handing over to-day. First leave party returned 1st day. Progress Reported to A.D.M.S.	KBB
"	"		Handed over Command of this unit to Major R Sloans R.A.M.C.	
			K.B.Baux Lt Colonel R.A.M.C.	

Army Form C. 2118

3

WAR DIARY
or
INTELLIGENCE SUMMARY.
(Erase heading not required.)

Instructions regarding War Diaries and Intelligence Summaries are contained in F. S. Regs., Part II. and the Staff Manual respectively. Title pages will be prepared in manuscript.

Place	Date	Hour	Summary of Events and Information	Remarks and references to Appendices
Witley	4/9/15	1 p.m.	Assumed Command of 63 Rd Aux'l & Vice Lt. Col. Bennett Rowe	RR/Appx
"	"	6 p.m	Orders received that all men on leave had leave stopped in 48 hours from 7 a.m. tomorrow. Progress reported to A.D.M.S.	RR
"	5.9.15	10 a.m	J.S. wagon & water carts received last night. Ordnance stores not received owing to enemy in sidings. Start draft stores in Africa with 3 J.S. wagons to Appx for them today. Progress reported.	RR
"	6.9.		Orders for departure of unit & not received. Ordnance equipment not yet to hand. Have despatched enlisted Officer Albert to draw all outstanding articles. Have also sent 3 dangerous miles to Remounts for exchange, & indent for one horse (heavy draught) to complete establishment.	RQ
"	"	10 a.m		
"	"	9 p.m	As out horse has been admitted Hospital Ordnance Stores complete with certain exceptions, a list of which is forwarded to A.D.M.S. – on draught have received.	RP
"	7.9	8 a.m	Advance Draught – OC Price finished for duty from 201 Southern General.	RR
"	"	9:30 a.m	Unit field dressings, presents or distributed to personnel. Harness inspected. Packing continued.	RS
"	"	2 p.m	Proposed surplus stations to O.C. British 63 Rd Aux't Liverpool	RR
"	"	10 p.m	The H. Amb. entrained in 2 parties – the first at 7 p.m. the 2 at 8 p.m. & marched to Milford station (in entrainment – & proceeded with the 1st train. First reached Southampton about 12 A.M., the second party arriving 2 hours later. Then men bilboed from marching out parade.	RS

2353 Wt. W.3514/1454 700,000 5/15 D.D. & L. A.D.S.S./Form/C. 2118.

Army Form C. 2118

WAR DIARY
or
INTELLIGENCE SUMMARY.
(Erase heading not required.)

Instructions regarding War Diaries and Intelligence Summaries are contained in F.S. Regs., Part II. and the Staff Manual respectively. Title pages will be prepared in manuscript.

Place	Date	Hour	Summary of Events and Information	Remarks and references to Appendices
Southampton	8.9.15	5.30pm	Embarked on H.T. "Achimilla" for Havre.	P.S.
Havre	9.9.15	12 pm	Disembarkation proceeding - one man sent to sick Hospital at Havre.	P.S.
		6.30pm	Marched to Rest Camp No 5. - Personal transport arrest	P.S.
Iroulle	11.9.15	9 AM	Arrived at S. Omer last night at 10 pm, & at once proceeded with the detrainment - this was completed about 12.45 A.M. the whole F.A. moved to march to the village of Iroulle, about 5 mile from S. Omer - Officers own billets	P.S.
"	12.9.15	10 AM	Yesterday was occupied in preparing the office, Q.R. Stores &c, in digging latrines & arranging for sanitation	P.S.
"	"	11 pm	ADMS 3rd Corps visited F.A. & ordered vehicles to be parked in better a line	P.S.
"	"	1 pm	Church parade 10.30. Equipment sorted out & re-packed	
"	"	6 pm	ADMS visited F.A.M.S., & ordered that an Officer should be sent to report to him daily.	P.S.
"	13 "	12 pm	Inspected unit at 8.45 AM - The work being done consists in unpacking, sorting, & repacking the wagons, shifting the horse lines & cleaning up: - 2 men of the unit admitted to hospital (A Section), & 2 of the 13th Northumberland Fus	P.S.
"	14. -	10 AM	B + C Sections, with Transport marched out on a route march.	P.S.
"	-	11 "	Inspected lines & billets.	P.S.
"	-	3 pm	Six Officers of the unit attended a conference of Officers of the F.O.C. of 5th Division held by Captain Nunkey Vans by the F.O. Field Ambulance.	P.S.
		3.45	4 Recruits reported	P.S.

Army Form C. 2118

WAR DIARY
or
INTELLIGENCE SUMMARY.
(Erase heading not required.)

Instructions regarding War Diaries and Intelligence Summaries are contained in F. S. Regs., Part II. and the Staff Manual respectively. Title pages will be prepared in manuscript.

Place	Date	Hour	Summary of Events and Information	Remarks and references to Appendices
Pradelles	15.9.	10 AM	Reported sick yesterday afternoon that 2 rifles belonging S.A.B. division are missing. From enquiry I held a preliminary investigation - placed the men concerned in arrest and reported the loss to the D.A.D.O.S. 2nd Division, & telegraphed to A.M.L.O. at Hazre. Route march for A&B section.	RS
		12.pm	S.O.G. 21st Division inspected F. Ambce.	RS
		2 pm	Unit paid.	RS
		6pm	A good many cases of scabies are being sent to us for disposal. I had 3 6 officers & 6 N.C.O.'s attended lecture on gas helmets, 0830, (rain afternoon)	RS
	16 -	10 am	Lieut. Westwood in hosp. Amb. admitted last night. Expecting him some hours, & sent to Mirror Hospital S. Omer	RS
	17 -	12 pm	Unit inspected by S.O.B. 11th Corps. Also A.D.M.S.	RS
		9.30pm	Lieut. Holman admitted 14th North Fusiliers. suffering from a kick from a mule & sent to S. Omer	RS
	18	11 AM	Conducted a party of 3 officers & 4 NCO's to 9 Fd Ambce at Borrelinghem, to receive instruction in preparing returns re general training of the unit route march for personnel & transport daily, stretcher drill + tent pitching exercises. Weather fine to moderate.	RP
				RS
	19.	10.30am	Church Parade for unit. The number of killed & wounded is out of all reason, and requires a fresh deal of health time - frequently have to employ 2 officers to help kill the work.	RS

WAR DIARY or INTELLIGENCE SUMMARY

Army Form C. 2118

Place	Date	Hour	Summary of Events and Information	Remarks and references to Appendices
Moulle	20.9.	7.30 a.m.	Received Preliminary order from H[ead] Q[uarters]. 62 Brigade with 2nd Div. Ammn. Column at junction S of E & T[illegible] at 9.10 p.m.; then orders received at 9.30 p.m. to commence packing proceedings —	RB
		6.30 p.m.	All in readiness to move off — both ambulances as to wire separated at midnight — a great deal of confusion & uncertainty. Clerking work has been caused by the regiments in our sending cases unable to travel, and as flat feet, bad sprains, bruises &c the T.A. at short intervals during the afternoon & evening; it would appear that the medical inspection of these battalions cannot have been properly carried out.	RB
Blaringhem	21.9.	9 A.M.	Reached here about 1.15 A.M. then morning — chateaux from Moulle about 16 miles. A very large number of men fell out during the march, far worse than could be taken in any of 3 horsed ambulances — the majority of these appeared to be suffering more from exhaustion than anything else, and it is stated by many of them that they had no food from breakfast till yesterday; marched out hungry. This march is bivouacked in a large field — weather fine — personnel & horses in good condition.	RB
Lierette	22.9.	9 A.M.	The Brigade marched from Blaringhem at 8.1. in last night. The actual starting point being at the level crossing ½ mile South of the S[tation] in S. Heater. Our front was reached at 8.30, & the subsequent route passed though Aire & S. Hilaire — very few men fell out. The distance being only about 12 miles — Arrived at about 12 a.m. — the wagons were billeted & horses & personnel in bivouac.	RB

Army Form C. 2118.

WAR DIARY
or
INTELLIGENCE SUMMARY.
(Erase heading not required.)

Instructions regarding War Diaries and Intelligence Summaries are contained in F. S. Regs., Part II. and the Staff Manual respectively. Title pages will be prepared in manuscript.

Place	Date	Hour	Summary of Events and Information	Remarks and references to Appendices
HAUT RIEUX	23.9.	9.AM	Marched from LIERETTE at 6.15 A.M. yesterday, the 63 Fd. Amb. to being the Brigade - a short march of about 6 miles. We are billeted in town, underly exposed the hardship is in a field at the other end of the village. The horses is difficult to supervise owing to the unit & the discipline has been excellent. Weather continues fine.	RB.
		4.P.M	Received 2 re-mounts, heavy draught, in lieu of one shot for paralysis & one in hospital.	RB.
"	24.9.	9.AM	Heavy rain in the night -	RB.
		12 P.M	Received following ordn. War Diary. Division will march tonight, the 62 Brigade lead marching and road war station of MARLES-LES-MINES at 7 A.M.	RB.
NOEUX LES MINES	25.9.	9.AM	Received orders yesterday afternoon that the Division was marching to the place - Wet day, & consequently trying march. - Reached our bivouac about 12 A.M. - Open ground, with no cover, for men or animals. Heaviest shrinking with distant 2½ miles & under suspicion. Horses watering about one mile distant - Attack on German trenches by us & Guards corps started at 6.30 A.M. - Our Division is General Reserve - Wet night - yesterday afternoon at 3 P.M. I also had a conference of A.H. Authorities commanders at this the 53rd Division, under Col. Stuart, ADMS.	RB.
	26.9	9AM	Reached this place last night, in pouring rain & having been previously parked for about 4 hours in a field close to R.9.2 gun & we were subjected to a certain amount of shelling from the enemy - about 3.30 A.M. I received	

WAR DIARY or INTELLIGENCE SUMMARY

Army Form C. 2118.

Place	Date	Hour	Summary of Events and Information	Remarks and references to Appendices
	26.	9 A.M.	Orders to establish a dressing station at HALTE (MAP C.36 square) with Head quarters at HALTE. A few casualties at once, & during the night. Cars were about but busied. Sent out A & B section bearers stretcher wounded. Kept bringing it in & fetching large numbers of walking cases, and from infront they are many serious cases & the knight is in. Have sent out all the mtr ambulance, with C section bearers stretcher wounded.	RS Obs
		2 P.M.	No. 8 A.C.C. evacuated but the lying down cases this morning, sent on all walking cases to a f/C ambs to Hazingart, as they were a good deal of confusion on the road, many stragglers retreating, a rested for 1 hour on our part (so reported)	RS
		10 P.M.	New chalk pit & this 500 wounded during the day, many serious cases. 6 & 8 M.A.C. has just evacuated 50 lying down cases.	RS
	27.	9 A.M.	Very busy night. Bearers out as usual. Strength in 118 wounded. Cars were awful. Kept here owing to heavy shell picking on.	RS
		2 P.M.	Dressing station & Head Quarters shelled this morning - One A.S.C. man attacked, wounded - Evacuated all patients in mtr ambulance to house & obtained Dressing Station in form of a school near the railway crossing.	RS
		7 P.M.	Shelling continued all day, few wounded brought in so far.	RS

WAR DIARY or INTELLIGENCE SUMMARY

Army Form C. 2118
9.

Place	Date	Hour	Summary of Events and Information	Remarks and references to Appendices
HALTE	28.9	9 AM	Quiet night last night — a few wounded and very tough to the morning. An open mts 6 ambulances began from the winch collected wounded from 2 o/s last night, & brought in about 100.	RS
			Shelled again at noon, but no damage done — Reeves ordrs front to BETHUNE, at 9 p.m. — The march took place in heavy rain though nearly ground, & there were many prolonged halts — arrived about 3 AM & went into billets.	RS
BETHUNE	29.9	12:30 pm	Lt Campbell left here, at Gite, to attack himself to H.F. Ambulance. Standing for orders	RS
		3 p.m.	Orders received to continue march, destination unknown, at 4.45 p.m.	RS
BLESSY	30.9	11 AM	Reached here at 3.15 AM the morning — had I travel about 18 miles in bright, windy, & rain. Charriots report checks in front, and as the men had cheifly been working on roofing, almost without sleep, for the last 6 days, they were supremely tired & completely misty which were picked up by our own ambulance wagons. The entire Div Division is being taken to the rear, for a rest, him the artillery and 14 field ambulances (Rivière).	RS
		6 p.m.	No orders for a move, as yet. Heavy downpour of rain.	RS
MORBECQUE	1.10.	3 pm	Received orders late last night, for the march. Started up at 7.30 a.m. and halted here after 1 ½ hrs — very poor roads & conditions	RS

121/7430

31/Brown

63rd Field Ambulance
to C : 2

Oct 15

Oct 19

Army Form C. 2118.

WAR DIARY
or
INTELLIGENCE SUMMARY.
(Erase heading not required.)

Instructions regarding War Diaries and Intelligence Summaries are contained in F.S. Regs., Part II. and the Staff Manual respectively. Title pages will be prepared in manuscript.

Place	Date	Hour	Summary of Events and Information	Remarks and references to Appendices
MORBECQUES	1/10	3 p.m	Lieut. Col. H. Brennan Reid (S.R.) joined for duty last night, Replace Lt. Campbell	Replace
STRAZEELE	2.10	4 p.m	Marched from MORBECQUES this stabing at 9.30 a.m. Billeted in a large farm about half a mile from the village. Walk round	R8.
"	3.10	9 a.m	20 others to reserve Trench today.	R9
"	4.10	11 a.m	Visit from Divisional Commander, who congratulated the unit on their useful work during the recent action. - Attended a meeting of C.O's of the Brigade, for an address from the Corps Commander. The 62 Brigade is now with the IInd Corps, II Army	R9
"	5.10	12. p.m	Took a party of officers, including regimental MO's & searchers to Ypres to inspect a sanitary exhibition at Head Quarters II Corps.	R9
"	"	2 p.m	2 sergeants & 1 driver of attached A.S.C. sent to hospital at HAZEBROUCK, for scabies.	R8.
"	6 "	10 AM	3 mules returned to hostile veterinary section, to await for slaughter knacker, one had heavy draught horse also sent, have wounded.	R8
"	7 "	8 p.m	Received 3 new mules from Remounts. Four letters to Ypres on Campaign in the Army, with particular reference to A.M.S.	R8
"	"	"	Practice route marches resumed today. Weather fine	
"	8.10	9 A.M.	2 water roller carts sent to Divisional Train for repairs.	R8.

2353 Wt. W2544/1454 700,000 5/15 D. D. & L. A.D.S.S.J/Forms/C. 2118.

Army Form C. 2118

WAR DIARY
or
INTELLIGENCE SUMMARY.
(Erase heading not required.)

Instructions regarding War Diaries and Intelligence Summaries are contained in F. S. Regs., Part II. and the Staff Manual respectively. Title pages will be prepared in manuscript.

Place	Date	Hour	Summary of Events and Information	Remarks and references to Appendices
STRAZEELES	11.10	4 p.m.	Transport & horses inspected by O.C. Answered from at 12 p.m.	RB
"	13.10	12 p.m.	The two ambulances returned from repair. The entire unit is being tallied, by means of a rail cloth in J.S. waggon, but water being procured by means of boiling in empty biscuit tins.	RB
"	14.10	2 p.m.	D.D.M.S., II Corps inspected the Field Ambulances at 10 A.M. today. The A.D.M.S. later sent for return the manner Field disinfector supplied from Divisional Head Quarters to disinfect blankets, as 2 of the C.S.E. drivers are suffering from lice; all straw in billets changed, & walls sprayed with creat solution.	RB
"	17.10	12 p.m.	The 62 Brigade moved up two days ago, ber Field Ambulance, 8 Yorkshires, the 63 Brigade arrived at STRAZEELES — Cases of measles and now being sent to 62 Field Ambulance at PRADELLES.	RB
"	18.10	10.30 a.m.	In pursuance of orders received from A.D.M.S., 84 Division, I despatched a party to ARMENTIERES consisting of 4 Officers, 4 N.C.O's, 20 men — They are to report to O.C. 2 Lancashire Field Ambulance, will receive instruction, for 4 days, in methods of evacuating wounded in trench warfare.	RB
"	20.10	12/—	One N.C.O. (L/Cpl Clement) sent to French School near MERRIS, for Company detached duty, by order of A.D.M.S.	RB

2353 Wt. W2544/1454 700,000 5/15 D. D. & L. A.D.S.S./Forms/C. 2118.

Army Form C. 2118

WAR DIARY
or
INTELLIGENCE SUMMARY.
(Erase heading not required.)

Instructions regarding War Diaries and Intelligence Summaries are contained in F.S. Regs., Part II. and the Staff Manual respectively. Title pages will be prepared in manuscript.

Place	Date	Hour	Summary of Events and Information	Remarks and references to Appendices
STRAZEELES	21.10.	6. p.m	Servant over to ARMENTIERES later, to 2/2 Midlesex Fd Amb of (T.F.) to obtain information about the working of a Field Ambulance in trench warfare	R.P
"	22.10	6. p.m	Party from ARMENTIERES returned today with the unit. I, with 3 officers the JO Embs attended a lecture by Col Anthony Bowlby, at BAILLEUL, on the early treatment of abdominal injuries. Lecture thought to have promoted caption.	R.P
"	23.10	10 A.M	Captain Sharples placed on Sick list. Today, by way of a change from CCS ordinary routine, and to give health exercise, athletic sports were held in this unit	R.P
"	25.10	10 A.M	Heavy rain and yesterday afternoon, after nearly 3 weeks dry weather. Sent a party, under an officer, at 9 A.M to LA MOTTE, to fetch wood from the forest officer. Captain Sharples transferred to No. 12 Casualty Clearing Station	R.P
"	"	12½ p.m		R.P
"	27 "	11 A.M	A party consisting of 1 officer & 25 NCOs men sent off to take part in a parade of the II Corps near BAILLEUL - wet day	R.P
"	28 "	4 p.m	Very heavy rain all day - parades cancelled - lectures to the men by Section Officers, & kit & health inspection at 2.15 p.m. I gave a lecture to all officers at 3 p.m on "the work performed by this unit during the recent action near LOOS, with criticisms" -	R.P

2353 Wt. W2544/1454 700,000 5/15 D.D.&L. A.D.S.S./Forms/C 2118.

Army Form C. 211

WAR DIARY
or
INTELLIGENCE SUMMARY.

(Erase heading not required.)

Instructions regarding War Diaries and Intelligence Summaries are contained in F. S. Regs., Part II. and the Staff Manual respectively. Title pages will be prepared in manuscript.

Place	Date	Hour	Summary of Events and Information	Remarks and references to Appendices
STRAZEELES	30.10.	10 AM	Sent 1/ orders to C.R.E. for wood, brackets & canvas, for erecting Company shelters for latrines, horse standings, & lean-tos for horses & ambulances.	R/Rs R/Rs Major Rowe OC 63 Field Ambulance

W K Warren

63 d. 2. a.
vol 3

121/7624

Nov 15.

Nov 15

Army Form C. 2118

WAR DIARY
INTELLIGENCE SUMMARY. 2/3 Field Ambulance

(Erase heading not required.)

Place	Date	Hour	Summary of Events and Information	Remarks and references to Appendices
STRAZEELES	1.11.15	12 p.m.	Rain continuing. Horse transport lines moved on account of muddy condition	RSplus
"	2.11.15	9 a.m.	4 Reinforcements arrived from the Base; below to officers on Sanitation generally at 6 p.m.	RS
"	3.11.15	6.30 p.m.	A good many cases of influenza are now being admitted.	RS
"	5 "	4 a.m.	3 New Recruits arrived, to replace casualties.	
"	"	9 a.m.	Our MT reinforcements arrived, to replace casualty.	RS
"	7.11.	3.30 p.m.	Orders received to reach ARMENTIERES on 9/11/15 to relieve 2/2 Highland Field Ambulance.	RS
"	8.11.	6 p.m.	Fine day – packing for tomorrow's work completed – Held meeting out parade this evening, followed by Officers route march.	RS
ARMENTIERES	9.11.	2 p.m.	Left STRAZEELES, less A Section, car 11.40 – Marched 14½ miles, arriving at Armentieres, treated at INSTITUTE ST JUDE – Hqrs 2/2 Highland Fd. Amb are A Section remains behind, to hand over to a section of the 6th when Fd Amb.	RS
"	10.11	12 p.m.	Took over buildings to form the Hillinchan Fd Amb.	
"	"	1 p.m.	Visited Advanced Dressing station treated at the BRICQUERIE at CHAPELLE D'ARMENTIERES. From it, a couple of accommodating about 2nd wounded.	RS
"	11.11	7 p.m.	Visited Regimental aid posts, on the road from CHAPELLE D'ARMENTIERES to the Duckbill.	RS

WAR DIARY
or
INTELLIGENCE SUMMARY.
(Erase heading not required.)

Army Form C. 2118

Place	Date	Hour	Summary of Events and Information	Remarks and references to Appendices
ARMENTIERES	11.11.15	10 AM	2/2 field Ambulance marked out. Unit cleaning up, & taking over billets - all day. One case of frost bite admitted; about 6 wounded admitted. Visited two lines at 2 p.m. - there are advanced posts the aid of NIEPPE; about 2 kilometres distant.	RB/ms
"	"	4 p.m.	2 cases of frost bite admitted - these have come increase in the amount of German shelling during the last 2 days.	RB
12.11		6 p.m.		
13.11		12 AM	Shells began to fall over this part of the town about 10 p.m. last night - Went over to the 7th Amb. head quarters, & found that one shell had burst over the hospital, slightly wounding one man of the unit - Shots afterwards on Ypres (the sanitary Ypres 2nd Division) was brought in, slightly wounded about head & face. In all about 20 shells appeared to fall; one struck Div. H.Q.', killed 6 men & wounded 7 others. 6 men were killed in their billets among 13th North'umbrians - few 150 Compound, few wounded. About 14 taken hed - Shelling ceased about 11 o'clock.	RB
"		12 p.m.	Visited Transport lines.	RB
"		3 p.m.	Visited head quarters of various units.	RB
14.11		5 p.m.	Visited Regtl Aid posts with A.D.M.S. also Advanced Dressing Station Sewin, Brewan Ravine, re-joined for duty.	RB

2353 Wt. W2544/1454 700,000 5/15 D. D. & L.   A.D.S.S./Forms/C. 2118.

Army Form C. 21

WAR DIARY
or
INTELLIGENCE SUMMARY.
(Erase heading not required.)

Instructions regarding War Diaries and Intelligence Summaries are contained in F. S. Regs., Part II. and the Staff Manual respectively. Title pages will be prepared in manuscript.

Place	Date	Hour	Summary of Events and Information	Remarks and references to Appendices
ARMENTIERES	15-11-15	11 AM	D.D.M.S. 3rd Corps visited the F.A. awaiting — Fus cases of self inflicted wounds at present in hospital, awaiting investigation	R.P.Chin
"	"	2 p.m.	Visited Asylum, which is the rendez-vous for motor ambulances in case of a general action. Transport Lain visited	R.P.
"	"	3 p.m.		
"	18 "	2.30	Town heavily shelled today — starting at 10.40 a.m., it continued till about 1.45 p.m. Two shells struck the F.A. Ambg, but there was no casualties among the personnel. All patients & personnel placed in cellars, except those on urgent duty above. I posted myself with the Adv. Offrs Arnveller & M.T. N.C.O at the signal office. — 15 casualties brought in during the day.	R.P.
"	19 "	12 p.m.	Visited Advanced Dressing Station	R.P.
"	22 "	7 p.m.	Proceeded to S. OMER & obtained a large supply of hospital comforts any necessaries from the Red Cross Society. Heavy firing last night.	R.P.
"	25 "	5 p.m.	7 severely wounded brought in from Art. aircraft gun section, a shell having made a direct hit on the gun. Visited Transport Lain at 12 p.m today.	R.P.
"	27 "	11 AM	Vicinity of F.A. Ambulance shelled again; 5 casualties brought in — 3 died, including one French civilian — G.O.C. 2. Division inspected the hospital whilst the shelling was proceeding.	R.P.
		11.45 AM		
"	28 "	6 p.m.	Weather has been very cold for last 5 days — hard frost, & water pipes frozen. The radiators of all cars (M.M.M. ambulance) are being kept empty except the car in waiting, which has its engine seen hourly.	R.P.

Army Form C. 21

WAR DIARY
or
INTELLIGENCE SUMMARY.
(Erase heading not required.)

Instructions regarding War Diaries and Intelligence Summaries are contained in F. S. Regs., Part II. and the Staff Manual respectively. Title pages will be prepared in manuscript.

Place	Date	Hour	Summary of Events and Information	Remarks and references to Appendices
ARMENTIERES	29.11	4 P.M.	Fairly heavy firing from our guns round the town all afternoon, partly replied to by the enemy. One soldier was brought in slightly wounded. One French woman severely wounded — a few shells have been passing over all day, at intervals.	RPHm
"	30.11	9 A.M.	Sudden thaw today, with torrents of rain. The town was fairly quiet throughout though the enemy's 8 inch gun of the 1st D.L.9 was brought in wounded about 3.15 a.m. One servo returned injury. Evacuated J. J. Stein in our motor ambulance to C.C.S. at BAILLEUL	RQ
		11 A.M.	Visited Transport offices Lindo.	RP

RPHm
Major Rawe

63rd F.a.
Vol. 4

121/7938

31st RW
———
F/1163/1

December 1915

Army Form C. 2118.

WAR DIARY
or
INTELLIGENCE SUMMARY.
(Erase heading not required.)

Instructions regarding War Diaries and Intelligence Summaries are contained in F. S. Regs., Part II. and the Staff Manual respectively. Title pages will be prepared in manuscript.

Place	Date	Hour	Summary of Events and Information	Remarks and references to Appendices
ARMENTIÈRES	2.12.15	10 p.m.	Town shelled - 2 wounded brought in. Weather very stormy now.	RB/ts
"	4.12	11.45 pm	Took ADMS to Advanced Dressing Station & Regimental Aid Post - The communication trench between those 2 points is now completed, but is at present waterlogged in parts.	RB
"	4.12	9.54 pm	Several shells fell in the town. 8 wounded brought back, including one French boy. No dead. Four cerebral injuries - Evacuated the remainder to BAILLEUL.	RB
"	5.12	4 pm	Fairly heavy shell fire over the town, but no casualties. Received one shrapnel wound from reinforcements.	RB
"	6.12	5 pm	Received 2 H.W.Draught horses from reinforcements.	RB
"	9.12	10.45	The 2d Army Commander visited the Field Ambulance.	RB
"	"	2 pm	Town heavily shelled - Two fell into the 1st Antres - one in the courtyard, did all explosive of tried shelf in soft earth - another amongst the chapel roof, 4 soldiers & 2 civilians treated as a result of this bombardment.	RB
"	10.12	10 pm	Received one heavy shrapnel horse & one mule from Remounts - one of my horses slightly horse wounded yesterday.	RB
"	11.12	6 pm	Heavy rain all day. The river LYS in flood.	RB
"	13.12	9.30 pm	Held Court of Enquiry as to HQ ltr of 21 Div Ambulance Workshops, a lorry by fire to a fleet.	RB
"	15.12	10.30 AM	Bombardment of enemy trenches by our heavy guns commenced. Despatched 40 bearers under Lt. [?] Kurin to Advanced Dressing Station, as reinforcements. They took with them dressings & blankets & wheeled stretchers.	RB

2353 Wt. W2544/1454 700,000 5/15 D. D. & L. A.D.S.S./Forms/C. 2118.

WAR DIARY
or
INTELLIGENCE SUMMARY.

(Erase heading not required.)

Army Form C. 2118

Instructions regarding War Diaries and Intelligence Summaries are contained in F. S. Regs., Part II. and the Staff Manual respectively. Title pages will be prepared in manuscript.

Place	Date	Hour	Summary of Events and Information	Remarks and references to Appendices
ARMENTIERES	15.12.15	11.45 AM	2 men of the R.F.A. brought in, both shattered legs. One died, the other evacuated to BAILLEUL, in motor amb. car.	Relieving Major Pring
"	16.12.15	8 A.M	Intense bombardment of enemy trenches commenced at 3.15 A.M, started about 4. A.M. — A company 18th Hussars R.I. attacked enemy trench. Snipers kept up heavy fire. Enemy bombarded our recent trenches, inflicting many casualties on 4th Middlesex & 18th Yorks Lancs regts. — Telephone message received from Regtl aid posts, asking for 3 motor ambulances. — 12 wounded brought in. — One died shortly after admission.	R.P.
"	"	9 AM	Visited Advanced Dressing Station. Our bearers have been working in trenches & between Aid Posts & Advanced Dressing Station since 5.30 A.M.	R.P.
"	"	12 P.M	Number of wounded admitted in last 24 hours is 65.	R.P.
"	19. "	10 AM	German bombardment of 63 Brigade trenches began at 7. A.M. — Message just received from O/C 4th Middlesex Regt. to send bearers. Staff being in 6 stretcher cases from Aid Post this morning.	R.P.
"	"	12 p.m	Six lying, 58 sitting cases brought in this morning.	
"	"	10.30 pm	Stink smell of asphyxiating gas in the atmosphere — sky clear, slow wind — This means a nw slowly drifted down from YPRES, where there was an enemy gas attack this evening.	R.P.
"	20.12.15	12 pm	Sent off a party of 60 men, under Lieut. Schwen, for duty at Divisional Baths.	R.P.
"	"	4 pm	Went with D.A.D.M.S. to STEENWERCKE to look for possible site for field ambulance in case of retirement — nothing settled.	R.P.

Army Form C. 2118

WAR DIARY
or
INTELLIGENCE SUMMARY.
(Erase heading not required.)

Instructions regarding War Diaries and Intelligence Summaries are contained in F. S. Regs., Part II. and the Staff Manual respectively. Title pages will be prepared in manuscript.

Place	Date	Hour	Summary of Events and Information	Remarks and references to Appendices
ARMENTIERES	21.12.	10.30 am	Board on 58 invalids & unfits for (1) fit for duty at the front (2) fit for duty at the Base — very wet day.	R&forms
"	22.12.	10.30 am	Board on unfits continued — Captain halton on 8 days leave to England	R.
"	"	2 p.m.	A.D.M.S. inspected Transport lines with me, & afterwards Armmil Batt.	
"	"	10 p.m.	Some enemy shells fell in the town, but not in the immediate vicinity of this Field Ambulance	R. R.
"	24.12	10 p.m.	Only 5 wounded in last 48 hours — very little sickness — weather wet.	
"	27.12	9.30 am	Visited Transport lines.	R.
"	"	12 p.m.	A good deal of shelling going on — 2 wounded in our Advanced Dressing Station	R.
"	29 "	12 P.M.	A.D.M.S. inspected Field Ambulance, seeing the piarced on parade —	R.
"	31 "	10 A.M.	Captain halton returned from leave, being but 24 hours overrun.	R.

R.P.Rau Major RAMC
O.C. 63 F.W. Amba.

2353 Wt. W2544/1454 700,000 5/15 D. D. & L. A.D.S.S./Forms/C. 2118.

63rd F.A.
Vol. 5

21st Div
F1163/2

63 F.A.

Jan 1916

5

Army Form C. 2118.

Instructions regarding War Diaries and Intelligence
Summaries are contained in F. S. Regs., Part II.
and the Staff Manual respectively. Title pages
will be prepared in manuscript.

WAR DIARY
or
INTELLIGENCE SUMMARY.
(Erase heading not required.)

Place	Date	Hour	Summary of Events and Information	Remarks and references to Appendices
ARMENTIERES	1.1.16	10 AM	Heavy shelling of enemy trenches to the morning at 3AM with consequent retaliation on our front line. 8.16 men of 4th Middlesex & 5 & 9 10th York & Lanc's admitted wounded. 1 dead	R.B/Ints
"	"	2 p.m	Visited Transport lines	RB
"	2.1.16	10 AM	9 wounded, from Middlesex & York & Lancs admitted during last 24 hrs.	RB
"	3.1.16	10 AM	Sgt. Maj. Vidolt proceeded on leave today. Driver Finn of ASC attached sent to Base as unfit for duties at the front.	RB
"	"	11.45 AM	Visited Advanced Dressing Station - No wounded. Pte Kennedy returned to duty from Punishment no 1 - 8 14 days. 6.13 for absence without leave - 3 days of Punishment no 1 - 814 days.	RB
"	4p.m Nov 12:30pm		Reported to 63 Brigade that bombs are being deposited at the Advanced Dressing Station , in use of the infantry.	RB
"	4.1.16	2:30pm	Visited Advanced Dressing Station also A.D.M.S., also Divisional Baths	RB
"	5.1.16	6 p.m	Nothing of interest. There has been an entire cessation of shelling in this party of the town for the past 3 weeks.	RB
"	6.1.	10 AM	Owing to the Cemetery behind the trenches being now closed, it has been arranged that all bodies be brought to the Advanced Dressing Station, and that a horsed Ambulance wagon be sent at night to take them from there to the Cemetery in the town. A party of drivers & ambulance wagon to be kept in the S. Aubin for this purpose	RB
"	8.1.	2.30 p.m.	Pte R.T. Harris ALC (attached) brought up on a charge of obtaining the	RB

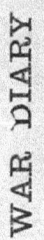

2353 Wt. W2544/1454 700,000 5/15 D.D. & L. A.D.S.S./Forms/C. 2118.

Army Form C. 2118.

WAR DIARY
or
INTELLIGENCE SUMMARY.
(Erase heading not required.)

Instructions regarding War Diaries and Intelligence Summaries are contained in F. S. Regs., Part II. and the Staff Manual respectively. Title pages will be prepared in manuscript.

Place	Date	Hour	Summary of Events and Information	Remarks and references to Appendices
			Report of a Consult. after investigation of sick and evacuees of Enteric, suspect for Court Martial.	RR Appx
ARMENTIERES	9.1.16	11.30 pm	Posted Advanced Dressing Station - very few wounded admitted for some days.	RR
"	11.1.16	6 pm	13 wounded from S' Sommet S.D. admitted this afternoon, of whom 8 were evacuated to C.C.S.	RR
"	12.1.16	2 AM	7 wounded admitted, making a total of 20 for past 12 hours - heavy bombardment of German trenches between 11.30 pm & midnight (11h 15" pm) followed by an attack by 62 nd Bgde - some Cuth. Casualties.	RR
"	"	11 AM	ADMS inspected Transport lines	RR
"	"	12 pm	Pvt. Harris acquitted by Field Gen. Court Martial - vide 8-1-16.	RR
"	15.1.16	10 pm	Enemy bombardment started about 6 pm, a stroll group an intermittent Shells have fallen in the Field Ambulance alf grep wounding two men, of whom Pvt Volpes of the Field Ambulance has a Compound Fractured extremity Bone of the left hand. Lieut. Price (Q hut) left on 7 days leave to England.	RR
"	16.1.	10 AM	Last night's bombardment lasted till about 1.30 AM this morning. one further shell struck our buildings, wrecking the ward on the East wing. only one man slightly wounded from the how.	RR
"	"		Yesterday the Transport was inspected at 10. AM. by OC Divisional Trans.	RR
"	17.1	10.30 AM	Inspected the school in the RUE MESSINES, with a view to taking it over as Field Ambulance - a suitable building except that it has no cellars, one place for putting motor ambulances & transport	RR

Army Form C. 2118.

WAR DIARY
or
INTELLIGENCE SUMMARY.
(Erase heading not required.)

Instructions regarding War Diaries and Intelligence Summaries are contained in F. S. Regs., Part II. and the Staff Manual respectively. Title pages will be prepared in manuscript.

Place	Date	Hour	Summary of Events and Information	Remarks and references to Appendices
ARMENTIERES	17.1.16	9 p.m.	Town bombarded. Two shells fell in the Ambulance – one soldier (surgeon in chief) and 8 wounded, 3 from 2s Div. Sanitary Section, the remainder from 90th & 2d G.R.E.	LeRoy
"	19.1.	10 A.M.	Recvd notice yesterday to move the Ambulance from its present site & the Ecole RUE MESSINES – therefore started to pack equipment down.	R8
"	"	4 p.m.	Transport teams all expected, having been 6 hours on a motor ambulance & one of emergency. Fired at & no emergency cellars in the new building, but several small cellars in the surrounding houses are available. Considerable shelling from both sides today.	R8
"	20.1.	11.30 A.M.	Visited Advanced Dressing Station.	
		3.30 p.m.	A.D.M.S. visited the Field Ambulance – everything is now in working order.	R8
"	23.1.	10 A.M.	Lieut & Qr. Mr. Price returned from leave last night.	R8
			Sgr. Major Viddler Rawe (unit S.M.) admitted – ? Tubercle.	R8
"	24.1.	11.30 A.M.	Major R Stops proceeded on leave this morning.	15th Mdlx
"	"	10.30 p.m.	Lieut. Bowman took up his duties as M.O. to the 8th Somersets.	9 p.m.
"	25.1.	4.30 p.m.	Staff Major Viddler R.A.M.C.T. evacuated to C.C.S. suffering from Pleurisy, Phthisis? Lt Coleman returned from his duties on the Transport being relieved by Lt Menzies of the 6/4th F. Amb.	9 p.m.
"	"	11 p.m.	At 6 p.m. went out with a Bearer Subdivision under Lt Mustiman and 3 Wheeler stretcher carriers to report to Lt Murphy M.O. 4th McLkinroos at 5 Dugouts. This was sent out to R.A.P. under Capt Going at 9.30. Had not returned yet –	9 p.m.

2353 Wt. W2544/1454 700,000 7/5/15 D. D. & L. A.D.S.S./Forms/C. 2118.

WAR DIARY or INTELLIGENCE SUMMARY.

Army Form C. 2118.

(Erase heading not required.)

Place	Date	Hour	Summary of Events and Information	Remarks and references to Appendices
ARMENTIERES	26.1.	3.30 AM	Enemy returned at 2 AM with 5 casualties. Bearer subdivision returned at 3.15 A.M.	J Mather Capt
"	"	9.30 PM	Weather very mild but dull.	9pm
"	27.1.	9.30 PM	Capt GARRETT. R.A.M.C. (T.C.) reported for duty from No. 11 M.A.C. The Germans have shelled our front line & support trenches very heavily today. 4th MIDDLESEX had a number of casualties.	9pm
"	28.1.	3.30 PM	1 Corp & 9 men R.A.M.C. reported for duty as reinforcements. Lieut MacKINNON left to take up his duties with No. 5 M.A.C.	9pm
"	"	10 PM	The Germans have again today heavily shelled our trenches. Very few casualties, only 3 slight cases. Pte Walmsley R.A.M.C. of this unit evacuated suffering from measles.	9pm
"	29.1.	10 PM	A.D.M.S. visited hospital. Weather fine but dull & misty at night.	9pm
"	30.1.	10.30 PM	Lieut CAMPBELL proceeded to home lines to relieve Lieut MENZIES. 7th & 64th F.Amb. Very quiet day.	9pm
"	31.1.		Sergt Griffiths 2nd/1st Borderer evacuated suffering from Neurasthenia & Debility.	9pm
"	31.1.	7 pm	Capt GARRATT R.A.M.C. (T.C.) detailed to take up his duties with the 63rd F.Amb.	9pm

J Mather Capt RAMC.T.
O/C 63rd F.Amb

63. J. A.
Vol. 6.
21st Dis.

Februar
5

Army Form C. 2118.

WAR DIARY
or
INTELLIGENCE SUMMARY.
(Erase heading not required.)

Instructions regarding War Diaries and Intelligence Summaries are contained in F. S. Regs., Part II. and the Staff Manual respectively. Title pages will be prepared in manuscript.

Place	Date	Hour	Summary of Events and Information	Remarks and references to Appendices
ARMENTIÈRES	1.2.	10.10 pm	Under orders from A.D.M.S. Capt THIERENS proceeded to a gas lecture held at OXELAERE. Quiet day. Weather mild. Interviewed East wind.	JMcArthur
"	3.2.16	10 AM	Lt. Col. Sloan R.A.M.C. returned from leave – Jazzthalle tent. Lt. Col. Helias commanding Field Ambulance, dated Jan. 27th.	R.S. for JMcArthur
"	4.2.16	11.30 am	Visited Transport Lines – is good order. Five weeks for past 7 days.	R.S.
"	"	4.1 pm	18 casualties have been admitted during the day, mainly from the 8th Lincolns. Lieut. Therens returned from 2 convoy / lectures on gas. Last night	R.S.
5.2."		11.30 am	Visited Advanced Dressing Station. All quiet. Captain Young R.A.M.C. Proceeded to England, on 7 days leave.	R.S.
7.2."		6.1 pm	No wounded today, very few sick except scabies patients, of whom there are 62 in the Ambulance at present. Weather fine & mild.	R.S.
9.2."		1.1 pm	Surgeon Bowlby (consulting surgeon to the Army) visited the Ambulance – Advanced Dressing Station visited – one abdominal wound sent to BAILLEUL.	R.S.
10.2."		2 pm	Col. Heringham (consulting physician) visited Ambulance – 4 slightly wounded today – still very few sick.	R.S.
		6 pm		
11.2."		6 pm	Town heavily shelled from 10 AM till about 4.30 pm today – one of casualty was received from one French woman with severe abdominal injury – apparently dying – & as relatives were unwilling for her to be evacuated to BAILLEUL or HAZEBROUCK	R.S.
12.2."		6 pm	Town again bombarded – Armoured Baths hit.	R.S.

WAR DIARY
or
INTELLIGENCE SUMMARY

Army Form C. 2118.

(Erase heading not required.)

Instructions regarding War Diaries and Intelligence Summaries are contained in F. S. Regs., Part II. and the Staff Manual respectively. Title pages will be prepared in manuscript.

Place	Date	Hour	Summary of Events and Information	Remarks and references to Appendices
ARMENTIERES	13.2.M	6 p.m	Hostile bombardment, 3 shells falling close to Actg Field Ambulance – 5 soldiers, and 2 civilians, with one French soldier killed. Commenced erecting sandbag shelter.	R.S. plan
"	14.2	9 AM	Captain J.P. Truin proceeded on leave. Captain W. Young has received 7 days extension.	R.S.
"	"	12 p.m	Captain Young telegraphs to say that he is ill, in bed.	
"	"	8 p.m	Quiet day – only 2 or 3 slightly wounded – Windmill close to Advanced Dressing Station hit today by 8" shell.	R.S.
"	15.2	12 p.m	Sand bagging of premises proceeding – Number of Seabrée sheets, which has been up to 5 to 6, is now reduced to 30.	R.S.
"	"	2 p.m	Visited A.D. Station, which was somewhat briskly shelled yesterday – windmill entirely destroyed.	R.S.
"	16.2	10 AM	Visited Transport lines – there are now much improved, the muddy surface having been constructed by brick standing, & bricked paths – weather very stormy for last few days, with exceptionally high wind.	R.S.
"	"	2 p.m	Sent our stretcher squad (4 men) up to Regtl Aid Post, for permanent duty between that point & Advanced Dressing Station.	R.S.
"	18.2	10 AM	Officer i/c Advanced Dressing Station reports rifle fire close to A.D.S. last night, 8 suspects a sniper near the Railway line – Reported to H.Q.R.S.	R.S.
"	"	2 p.m	Visited Advanced Dressing Station – all correct	R.S.
"	19.2	10 AM	4 wounded admitted during night – no dangerous. Inspected Transport Lines – very muddy, one H.D. hrs sick – m T 2457 6 Pte Stevens A.S.C. appointed acting Sergeant.	R.S.

2353 Wt. W2544/1454 700,000 5/15 D.D.&L. A.D.S.S./Forms/C. 2118.

Army Form C. 2118.

WAR DIARY
or
INTELLIGENCE SUMMARY.
(Erase heading not required.)

Instructions regarding War Diaries and Intelligence Summaries are contained in F. S. Regs., Part II. and the Staff Manual respectively. Title pages will be prepared in manuscript.

Place	Date	Hour	Summary of Events and Information	Remarks and references to Appendices
ARMENTIERES	21.2.16	10 AM	ADMS inspected the Field Ambulance - an aeroplane tent dropped within 100 yards. Fine, weather clear & frosty.	R8 etc
"	22.2.16	6 PM	Lieut. Grierson returned from Leave, & given charge 1 Divisional Baths, vice Capt. C. J. Schurr.	R8.
"	23.2.16	10 AM	Capt. Young returned from Leave, having been detained by sickness. Hard frost last night.	R8.
"	"	7 PM	Much snow today - no wounded admitted for last 24 hours —	R8
"	24	2 PM	Inspected Advanced Dressing Station, & Transport Lines - Several Horses (Heavy Draughts) suffering from lice.	R8
"	"	6 PM	All leave temporarily stopped, by telegram - 10 degrees of frost today.	R8
"	26	10 AM	Received information from ADMS that the unit will move to PRADELLES on head	R8
"	"	11 AM	Proceeded to PRADELLES to arrange for taking over buildings there	R8
"	"	6.30 PM	Approaching move to PRADELLES postponed indefinitely	R8
"	27	10 AM	Gas alarm last night about 12 midnight, signalled from the trenches by horns & bells - false alarm	R8
"	"	10 PM	Lieut. R.T. Raine, R.A.M.C. arrived in relief of Captain C.J. Schurr Raine. Transport in, after several days frost — A good deal of shelling this morn.	R8

WAR DIARY
or
INTELLIGENCE SUMMARY.

(Erase heading not required.)

Army Form C. 2118.

Instructions regarding War Diaries and Intelligence Summaries are contained in F. S. Regs., Part II. and the Staff Manual respectively. Title pages will be prepared in manuscript.

Place	Date	Hour	Summary of Events and Information	Remarks and references to Appendices
ARMENTIERES	28.2.16	10 AM	Captain G. J. Selwyn reported his departure for No. 20 Ambulance Train.	R.J. Jones

R.J. Jones
Lt. Col. R.A.M.C.
S.C. 63 Brd. Army

63 J Amb
Vol 7th
26 Dec

COMMITTEE FOR THE
MEDICAL HISTORY OF THE WAR
Date 9 - JUN. 1915

March 1916
October 1916
S.

WAR DIARY
or
INTELLIGENCE SUMMARY.
(Erase heading not required.)

Army Form C. 2118.

Instructions regarding War Diaries and Intelligence Summaries are contained in F. S. Regs., Part II. and the Staff Manual respectively. Title pages will be prepared in manuscript.

Place	Date	Hour	Summary of Events and Information	Remarks and references to Appendices
ARMENTIERES	29.2.16	11 Am	Lieut. G.M.J. Ross RAMC reported for duty, last injury in relief of Lieut. W.E. Campbell	Reflns
"	1/3/16	7.30 Am	Lieut. Campbell departed to report ADMS, Rouen.	RP
"	"	2 pm	Visited Advanced Dressing Station	RP
"	3.3.	10-30 am	Visited Transport lines - heavy rain & sleet all the afternoon	RP
"	4.3	2 pm	Heavy snow fall, with thaw.	
"	"	6 pm	Town bombarded this afternoon, for a quarter of an hour, from 5.15 to 5.30 pm, the projectiles coming in very thickly during that time	RP
"	5.3.	3.30	One NCO & one female of this unit killed, two privates of this unit & one gftr. to be field Ambulance wounded owing to the accidental explosion of a small shell in possession of Pte. Kennedy, one of the wounded. Reported matter to Div. # 9	RP
"	6.3	11 Am	Reported Held Court of Enquiry on yesterday's explosion & funeral procedure to A.D.M.S.	RP
"	"	4 pm	Funeral of Cpl. Jeffreys & Pte. Rodrigin, killed by the explosion yesterday, and aeroplane (a tink hose) & an unexploded anti-aircraft shell fell near this Ambulance	RP
"	"	5.30 pm	Reported the absence off leave of no. 1676 Pte. O'Neill of this unit - the shortest have reported on march 1st.	RP
"	8.3	2 pm	Visited A. Dressing Station. DDMS 2nd Corps inspected the Field Ambulance at 11 Am	RP
"	10.3	4 pm	4 reinforcements (bearers) RAMC arrived - much snow & sleet.	RP
"	11.3	6 pm	2 A.S.C. drivers (horse transport) & 2 M.T. drivers arrived - fine day	RP

Army Form C. 2118.

WAR DIARY
or
INTELLIGENCE SUMMARY.
(Erase heading not required.)

Instructions regarding War Diaries and Intelligence Summaries are contained in F.S. Regs., Part II. and the Staff Manual respectively. Title pages will be prepared in manuscript.

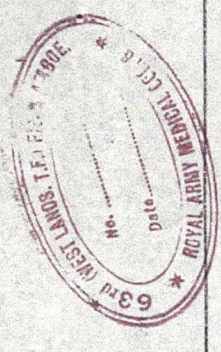

Place	Date	Hour	Summary of Events and Information	Remarks and references to Appendices
ARMENTIERES	12-3-16	11 AM	Proceeded to HQ 2nd Army to see DMS, who informed us that two FA appointed to DADMS 6th Division.	RS/John
"	"	8 p.m.	Practically no wounded admitted last week, very few sick, except Influenza	RS
"	13.3	10 AM	DDMS 2nd Corps inspected Advanced Dressing Station	RS
"	"	6.p.m	Received orders that one section of the Fd Amby will move to STRAZEELE on March 17th, the remaining 2 on the 22nd March.	RS
"	14.11	10.30 am	Captain J. Matter proceeded to STRAZEELE to arrange with the outgoing Field Ambulance about billets, equipment &	RS
"	15 "	10.30 am	Visited ADS Station & Transport lines	RS
"	16 "	8.30p	Captain E.J. Kavanagh RAMC arrived, b/che over command.	RS
"	"		Lunch stelling today	RS
"	17."	8. AM	B Section (Captain Young) marched out to BAILLEUL for STRAZEELE	RP
"	"	9 a.m	Commenced to hand over to Captain Kavanagh	
"	"	11. AM	Visited Transport Lines	
"	"	2 p.m	" Dressing Station	RS
	18th		Took over command on 17th inst. Visited A.D.S. & horse lines. 2 sections 52 Fd Ambce	RP Amber
			arrived to take over from us. wounded	xx
	19th		activities to hospital — Evacuated 9 to 58 CCS BAILLEUL and 2 to D.R. Station	
			and 9 sick to 58 C.C.S. and 10 sick to D.R. Station	

WAR DIARY or INTELLIGENCE SUMMARY

Army Form C. 2118.

Place	Date	Hour	Summary of Events and Information	Remarks and references to Appendices
ARMENTIERES	19th		Handed over A.D.S. to 51st Field Ambce.	E.9.K
	20th		1 N.C.O + 14 men detached for duty at Stone Yard. Handed over hospital equipment at new evening station to 52nd F. Ambce. Evacuated 3 wounded + 8 sick to No 2 CCS and 8 sick to Div. Rest Stat. Visited baths.	E.9.K
			Evacuated 1 French civilian attached to R.E. 97 who was wounded to No 2 CCS. Capt. Brennan proceeded on 10 Days leave.	E.9.K
	21st		Handed over hospital to 52nd Field Ambce at 3 P.M. Evacuated 1 wounded to No 2 CCS.	E.9.K
	22nd		Marched from ARMENTIERES and proceeded to BAILLEUL where we billeted for the night.	E.9.K
STRAZEELE	23rd		Arrived at STRAZEELE. Evacuated 1 sick officer and 1 OR to No 2 CCS + 1 OR to No 50 CCS	E.9.K
	24th		Remained in billets. Heavy snow storm. Evacuated 3 sick to 8 CCS and 2 Scabies to No 50 C.C.S. Capt Thienus reported his arrival from leave at ARMENTIERES	E.9.K
	25th		Remained in billets. Evacuated 3 scabies cases to No 50 C.C.S. Received order to transfer St. Ross to 21 D.A.C.	E.9.K

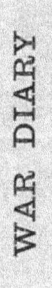

Army Form C. 2118.

WAR DIARY
or
INTELLIGENCE SUMMARY.

(Erase heading not required.)

Instructions regarding War Diaries and Intelligence Summaries are contained in F.S. Regs., Part II. and the Staff Manual respectively. Title pages will be prepared in manuscript.

Place	Date	Hour	Summary of Events and Information	Remarks and references to Appendices
STRAZEELE	26		St Ross proceeded to 21 D.A.C. St Bain RAMC reported to annul formats. Evacuated 1 sick No PCCS and 2 Scabies to 50 CCS.	S.M.
	27th		St Bain proceeded to 4th Middlesex Regt for temporary duty. One reinforcement RAMC(T) arrived. Evacuated 3 sick (scabies) to 5 FCS and 3 Scarlet Cases to No 8 CCS. Held Court of enquiry on death of Cap'l Jeffrey & Pte Robinson (both RAMC(T)) of this unit on March 5th	S.M.
	28th		Evacuated 4 sick to No 8 CCS & 5 sick to No 50 CCS. One reinforcement (M.T.) arrived.	S.M.
	29th		Evacuated one Officer sick to No 1 CCS and Six OR & No 8 & 1 CCS and 30 OR to No 50 ECS.	S.M.
	30th		Capt Thieum, interpreter and one cyclist went on advance party to new billeting area according to orders.	S.M.
	31st		Marched out billet at 8 AM to GODEWAERSVELDE station where we entrained and left it at 1:53 P.M. Detrained at LONGEAU about midnight and marched to village of POULAINVILLE where we billeted on arrival 6 AM on April 1st	S.K.

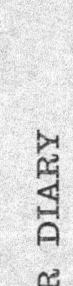

R. J. Kavanagh
Capt RAMC

63 F Amb
Vol 8

Army Form C. 2118.

WAR DIARY
or
INTELLIGENCE SUMMARY.
(Erase heading not required.)

Place	Date	Hour	Summary of Events and Information	Remarks and references to Appendices
POULAINVILLE	April 1st		Arrived here at 6 A.M. Erected tent hospital. Capt Brennan returned from leave. Capt. S. Sharples reported his arrival for duty. Motor ambulances arrived about 5.P.M.	E.J.K.
"	2nd		Remained in billets. No sick evacuated.	E.M.
"	3rd		Remained in billets. No sick evacuated. Found suspected "scabies" in one. Sacks "scabies". Re Journeyed to 62nd Bde H.Q.	J.M.
"	4th		Remained in billets. Evacuated 4 sick to No 21 C.C.S.	E.J.K.
"	5th		Remained in billets. Evacuated 1 sick to No CCS	E.J.K.
"	6th		Marched from POULAINVILLE at 7AM to AUBIGNY and arrived at 12:30 PM. Self Capt Young, two horse ambulances and one motor ambulance for duty with 62 Bde. (+3 RAMC mks) took over baths at LA NEVILLE from 65 to Maker Field Amb. on temporary duty with 4th Middlesex Regt.	E.J.K.
AUBIGNY	7th		Remained in billets. Lieut Bain reported his arrival from 3rd Sanitary Section reported their arrival for 7 sanitary duties.	E.M.
"	8th		One sergeant + 3 O.R. from 64 Field Ambulance. Capt Young, 2 horse ambulances evacuated one sick to 5 C.C.S. Lt Bain transferred for duty with 64 Field Ambulance. Evacuated no sick to C.C.S. one motor ambulance returned this day.	E.J.K.
"	9th		St Adaman proceeded on leave. Capt Thienn went to 8th Lincoln on temporary duty at 126 Field Co. R.E. at Capt Brennan attended Funeral of pring at 126 Field Co. R.E. to burial of Co. Sgt major Spondowth R.E. by evening on Jan 15/16.	E.J.K.

WAR DIARY
or
INTELLIGENCE SUMMARY.
(Erase heading not required.)

Army Form C. 2118.

Place	Date	Hour	Summary of Events and Information	Remarks and references to Appendices
AUBIGNY	9th		Reassembled Court of Inquiry on death of Corpl Jeffreys & Pte Robinson. A.D.M.S. inspected Camp. Evacuates one officer (venereal air vac) to No 5 CCS	fax
"	10th		Capt Young relieves Capt Thienen who is recalled to find "gas" lecture. Dr McKay RFA 95th Bde reported here for an-day in re anaesthetics. Evacuate 1 no sick.	E.J.X.
"	11th		Evacuates no sick. Capt Greig reports his arrival from temporary out-work 1st C.M.R/4th 11C.M.R.	E.J.K.
"	12th		Evacuates no sick.	E.J.X.
"	13th		Evacuates no sick. D.D.M.S. XIII Corps inspected unit. Two reinforcements (RAMC) Dr Adamson and one new orderly from leave of absence received this morn. arrived for duty.	E.J.X. E.J.X.
"	14th		Evacuates one sick to No 21 C.C.S.	E.J.K.
"	15th		Held medical board on men of 10th Yorks, 1st Lincoln, 1st Div proceeding on leave. A.D.M.S. inspects men afterwards. Proceedings forwarded to A.D.M.S. 21st Div = Capt Thienen proceeds on afternoon pass by rail for demonstration purposes.	P.B. B.J.X.
"	16-		Evacuates 1 sick to 5 CCS & 1 to 21 C.C.S. Evacuates 1 sick to 5 C.C.S.	fox
"	17-		Evacuates 1 sick to 5 C.C.S.	fox

Army Form C. 2118.

WAR DIARY
or
INTELLIGENCE SUMMARY.
(Erase heading not required.)

Instructions regarding War Diaries and Intelligence Summaries are contained in F.S. Regs., Part II. and the Staff Manual respectively. Title pages will be prepared in manuscript.

Place	Date	Hour	Summary of Events and Information	Remarks and references to Appendices
AUBIGNY	18th		Evacuated two sick Officers to 21 CCS and one OR & 4 CCS. Sent 2 NCOs & 28 men Dvr temporary duty to 36 CCS. St Adam returned from leave having been measles.	FM
"	19th		St Reine detailed for temporary duty with 15th D.L.I. Capt Thieves sent for lectures and demonstration to unit of 64th Bde. Evacuates one German measles case to Highland Casualty C.S. Villers-Bocage.	SM SM SM
"	20th		Capt Thieves continues lectures. Evacuates one Officer & 5 OR. to 21 CCS.	SM
"	21st		Evacuates 2 sick to 5 CCS. Capt Thieves continued his lectures.	SM
"	22nd		Evacuates one Officer and 2 OR to 21 CCS. Capt Tuny reported from temporary duty with 8th Lincolns	SM
"	23rd		Evacuates 1 sick to 5 CCS.	SM
"	24th		Evacuates 1 sick to 21 CCS. St Reine reported his arrival from temporary out duty	SM
"	25th		Evacuates 5 sick to No 5 CCS with 15th D.L.I.	SM
"	26th		Evacuates 1 sick to 5 CCS. tour OR	SM
"	27th		Evacuates 1 Officer (German measles) to Highland Casualty C.S. Villers-Bocage & 10 OR to 21 CCS & 2 OR to 5 CCS.	SM

Army Form C. 2118.

WAR DIARY
or
INTELLIGENCE SUMMARY.
(Erase heading not required.)

Instructions regarding War Diaries and Intelligence Summaries are contained in F. S. Regs., Part II. and the Staff Manual respectively. Title pages will be prepared in manuscript.

Place	Date	Hour	Summary of Events and Information	Remarks and references to Appendices
ALBION	April 28th		Evacuated 2 cases German measles to Highland Casualty C.S. FILLERS-BOCAGE and 3 sick to 21 CCS.	8M
	29th		Sent advance party 2 Officers + 15 O.R. to take over D.R.S from 97th Field Ambulance at ALLONVILLE. Evacuated 3 sick to 5 ECS Corbie.	8M
ALLONVILLE	30th		Marched from Vellet at 7AM and reached chateau at ALLONVILLE at 10:30 AM took over D.R.S. Left Capt Mather Major Thierre with tent-sub-division at our Vellets to look after sick in our old area, and to keep in baths.	1PM.

E.J. Kavanagh
Capt. RAMC
O.C. 63rd Field Ambulance

21st Div

May 1916.

No. 43 F. Amb

COMMITTEE FOR
MEDICAL HISTORY C...
Date 26 JUN. 1915

63. Fanb
Vol 9

WAR DIARY or INTELLIGENCE SUMMARY

Army Form C. 2118.

63rd (WEST LANCS. T.F.) FIELD AMB.GE.
ROYAL ARMY MEDICAL CORPS

Place	Date	Hour	Summary of Events and Information	Remarks and references to Appendices
ALLONVILLE	May 1st		Remained in billets and arranged hospital. Admits 4 cases	fm
"	2nd		Admits 5 cases	fm
"	3rd		Admits 7 cases. Evacuates 2 cases venereal to Highland CCS - one man to own unit. Went to Red Cross stores at ABBEVILLE for hospital stores	fm
"	4th		Admits 16 sick to hospital. Lt McCaughey RAMC reporting duty to relieve Capt Sharples proceeds to 8th MR Rouen for duty. Admits an Officer R.F. Corp	fx
"	5th		Admits 1 Officer + 17 O.R to hospital. Capt Sharples departs for ROUEN. Received 50 tents to extend hospital. Capt Young sent to own unit sub division at AUBIGNY for medical board. Pitched 50 tents to extend hospital.	fm SOK
"	6th		Admits 2 Officers + 7 O.R to Hosp. DDMS XI Corps inspected ambulance.	fx
"	7th		Admits 30 O.R to hospital. 1st Day that patients arrived from 7th Div.	fx
"	8th		Discharged 10 Officers to duty. Evacuates 4 to 21 CCS. Admits 10 Officers + 14 O.R to hospital. Evacuates 4 sick to 21 CCS	fm
"	9th		Admitted 1 Officer + 9 O.R to hospital Capt D+THR left for Amiens but with 9th ROYL. + Capt Young replaces him at LA NEUVILLE farm	S.G.K.
"	10th		Admits 11 sick to hospital	fm

Army Form C. 2118.

WAR DIARY
or
INTELLIGENCE SUMMARY.
(Erase heading not required.)

Instructions regarding War Diaries and Intelligence Summaries are contained in F.S. Regs., Part II. and the Staff Manual respectively. Title pages will be prepared in manuscript.

[Stamp: 63rd (WEST LANCS.) T.F. FIELD AMBCE. ROYAL ARMY MEDICAL CORPS]

Place	Date	Hour	Summary of Events and Information	Remarks and references to Appendices
ALLONVILLE	Nov 11th		Admits 10 sick to hospital, discharges 3 to duty.	J.M.
"	12th		Appoints Capt Greig RN in general charge of No 4 Bn Group being on leave & relieving D.O. of that unit. Admitted 1 Officer & 12 O.R. to hospital. D.O.H. Inspects tent hospital. Returned 1 O.R. to duty.	J.M.
"	13th		Admits 30 O.R. to hospital. Discharged 2 Officers and 9 O.R. to duty.	S.M.
"	14		Admits 17 sick to hospital. Discharges 11 O.R. to duty	J.J.K.
"	15th		Admits 1 Officer & 21 O.R. to hospital. Discharged 7 to duty & evacuates 2 to 5 C.C.S.	S.J.K.
"	16		Admits 17 O.R. to hospital, discharges 7 O.R. to duty & evacuates 1 Officer & 1 O.R. to 21 C.C.S.	J.M.
"	17		Inspects Sg blkts & Saffs of unit. Discharges 11 to duty & evacuates 1 Officer & 11 O.R. to hospital.	J.M.
"	18		Admits 14 O.R. to hospital. Discharged 1 Officer & 9 O.R. to duty. Evacuates 1 Officer & 17 O.R. to 21 C.C.S.	J.M.
"	19		Admits 19 sick to hospital, discharges 16 to duty & evacuates 3 to 5 C.C.S.	J.M.

WAR DIARY or INTELLIGENCE SUMMARY

Army Form C. 2118.

Place	Date May	Hour	Summary of Events and Information	Remarks and references to Appendices
HUMMEL	21st		admits 2 sick, discharges 18 duty, evacuates 4 to 21 C.C.S.	
			Received order to receive H.T.'s on rest, at strength, and one Group	
			strength horse and one H.T. Sergeant, and one driver H.T. order XI Corps	
		4pm	No D.C./413. 4th Army D.C.(420) 8/150/015 + A2015/11/16	
	22nd		admits 7 B sick, evacuates 3 to 5 CCS + discharges 22 to duty	
			admits 26 to hosp - evacuates 4 to 21 CCS + discharges 10 to duty	
			Sent 2 Horse Ambulances to 6th War Yorkshire Regt for ten days march	
	23rd		Received orders to return the motor bicycle to Army supply column +	
			sent one Corporal M.T. to base. admitted 11 to hosp, evacuates 5 to 5 CCS	
			+ discharges 9 to duty	
	24th		admits 18 to hospital, evacuates 3 to 5 CCS + discharges 14 O.R. to duty	
			3 21	
			Evacuates 1 one German measles to 39 C.C.S	
	25th		admits 19 to Hosp, discharges 11 to duty + evacuates 1 German measles to 39 C.C.S	
			D.D.M.S. inspects and gave verbal order about over camp hospital on	
			29 in. X L22 FA	
	26th		Corps General. Apl. 21st Nov + A+B D.G. 21st Div inspects hospital	
			admits 15 to hospital, discharges 26 to duty, evacuates 5 to 21 CCS	
	27th		admits 16 + discharges 20 to duty. Evacuates 5 O.R. to 5 C.C.S. D.M.S. 4th Army inspects	
			us. D.A.D.M.S. XI Corps also inspects	

WAR DIARY
or
INTELLIGENCE SUMMARY.
(Erase heading not required.)

Army Form C. 2118.

Place	Date	Hour	Summary of Events and Information	Remarks and references to Appendices
ALLOUAGNE	Aug 27		Capt Young transferred to 21st Div. Train. Capt North reports from duty with 9th Ry Lt.	MK
"	28th		Admits 10 Officers & 19 OR Hospital. Evacuates 15 to 21 CCS & discharged 28 to duty	MK
"	29th		Advanced party of 22nd FA arrived. Took over camp. Admits 18 to hospital. Discharged 32 to duty. Evacuated 2 to 5 CCS. Transferred 1 to DRS (?7th Div)	EJK
"	30th		Admits 1 Off & 14 OR hospital. Discharged 18 to duty & evacuates 15 to CCS. Sheeho disinfector arrived from 110th Fd Amb.	EJK
"	31st		Admits 13 OR & 2 Officers. Evacuates 4 to 5 CCS & discharges 13 to duty.	EJK

E.J. Kavanagh
Capt R.A.M.C.
O.C. 6/3 W. La. F.A.

COMMITTEE FOR THE
MEDICAL HISTORY OF THE WAR
Date 5 AUG. 1915

No. 63 7.0.

June 1916.
51

D.A.G's Office
GHQ
 Base

[Stamp: 63rd (WEST LANCS. T.F.) FIELD AMBCE. No. FA912 Date 30/6/16 ROYAL ARMY MEDICAL CORPS]

Enclosed please find "War Diary" of this Unit for month of June please.

J. Mather.
Capt RAMC
for O C 63rd F Amb

WAR DIARY or INTELLIGENCE SUMMARY

63 F Amb
Vol 10
June

Army Form C. 2118

Place	Date June	Hour	Summary of Events and Information	Remarks and references to Appendices
ALNWICK	1st		admits 8 to hospital, discharges 4 to duty and evacuates 2 to 21 C.C.S. Inspected Sub-section at LA NEUVILLE.	P.K.
"	2nd		admits 1 Officer + 14 O.R. to hospital, discharges 1 Officer + 7 O.R. to duty.	S.J.K.
"	3rd		admits 14 to hospital, discharges 10 to duty and evacuates 2 to 21 C.C.S. Capt Thoren to report to 13th Northumberland Fus for temporary duty.	S.J.K.
"	4th		Capt Hetherington on leave. Capt Grey + St MacCarthy proceed to sub section. admits 10 to hospital, discharges 10 Officer + 12 O.R. to duty, evacuates 2 to 5 C.C.S. St A.D.C. MacC reports arrived from temporary duty with 13th Y/OR Fus Lancaster Regt.	P.J.K.
"	5th		admits 17 sick to hospital, discharges 14 to duty & evacuates 7 to 21. C.C.S.	K.Z.
"	6th		admits 27 to hospital, discharges 2 Officers + 7 O.R. to duty, evacuates 3 to 5 C.C.S. Also admits 1 Officer to hospital	T.K. K.Z.
"	7th		admits 15 to hospital, discharges 11 to duty, evacuates 2 to 21 C.C.S. St Bennett (T.C.) reports for duty with the unit. 4 Reinforcements arrived.	K.K.
"	8th		admits 1 Officer + 30 O.R. to hospital, discharges 16 to duty, evacuates 10 Officer + 1 O.R. to 5 C.C.S.	S.J.K.
"	9th		admits 1 Officer + 30 O.R. to hospital. ADMS 1st XV Corps inspected St MacCarthy went on temporary duty to 21st H.A. Group. St Bennett went to sub section 3 to 21 C.C.S. admits 13 to hospital, discharges 6 to duty + evacuates 3 to 21 C.C.S.	P.K.

WAR DIARY or INTELLIGENCE SUMMARY

Army Form C. 2118.

Place	Date	Hour	Summary of Events and Information	Remarks and references to Appendices
ALLONVILLE	June 10th		Admitted 1 O.R. hospital, undergoing 1 yr. out. S' Adrason reports his departure on expiration of yearn service to join C.A.M.C.	S.M.
	June 11		Admitted to hospital 14. O.R. — Discharged to duty 20. O.R. — Evacuated to No. 21. C.C.S. 4 sick. One driver soldier sent from Divisional Train in exchange for one driver.	C.H.B.
	12	8 A.M.	Capt Kavanagh proceeded on leave. Admitted to hospital 21 O.R. Discharged to duty 11 O.R. Evacuated to No 5 C.C.S. 2 O.R. and 39 C.C.S. 1 O.R. D.D.M.S. XV Corps visited Rest Station and gave verbal instructions to Capt Bennett that the patients were to be evacuated quickly so that the hospital would be cleared within a fortnight. He wished to be carried out in a manner which would not arouse enquires as to the numbers being evacuated. Weather unseasonably cold and showery.	C.H.B.
	13th		Admitted 1 Officer and 23 O.R. Discharged to duty 12 O.R and evacuated to No 21 C.C.S. 13 O.R.. Capt Hather returned from leave. Col. M c Cowen Div. Train inspected transport. Memorial service for Field Marshall Lord Kitchener held in R.F.C. ground at 12 noon. Received letter from A.D.M.S. giving instructions to evacuate gradually all cases except Scabies not likely to be able to rejoin the ranks within a week and reduce number to a minimum. Scabies to be kept in as short a time as possible. Capt Greg returned from farm at La NEUVILLE for duty at Chateau ALLONVILLE.	C.H.B.
		7:30 PM		C.H.B.

Army Form C. 2118.

WAR DIARY
or
INTELLIGENCE SUMMARY.
(Erase heading not required.)

Instructions regarding War Diaries and Intelligence Summaries are contained in F. S. Regs., Part II. and the Staff Manual respectively. Title pages will be prepared in manuscript.

Place	Date	Hour	Summary of Events and Information	Remarks and references to Appendices
	14th		Admitted 1 Officer 17 O.R.. Discharged to duty 10 O.R.. Evacuated to No 5 (W) 17 O.R.. Instructions received from A.D.M.S. to have equipment as much as possible packed up to enable the unit to move at short notice. Instructions received also that the armies in France will adopt the same time as ordered by recent decree of French Government and at 11 P.M. on this date time will be advanced 60 minutes and 11 P.M. will become 12 midnight. Instructions carried out.	C.H.B.
	15th		D.D.M.S. XVth Corps visited the Chateau and confirmed his orders of a previous date with to evacuations of patients. Notification from A.D.M.S. asking for two officers daily to report at 2.30 P.M. to O.C. 64 F.A.M.B. for purpose of being shown over ground at present held by Division. Admitted 21 O.R. Discharged to duty 10 O.R. Evacuated to No 2 C.C.S. 9 O.R.. Captains Mather and Raine reported to O.C. 64 F.A.M.B. as per instructions from A.D.M.S.. A.D.M.S. visited the Chateau.	C.H.B.
	16th		Admitted 19 O.R.. Discharged to duty 9 O.R.. Evacuated to No 5 C.C.S. 6 O.R.. Capt. Holden 64 F.A.M.B. visited the Chateau to arrange for transfer of material for use of 64 F.A.M.B. (hospital equipment) Capt Grieg and Lieut Bewlet reported to O.C. 64 F.A.M.B. for purpose of being shown over ground at present held by the Division	C.H.B.

WAR DIARY
or
INTELLIGENCE SUMMARY.
(Erase heading not required.)

Army Form C. 2118.

Place	Date	Hour	Summary of Events and Information	Remarks and references to Appendices
	17th		Admitted officers 1 - 10 O.R.. Discharged to duty 12 O.R. Evacuated to No 21 C.C.S. 9 O.R.. Received instructions from A.D.M.S. to detail Capt. THEIRENS for permanent duty with 21 Div. Engineers. Capt GREEG sent to relieve Capt THEIRENS from 13 North'd Fus. Capt BRENNAN and Lieut PRICE reported at 21.30 P.M. to O.C. 64 F.AMB. for purpose of being shown the area at present held by the Division. Major THOMSON D.A.D.M.S. 21 Div. visited the Chateau and gave instructions that patients must be evacuated as soon as possible. Lieut RICE warned to attend F.G.C.M. and Capt MATHER (in the absence of Capt KAVANAGH (who was also to have been present) and Lieut PRICE will attend the F.G.C.M. of No 1757 Cpl CHALLENOR A. R.A.M.C. to be held on 18th inst. 	C.K.B.
	18th		Admitted 1 officer 2 O.R. Discharged to duty 23 O.R.. 1 officer to No 5 C.C.S. and 1 officer and 28 O.R. Convalescents to be sent tomorrow to No 45 C.C.S. Verbal instructions given by Major THOMSON D.A.D.M.S. 21 Div. to VECQUEMONT to act as fatigues in that C.C.S. Sur. Gen. MacPHERSON and D.D.M.S. XVth Corps visited Chateau informed us that we were handing over REST STATION on Tuesday 20th inst. to Sub Lieut div. of 51st F.AMB. Preparations and packing proceeded with. Three H.D. horses sent to 3B M.V.S. having been diagnosed as suffering from Mange. Capt MATHER and Lieut PRICE attended as witnesses at	C.K.B.
		5 P.M.	proceedings F.G.C.M. of No 1757 Cpl. CHALLENOR. 1 Cpl. CHALLENOR arrived with escort and was handed over awaiting	

WAR DIARY or INTELLIGENCE SUMMARY

Army Form C. 2118.

Place	Date	Hour	Summary of Events and Information	Remarks and references to Appendices
ALLONVILLE	18th 19th	9 A.M.	the promulgation of his sentence. 1 Officer and 28 O.R. of Convalescent Platoon proceeded to No 45 C.C.S. as per instructions given verbally by Major Thomson. Received note from A.D.M.S. confirming instructions received from D.D.M.S. XVth Corps viz. that we are to hand over the Rest Station to 1 Officer and tent sub. div. of 51 Field Ambulance (17th Div.) on 20 inst. and we are to hold ourselves in readiness from that date to move at short notice. Admitted Officers 1. O.R. - Discharged to duty 1 Officer 36 O.R. Evacuated to No. 3 & C.C.S. 9 O.R.. D.D.M.S. XVth Corps visited Chateau but gave no further instructions. Capt Compo to remain until discharged for duty as per instructions received from A.D.M.S. 17th Div. Capt. _____ in the absence of O.C. 51st F.Amb. came over to Chateau in order to inspect before taking over with his 1 Sect Amb. Div. Major McDonnell A.D.V.S. 27th Div. inspected and examined horses and gave instructions for 6 mule horses here to be evacuated to 33 M.V.S. designated "mange", the grooms (3) to accompany these horses together with their kits and saddlery which must be disinfected. The horses will be returned when cured. Also gave instructions that those lines and all harness and saddlery were to be disinfected.	C.H.S

Army Form C. 2118.

WAR DIARY
or
INTELLIGENCE SUMMARY.
(Erase heading not required.)

Instructions regarding War Diaries and Intelligence Summaries are contained in F. S. Regs., Part II. and the Staff Manual respectively. Title pages will be prepared in manuscript.

Place	Date June	Hour	Summary of Events and Information	Remarks and references to Appendices
ALLONVILLE	20		Returned from leave. Admitts 5, hospital, discharged 6, to duty. Evacuates 1 Officer + 2 O.R. to 5 C.C.S. Rifles ammn for A.S.C. (35)	P.J.K.
"	21st		Admitts 1, hospital, discharges 1 Officer to duty + evacuates to 34 C.C.S. 1 O.R.	E.J.K.
"	22nd		Admitts 1 Officer + 5 O.R. to hospital, discharges 10 to Duty. Visits trench recoy by 21st Div.	E.J.K.
"	23rd		No admissions, discharges to duty 50 and evacuates to 34 C.C.S, 2 O.R. Received in hospital Officers 4 + O.R. 28. Handed over cases to 51st F. Amb. Ambulance. Visits Depn 1 XV Corps.	P.J.K.
BUIRE	24th		Marched from ALLONVILLE at 6:30 A.M. to BUIRE. Arrived 11 A.M. Evacuates 3 sick to 5 C.C.S.	E.J.K.
"	25th		3 Officers, 8 NCOs + 20 men proceeded in temporary out to 34 C.C.S. Evacuates 9 officers (Scarlet Fever) + 5 to 39 C.C.S. Inspect in ration of unit. Sent billets, latrines, Septic pans, trenches to 64 F.A. for clean moving station. Car Kled inspector at 8.45 A.M. Sent 3 to D.R.S. at ALLONVILLE, Transferred 1 to 64 F.A. admitts + FA. 7 + discharged 1 to duty. Car called out to collect	E.J.K.
"	26th		wounded in a tiller at VILLE — Can brought cases to 64 FA direct. Warned that our Gas attack which took place at 11:30 A.M + V by 3rd Corps attack at 6 P.M. Had whole unit ready with Gas helmets. Sent car to VILLE to convey wounded front where to evac hospital, HERISSART. Sent 1 NCO + 10 men for Sanitary duties Bn at MERICOURT.	E.J.K.

WAR DIARY or INTELLIGENCE SUMMARY.

Army Form C. 2118.

Place	Date	Hour	Summary of Events and Information	Remarks and references to Appendices
BUIRE	27th		Sent horse ambulance to 8th Lincoln for their march to LA NEUVILLE. 1 NCO + 8 men sent for duty at Baths at VILLE. LIEUT P.G. FOWKES reports for duty. Sir J.H. Egbert (T.C.) reports for duty. 2nd Lt McCauley reports his arrival from temporary duty with 21 H.A.G. Sent motor ambulance to Amiens with sick French Offr. Sent 2 horse ambulances to 8th Lincoln for their march. Admitted 176 O.R. 2nd 8 to D.R.S. SAILLOUVILLE and discharged Capt J.A. Gill to duty.	E.J.K.
"	28th		Detached from LA NEUVILLE arrived at 1 A.M. to 64 F.A. a spare team for our horse ambulance. Sent 6 horses & 4 mules to 64 F.A. since R.E. Capt J.A. Gill reported for duty. Sent temporary add run our horse ambulance. Capt Thuron reported our add run at 9 P.M. at VILLE MILL. Three horse ambulance & 2 G.S. wagon filled with ambulance under the order is cancelled. Three horse ambulance to 64 FA & horse ambulance to VILLEMILE. Movements 21st to 17 D.R.S. Tonghene. Return horse & 64 FA. Discharged 4 OR to duty. Movements 2 to S.C.C.S. Half 1 Offr to 64 FA movements 2 to S.C.C.S. Received orders that operations intended have been postponed for 48 hours.	E.J.K.
"	29		Capts Brown & Ruine returned from 34 CCS and were replaced by Lts Egbert & Fowkes. 1 Acutts 1 Officer & 50 R. Movements 1 Officer & 50 R. to D.R.S., 50 R. to 34 CCS & 1 measles case to 39 CCS St. Ouen. Discharges 2 to duty. Capt Gill transferred to 64 Field Amble.	P.G.F.

Army Form C. 2118.

WAR DIARY
or
INTELLIGENCE SUMMARY.
(Erase heading not required.)

Place	Date	Hour	Summary of Events and Information	Remarks and references to Appendices
BULRE	June 30		Admtts Offrs + 96 OR. Evauts 1 Offr + 130 R + 130 R + 150 R DRs. 5 C.C.S. Evacuations 3 Bats. Horse ambulances (3) + 2 g.S Wagons (converted to ambulance) went to VILLE NILL as P.D. 5/one pair for amn went to 64 F.A an 5. P.N. also one M.T. amn. 2 N.C.O Th.O.R. proceeded as temp" orrt to 64 F.A.	

G. Kavanagh
C. Capt. & and
D.C. 63rd F.A.

21st. Division

63rd Field Ambulance

COMMITTEE FOR THE
MEDICAL HISTORY OF THE WAR
Date 5 - SEP 1916

July 1916

WAR DIARY or INTELLIGENCE SUMMARY

Army Form C. 2118.

MEDICAL

Vol II

Place	Date	Hour	Summary of Events and Information	Remarks and references to Appendices
BUIRE	July 1st		Sent 7 motor ambulances to A.D.S. of 65th Field Amb¢e Proceeded to collect footgear at trucks to arrange evacuation of casualties. Sent Capt. Brennan + Raine, 3 NCO + 36 OR to trucks to collect & carry back wounded. Capt Thirner, + Lt McCauley went to 64 F. Ambulance for day at rain dump station to. Later sent Capt Grig + 2 OR to trucks to collect wounded.	F.K.
	2nd		Sent Capt Mather, 10 NCOs, 12 men to 64 Field Amb¢ for duty. 2 NCOs came back. 1 NCO + 8 men transferred from Veith at VILLE to 64th FA for duty. Slightly wounded O.R.s walked + returned toward the transfer to 64 FA Adler job arrived. They were not back in our lorries. Received orders to send wounded prisoners + wa + Prisoners Field Ambulance at MORLANCOURT.	F.R.
	3rd		all slightly wounded cases transferred to 64 F.A. Found our unit wounded	P.K.
	4th		All men, Officers + NCOs returned to our billets at BUIRE from trucks and 64th FA. Capt Fox Motor ambulance also returned. Left BUIRE at 9:15 AM + entrained at DERNACOURT at 8 PM and arrived at AILLY SUR SOMME at 12:30 AM on 5th inst.	F.R.

WAR DIARY
or
INTELLIGENCE SUMMARY.
(Erase heading not required.)

Army Form C. 2118.

Place	Date	Hour	Summary of Events and Information	Remarks and references to Appendices.
BUIRE	July 4th		Horse transport under Capt BRENNAN proceeded by road to ST SAUVEUR as per the motor ambulances – former arrived 6 PM, latter at 3:30 PM. Arrived at 1:30 AM. Capt Thurnam returned to Divisional R. Engineers. Admitted 2 to F.A.	PK
ST SAUVEUR	6th		Capts Nathan, Brennan + Lt McCaughey went to OR. & proceeded to take over new station at ALLONVILLE. One officer & 6 Daily see 2 Co train at Car VAUX	P.J.K
"	7th		Sent Officer to D.R. & R.O.R. Inoculated OR to C.C.S. (Southolm) Left ST SAUVEUR at 3 PM + marched to SAISSEVAL where we arrived 5:30 PM. One reinforcement arrived from base.	P.J.K
SAISSEVAL	8th		Admitted 7, sent one to S. Midland CCS. A.D.M.S. visited F.A. Received instruction that transport would move tomorrow.	PK
"	9th		Sent # 1 to Rest Station 1 Officer + 1 OR to S. Midland CCS. Transport effry road to march to QUERRIEU.	PK
"	10th		Unit left at 7:30 AM + entrained at AILLY-SUR-SOMME at 4 PM returned at CORBIE at 6:30 PM arrived at Saleux BECORDEL (with all transport which 10R Party at ALLONVILLE left at 10 AM turned over to S. Midland CCS. 1 OR at VILLE-SUR-ANCRE) at 4:30 PM were att. 1 Officer to S. Midland CCS. 1 OR MEAULTE Sent 13 OR. Rest Station	PK

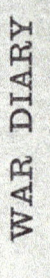

WAR DIARY or INTELLIGENCE SUMMARY

Army Form C. 2118.

Place	Date	Hour	Summary of Events and Information	Remarks and references to Appendices
BECORDEL	July 11		Took over bearing station from 53 Field Ambulance. Also took over collecting post at FRICOURT – Sent 30 Officers & OR including 2 Officers and OR from 64 F.A. Sent 1 Officer & 16 OR to Queen's Redoubt. Not counting cases we saw A & D Bosh but evacuating all on 65th Divisional Collecting post and 64th main bearing station. Three Officers from 65th FA arrived for evacuation. Seven 2 Officers of 64 FA to this unit. 	f.k.
"	12th		1 reinforcement examined. Changed ADS from FRICOURT to DANETZ. DDMS XV Corps inspected us. Pitches tent at DANETZ & sent Capt. Brennan, Greig, Rains, & Shanks & 65th FA. Sent 120 NCOs & men. Poole – Battle Two Officers from 65th FA.	f.k.
"	13th		Went to DANETZ to take overcharge. Brought St Baine & the remaining 10 men from FRICOURT to DANETZ. Had all horse ambulance & Field Ambulance of Division to evacuate wounded. Got 2 motor lorries to help to evacuate the wounded. 97 HAC came direct to BECORDEL to evacuate cases.	f.k.
"	14th		Sent another 100 NCOs & men from 64 & 65 F.A. to DANETZ. Also for home transport to Field Ambulance of 33rd Division to evacuate cases. War Informed 2 cases of 2 cases were shell on a become omission to work 19th 7701st F.A. in case of recoup.	f.k.

WAR DIARY
or
INTELLIGENCE SUMMARY.

Army Form C. 2118.

Place	Date	Hour	Summary of Events and Information	Remarks and references to Appendices
BECORDEL	July 15th		Nothing special to record. 6 wounded received. Most cases up from 335 Bde.	P/x
"	16th		Reinforced 65th F.A. Sent train bearers of wounded prisoners.	P/x
"	17th		Received instructions that 99th F.A. would take over at BECORDEL and 101st F.A. at NANETZ. Handing over at NANETZ took place at 1:10 P.M. 18th Jan. BECORDEL at 6 A.H. – 18th 3 marches personnel from NANETZ reached BECORDEL at 2 A.M. Remainder at BECORDEL at 6 A.M. & marched	S/x
"	18th		Unit marches from BECORDEL at 6 A.M. & reached BUIRE at 8:30 A.M.	P/x
BUIRE	18th			P/x
ALLONVILLE	19th		Marched at 5 P.M. & reached ALLONVILLE at 9.20 P.M.	P/x
RIENCOURT	20th		Marched at 9 P.M. and arrived at RIENCOURT at 10.40 P.M. Sent motor ambulance to SAIEUX to fetch Hurst Camp & Staff Sergeant Capt RAINE, 2 M.N.	P/x
"	21st		Remained in billets. 6 reinforcements arrived.	P/x
"	22nd		Marched to LONGEAU & entrained wth 3 motor ambulances & lettering Station at 1:30 A.M. & PETIT HOUVIN to billets Bruges on 23rd motor entrained by road – reporting at STPOL	P/x
TERMAS	23rd		Detrained at ST. POL at 7:30 A.M. & marched to TERMAS – arriving at 9:45 A.M.	P/x

Army Form C. 2118.

WAR DIARY
or
INTELLIGENCE SUMMARY.
(Erase heading not required.)

Instructions regarding War Diaries and Intelligence Summaries are contained in F. S. Regs., Part II. and the Staff Manual respectively. Title pages will be prepared in manuscript.

Place	Date	Hour	Summary of Events and Information	Remarks and references to Appendices
TERNAS	July 24		Received orders to march off at 4 P.M. to GIVENCHY-LE-NOBLE. March with 6 P.M. trucked billets at 8.15 P.M. Evacuate 1 Officer + 10 O.R. to 37 C.C.S.	S.J.R. S.J.R.
GIVENCHY LE NOBLE	25th		Remained in billets. Evacuate 2 sick to 14 Dis. Rest Station.	S.J.R.
"	26th		Remained in billets. Sent advanced party of 1 Officer + 12 O.R. to HABARCQ. Establish horse lines & special hospital + main dressing station. Evacuate 1 Officer + 9 O.R. to Rest Station. 7 O.R. to 37 C.C.S.	S.J.R.
"	27th		Remained in billets. Capt Brennan sent on temporary duty to 12 Northumb'd Fusiliers. Lieut Bennett + 2 O.R. tk medical inspector room at Du15 A.M.S. Evacuate 1 Officer + 14 Dis. Rest Station, 2 O.R. to 37 C.C.S. + 1 to 12 Stationary Hosp.	S.J.R.
HABARCQ	28		Marched at 1.80 P.M. + arrived at 8.15 P.M. Took over from 48th Field Ambulence. Surgical specialist + nursing sisters attached, Capt Natter proceeded to III Army for School for Instructors.	S.J.R.

WAR DIARY
or
INTELLIGENCE SUMMARY.

Army Form C. 2118.

Place	Date	Hour	Summary of Events and Information	Remarks and references to Appendices
HABARCQ	29th		Admitted Officer 3 + OR 66. Evacuated CCS Officer 2, OR 16	AMcK
"	30		Discharged out O.R. 6. Transferred to 64 Field Amber G.I.O.R from this hospital. Received in exchange from Rear Stores at H.E.M. to get necessary stores.	AMcK
"	31st		Noted Rear Stores at H.E.M. one Officer Admitted 1 Officer + 43 O.R. Transferred to Officer Rest Station Evacuated to 12 CCS 1 Case Scarlet fever, + 3 wounded to No 42 CCS, + 2 sick to 12 CCS.	T.McK

G. Newsome
Capt RAMC
OC 63rd Field Ambulance

21st Div.

63rd (W. Lanc). F.A.

Aug. 1916.

S/1

COMMITTEE FOR THE
MEDICAL HISTORY OF THE WAR
Date -5 OCT. 1916

WAR DIARY
or
INTELLIGENCE SUMMARY.
(Erase heading not required.)

Army Form C. 2118.

Place	Date	Hour	Summary of Events and Information	Remarks and references to Appendices
HABARCQ	Aug 1st 1918		Evacuated 1 Officer & 12 OR to 37 CCS. Discharged 2 Sick OR. Retained 1 2 OR. for treatment at Field Ambulance. One man (abdominal) died.	E.J.R.
"	2nd		DDMS VII Army, ADMS VII Corps inspected ambulance. Admitted 1 Officer & 39 OR. Discharged 20 to Duty. Evacuated to Officers Rest Str 1 Officer [crossed out] 11 OR to 37 CCS. Mr Pike OC. District Red Cross Stores. One man died after operation. Came to see relatives in hospital.	J.R.
"	3rd		Capt Heath & Brennan reported from temporary duty. One man died from abdominal wound in Special Hospital. Admitted 1 Officer & 38 OR. (2 wounded) Discharged 12 OR to duty. Evacuated 11 to 37 CCS.	E.J.R.
"	4th		Admitted 9 Sick & 1 wounded. Discharged to Duty 22, Evacuated 7 OR. to 37 CCS. 1 Officer & OR Rest Station, + 54 OR to Rear Station + 1 OR wounded to 42 CCS. 1 Officer to Officers Rest Camp at Beauvois. Sent Officer to inspect German prisoners between Corps HD Qrts BELLAVESNES.	J.R.

WAR DIARY or INTELLIGENCE SUMMARY

Army Form C. 2118.

Place	Date	Hour	Summary of Events and Information	Remarks and references to Appendices
HABARCO	Aug 5th		Admitted 2 sick & 1 wounded Officers, & O.R. 23 sick & 15 wounded. Sent to D.R.S. 20 O.R. & 57 CCS 9 sick & 30 C.C.S. 3 wounded. Discharged to duty 7.O.R.	E.D.K.
"	6th		Scarpt. Egypt. Admitted 1 Officer, 137 sick & 6 wounded O.R. Discharged 22 O.R. to duty. Evacuated 2 sick & 37 CCS & 1 sick & 1 wounded to 42 CCS, 118 sick & 4 wounded to D.R.S. & 1 Officer & 1 Officer & green R. Statn. Capt. Rawlinson left for 19 C.C.S. as Lieut. K. M. Walker returned to take over Duties of Surgical Specialist at Special Hospital	E.D.K.
"	7th		Admitted 2 Officers sick & 1 wounded. O.R. 29 sick & 1 wounded. Discharged to duty 3 O.R. Evacuated to 37 C.C.S. O.R. sick & 1 Officer wounded. Sent to Stationy for 42 C.C.S. 1 Officer & 2 Officers & D.R. S. nil. Sent Officer Red Staten 2 Officers & D.R. S. nil.	E.D.K.

WAR DIARY or INTELLIGENCE SUMMARY

Army Form C. 2118.

Place	Date	Hour	Summary of Events and Information	Remarks and references to Appendices
HABARCQ	August 8th		Admitted 4 Officers sick, 8 O.R. 28 sick & 5 wounded. Discharged 4 O.R. to duty. Evacuated 3 Officers & 8 O.R. to 37 CCS & 5 O.R. to 42 CCS.	S/W
"	9th		Admitted 1 Officer sick, 36 O.R. sick & 2 wounded. Discharged 1 O.R. to duty. Evacuated 2 Officers to Officers Rest Station, 4 O.R. to 37 CCS. Rest Stat. 1 (64th & Amb.) 4 wounded to 30 CCS, 6 sick to 37 CCS.	O.K.
"	10th		Admitted 1 Officer sick & 1 wounded, 36 O.R. sick & 2 wounded. Sent 4 cases to 6 Stationary Hosp. for eye treatment 2 cases (ear) to 12 Stationary Hosp. Evacuated 2 sick Officers to O.R. Rest & 37 CCS wounded & 2 O.R. sick to 42 CCS.	
"	11th		Admitted 1 Officer sick, 34 O.R. sick & 1 wounded. Discharged 5 O.R. to duty. Sent to D.R.S. ((64 & 7 A)) 39 sick & 1 wounded. Evacuated 4 sick O.R. to 37 CCS. 1 O.R. sick to 12 Stationary Hosp., 2 O.R. wounded to 30 CCS. 1 Officer died (Capt McCluckie 3rd Argyll & Sutherland Highrs attd 9 W. York Regt)	

2353 Wt. W2544/1454 700,000 5/15 D. D. & L. A.D.S.S./Forms/C. 2118.

WAR DIARY
INTELLIGENCE SUMMARY

Army Form C. 2118.

Place	Date	Hour	Summary of Events and Information	Remarks and references to Appendices
HABARCQ	August 12th		admits 1 Officer sick, 11 OR sick & 3 wounded. Discharged 4 OR to duty. Sent 330 R to D.R.S (65th FA) Evacuate 1 Officer & 8 O.R. to 37 C.C.S, 2 OR to 12 Stationary Hosp St Pol, 1 + 2 wounded to 42 C.C.S.	M
"	13th		admits 40 sick + 9 wounded. Discharged 5 to duty. Evacuate 3 to 37 CCS. 8 wounded to 30 CCS + 54 to D.R.S (40 to 65 FA + 14 to 64 FA) Col. RAINE appointed town major.	M
"	14th		admits 2 Officers sick, 1 wounded, 41 OR sick + 4 wounded. Discharged 1 to duty, 4 O.R. Evacuate 1 [mr] to 6 OR to 37 CCS, 2 OR to 6 Stationary Hosp, 2 Officers + Officers Rest Sta 42 C.C.S. 7 D.R. to 6 Stationary Hosp, 2 Officers to Officers Rest Station, 15 OR to D.R.S (65th FA) + 13 OR to D.R.S (64th FA) Capt Mather went on temporary duty to 1 Lincoln Regt.	M
"	15th		admits 1 Officer sick, 27 O.R. sick + 4 wounded. Discharged to duty 17 O.R. Evacuate to 37 CCS 1 Officer + 2 O.R., to 30 CCS 6 OR wounded, + to 12 Stationary Hosp 4 O.R.	M

Army Form C. 2118.

WAR DIARY
or
INTELLIGENCE SUMMARY.
(Erase heading not required.)

Instructions regarding War Diaries and Intelligence Summaries are contained in F.S. Regs., Part II. and the Staff Manual respectively. Title pages will be prepared in manuscript.

Place	Date	Hour	Summary of Events and Information	Remarks and references to Appendices
HABARCQ	16th		Admitted 10 Officer wounded + 50 O.R. sick + 20 R wounded. Sent 1 officer + officers Rest Station, 25 O.R. to D.R.S (64th F.A.) + 30 O.R. to D.R.S (65th F.A). Evacuate 6 O.R sick to 37 CCS. A.D.M.S VI Corps inspected Special Hospital + Field Ambulance. Capt. Kavanagh appointed Town Major vice Capt. Raine.	E.J.K
"	17th		Lieut Eglinton detailed for temporary duty with 13th Northumberland Fusiliers. Attended conference at D.D.M.S VI Corps.	E.J.K
"			Admitted 5 officer wounded, 38 O.R sick + 20 R wounded. Sent to Officer Rest Station one officer, discharged to unit 14 O.R. Evacuates to 37 CCS 3 O.R, to 12 Stationary Hospl 4 O.R, to 6 Stationary Hosp 7 O.R. + 30 CCS. 1 O.R wounded.	E.J.K
"	18th		Admitted 11 officer wounded, 28 O.R. sick + 3 O.R. wounded. Discharged 7 O.R to duty. Self 20 O.R to D.R.S (64th FA) + 15 O.R to D.R.S (65th FA) Evacuates 1 officer 17 O.R to 42 CCS + 5 O.R. to 37 CCS. One man died after operation.	E.J.K

WAR DIARY

or

INTELLIGENCE SUMMARY

Army Form C. 2118.

Place	Date	Hour	Summary of Events and Information	Remarks and references to Appendices
HABARCQ	August 19th		Admitted 29 sick + 10 wounded. Discharged 1 Officer + 7 OR to Unit. Evacuated 5 OR to 37 CCS & 5 OR to 30 CCS. Lt. Walker returned on furlough.	EJR.
"	20th		Lt Walker Surgical specialist went for temporary duty at 9 K.O. Jok. L.I. Replaced temporarily by Capt. R. Wilson. Capt. Dickie went to II Corps Lt Fowler, Sgt Brewer + Cpl ? R.A.M.C. School of Instruction. Admitted One Officer sick, 35 OR sick, 1 wounded. New 3O OR to II OR S (65th Field A) + 2O OR to 2 RS (64th FA) Evacuated 3 OR sick + 2 OR wounded to 37 CCS + 2 OR wounded to 30 CCS, 2 OR sick + 2 OR wounded to 42 CCS. Discharged 9O OR to duty.	EJR.
"	21st		Admitted 2 Officers sick, 5O OR sick + 1 wounded. Evacuated to 4 CCS 1 Officer wounded. 1 Officer sick + 57 CCS. 1 Officer sick + 5 J.R. Sent to 6 Stationary Hospital 1 Officer sick + 1 Officer R.A.F. Platus 1 Officer. Sent to 12 O.R. Sent to Officers sick + 12 O.R. Sent 8 B.R. 1872 Cpl J. Moloney went to Returned 6 mules field Kitchen in us in the ambulance as (or Head Quarters) to mules field Kitchen model for the division	SBR.

WAR DIARY or INTELLIGENCE SUMMARY

Army Form C. 2118.

Place	Date	Hour	Summary of Events and Information	Remarks and references to Appendices
HABARCQ	Aug 22nd		J.O.C. 21st Divr inspected Special Hosp & Field Ambulance. Admitted 1 Officer wounded & 3 O.R. wounded. One Officer sick & 45 O.R. sick. Discharged 13 O.R. to duty. Sent 3 O.R. to DRS (65th F.A.) & 3 O.R. to DRS (64th F.A.) evacuated 1 Officer to 3 CCS & 8 O.R. to 42 CCS & 30 CCS 1 O.R. 1 Officer & 3 O.R. & 30 CCS 1 O.R.	E.J.K.
"	23rd		Admitted 3 Officers sick, 31 O.R. sick & 1 wounded. Discharged 4 to duty. Sent 1 Officer to Officers Rest Station evacuated 1 wounded to 30 CCS. 1 wounded to 26 General Hospital Etaples	E.J.K.
"	24th		Admitted & Sick Officers, 33 O.R. sick & 2 O.R. wounded. Discharged 4 to duty, evacuated 5 O.R. sick to 37 CCS. Sent 3 Officers sick to Officers Rest Station & 3 O.R. to DRS (65th F.A.)	E.J.K.

WAR DIARY
or
INTELLIGENCE SUMMARY.
(Erase heading not required.)

Army Form C. 2118.

Place	Date	Hour	Summary of Events and Information	Remarks and references to Appendices
HASARLO	August 25th		Capt Mather reported from temporary duty. Admits 5 Officers sick, 27 O.R. sick & 7 O.R. wounded. Discharged & sent 14 O.R. sick. Officers Rest Station 3 Officers. To D.R.S. (65th F.A) 2 O.R. Evacuate to 37 CCS 2 Officers & 2 O.R. To 30 CCS 60 wounded. To 6 Stationary Hospl 2 (eye cases) OR, & 12 Stationary Hospl 1 Gunner Prisoner	E.J.K.
"	26th		Admits 2 Officers sick, 27 O.R. sick & 7 O.R. wounded. Discharged 7 O.R. wounded. Evacuate to 37 CCS 6 O.R. 67 CCS 1 Officer wounded & 8 O.R. wounded. Sent 2 Officers to Officers Rest Station. 1 Officer & 2 O.R. to D.R.S. (65th F.A) & 2 1 O.R. to R.R.S. (65th F.A) St Fouekis. 4 2 NCOs reported from VI Corps RAMC School of Instruction. Pte PARKIN went to III Army Cooking School for instruction.	S.J.T.
"	27th		Admits 1 Officer & 27 O.R. sick, 17 O.R. wounded. Discharged 5 O.R. Sent 2 Officers to Officers Rest Station, 1 & 19 O.R to D.R.S. (65th F.A). Evacuate 2 O.R sick to 37 CCS & 40 R wounded to 30 CCS. G.O.C. VI Corps inspected Special Hospital & Field Ambulance	E.J.K.

WAR DIARY
or
INTELLIGENCE SUMMARY
(Erase heading not required.)

Army Form C. 2118.

Place	Date	Hour	Summary of Events and Information	Remarks and references to Appendices
HAZEBROUCK	August 28		Admitted 1 Officer & 24 O.R. sick & 5 O.R. wounded. Discharged per Lant: Sent 20 O.R. to D.R.S (65th FA) Evacuated 2 O.R. sick 27 C.C.S. & 10 R. wounded to 42 C.C.S. Evacuated Officer to 6 Stationary Hosp. Sr. H.S. MOORE reported his arrival for duty with this unit.	E.J.K.
"	29th		Capt. Raine went on temporary duty to 9th Evacn. Rept. Admitted 2 Officers sick, 26 O.R. sick & 3 O.R. wounded. Evacuated 7 O.R. duty. Sent 13 O.R. to D.R.S (65th FA) Evacuated 3 O.R. (eye cases) to 6 Stationary Hospital, 37 C.C.S., 2 O.R. wounded to 30 C.C.S. 3 O.R (eye cases) to 6 Stationary Hospital 2 O.R. wounded to 26 General Hospital	E.J.K.
"	30		Admitted 2 Officers sick, 38 O.R. sick & 2 O.R. wounded. Discharged to duty 110 R. Sent Officers Rest Station. 4 Officers sick to D.R.S (65th FA) 30 O.R. Evacuated 2 O.R. sick to 37 C.C.S. & 2 O.R. wounded to 42 C.C.S. O.C VII Corps inspected our proposed improvement for coming winter. We have made Horse Standings.	E.J.K.
"	31st		Admitted 3 wounded Officers, 20 O.R. wounded & 31 O.R. sick. Discharged 6 O.R. to duty. Sent 23 O.R. to D.R.S (65th FA). Evacuated 30 R. to 37 C.C.S. 14 O.R to 30 C.C.S, 2 Officers to 42 C.C.S., 10 R. wounded to 6 Stationary Hosp. + also 1 German Prisoner to 6 Stationary Hosp.	E.J.K.

E.J. Kavanagh
O.C. 63rd F. Ambulance

140/1734

21st Division

63rd Field Ambulance.

Mk 1916

51

COMMITTEE FOR THE MEDICAL HISTORY OF THE WAR
Date **30 OCT. 1916**

WAR DIARY
or
INTELLIGENCE SUMMARY.

Army Form C. 2118.

Place	Date September	Hour	Summary of Events and Information	Remarks and references to Appendices
HARAR(?)	1st		Admits 1 Officer sick, 1 Officer wounded, 37 O.R. sick + 3 O.R. wounded. Sent 1 Officer to Main Rest Station, 20 O.R. to D.R.S. (64 F.A.) Evacuates 3 O.R. to 37 C.C.S. 1 Officer wounded 1 4 O.R. wounded to 42 C.C.S. Capt E. B. EGERTON 17th Lancers died of wounds in Special Hospital.	S.M.
"	2nd		106th Field Ambulance reached and we handed over at 6 P.M. Hangover use 1 Officer + 93 O.R. to Green Ambulance. Lt. Eghurt reports his arrival from Temporary duty.	M
TLEL LES HAMEAU	3rd		Marched out at 9:15 A.M. reached ITEL-LES-HAMEAU at 10:45 A.M. Capt. Brennan admitted to 106th Field Ambulance Sick. St. McCaughey proceeded on Temporary duty with 1st Lincolns. St. Moore, 2 Sgt + 15 O/R went to VI Corps School of Instruction. Admits 4 Sick. Evacuates 1 to 37 C.C.S.	
"	4th		Sick 1 case (scabies) to 106th F.A. + 2 cases to D.R.S. (64th F.A)	S.M.
"	5th		Remains in billets. Admits to FA 13 sick. Sent 8 to DRS + evacuates 1 to 37 C.C.S.	S.M.

Army Form C. 2118.

WAR DIARY
or
INTELLIGENCE SUMMARY.
(Erase heading not required.)

Instructions regarding War Diaries and Intelligence Summaries are contained in F. S. Regs., Part II. and the Staff Manual respectively. Title pages will be prepared in manuscript.

Place	Date	Hour	Summary of Events and Information	Remarks and references to Appendices
MELLES-HANEAU	Sept 6th		Units 12, Sect 116 DRS (64 FA) + 2 & 106th FA. Remained in billets	E.P.K.
"	7th		Remained in billets. Aeroplane 96 lies Amber Capt Greig + Pte Greater attended. Court-martial at 64 Yorks.	E.P.K.
"	8th		Remained in billets. Capt Raine reported arrived from attached duty.	F.P.K.
"	9th		Medical boards held on P.B. men of 64th Bn. Lieut nett Capt Greig, Lt. Fowler + Lt Bircham to P'ville and "A" sect. Entrained at TINQUES. Train left at 5:30 PM.	E.P.R.
On route	10th		Reached ABBEVILLE about midnight + remained in train. Train left at 8:30 PM	E.P.K.
BECORDEL	11th		Detrained at HEILLY at 11:30 A.M. + proceeded to BECORDEL	P.P.X.
"	12th		Took over Main Dressing Station XV Corps at midday from 2nd, 3rd Field Ambulance. We have attached one sub-division of 2nd New Zealand, 2nd + 3rd N.Z. F° Amb., 138th F.A. 140th F.A. 42nd F.A. 44th F.A. 1/3 West Lancashire F.A. 2/1st Wessex F.A.	E.P.K.

WAR DIARY
or
INTELLIGENCE SUMMARY.

(Erase heading not required.)

Army Form C. 2118.

Place	Date	Hour	Summary of Events and Information	Remarks and references to Appendices
BECORDEL	Aug 13th		Remainder of Ambulance reached in at 10 P.M.	F.M.
"	14th		Evacuated the casualties.	M.
"	15th		Large number of casualty evacuated. D.M.S. VII Army inspected Dressing Station. General our Capt (Surg of OC) XV Corps inspected. D.M.S VII Army here Director General who inspected CCS receiption of wounded. CCS was closed. Large number of casualties evacuated. 10:30 P.M.	P.M. E.M.
"	16			E.M.
"	17th		Sent 2 Bearer Sub division to 21st Div. Coll. Sta. Point also 3 horse ambulances. Evacuated a large number of wounded. CCS was closed. In consequence of closing of 10th CCS perception of cases was slowed collected. C.C.S.	M.
"	18th		Evacuated less casualties. DADMS XV Corps inspected Dressing Station	E.M.
"	19th		Less casualties. Sent 2 O stretcher bearers to relieve men at 64th F.A.	B.M.
"	20th		New casualties. Nothing of importance. Brick drying room protected as weather very wet.	B.M.
"	21st		Capt Raine proceeded to 1 East York Regt to replace Capt J.B. Winfield (T.C.) who came to this unit for duty. One tent sub division of ambulance SB 14th Division rejoined their unit. Evacuated some casualties	

Army Form C. 2118.

WAR DIARY
or
INTELLIGENCE SUMMARY.
(Erase heading not required.)

Instructions regarding War Diaries and Intelligence Summaries are contained in F. S. Regs., Part II. and the Staff Manual respectively. Title pages will be prepared in manuscript.

Place	Date	Hour	Summary of Events and Information	Remarks and references to Appendices
BECORDEL	Sept 22		Evacuates Casualties	M.K. W.K.
"	23rd		Surg-Genl Sir A. Bowlby inspects Dressing Station. Genl Lord Woodroffe (G.H.Q.) visited Dressing Station	
"	24th		Evacuates Casualties. Surgical specialists of 36 & 38 C.C.S. came to see work of Dressing Station. Sent Capt Greig, S/S Foulkes T. Moore with 3 O.R. & 64 F.A. (Advanced) Dressing Station) under orders from A.D.M.S. 21st Div Evacuates Casualties. Capt Mather of this unit to C.C.S.	P.J.K.
"	25		Surg-Genl Macpherson visits Main Dressing Evacuates Main Casualties Station.	E.J.K. E.J.K.
"	26		Evacuates many Casualties. Capt. Young, Hardy & Taylor being temporary out of Dressing Station	
"	27th		Evacuates Casualties. D.M.S. IV Army inspects Dressing Station Aeroplane toppled us about 11 P.M. throwing three bombs that fell in the camp. Two horses only slightly wounded.	E.J.K.
"	28th		Evacuates Casualties. A.D.M.S. 41st Div came to see our Dressing Station.	P.J.K.

2353 Wt. W2544/1454 700,000 5/15 D. D. & L. A.D.S.S./Forms/C. 2118.

Army Form C. 2118.

WAR DIARY
or
INTELLIGENCE SUMMARY.
(Erase heading not required.)

Instructions regarding War Diaries and Intelligence Summaries are contained in F. S. Regs., Part II. and the Staff Manual respectively. Title pages will be prepared in manuscript.

Place	Date	Hour	Summary of Events and Information	Remarks and references to Appendices
BECORDEL	Sept 29th		Under orders from D.D.M.S XV Corps the transport attached here of 2/1 Wessex F.A & 1/13# West Lancs F.A. marched to RIBEMONT to report to DC. 2/1 W. Lancs F.A.	Appx
"	30th		Lieut W.M. Perry(?) reports for duty with this ambulance and is taken on the strength. Sent return in of 38# F.A marched in at 1.45PM & that of 2/1 Wessex F.A. marched out immediately that of 36 F.A at 2.10 PM & 1/3 W. Lancs marched out. Evacuated casualties	EYK

E. Y. Kavanagh
Capt. in charge
of 63 Field Amb

140/171

21st Div.

63rd Field Ambulance

Oct. 1916

COMMITTEE FOR THE
MEDICAL HISTORY OF THE WAR
Date -9 DEC. 1916

Army Form C. 2118.

MEDICAL

WAR DIARY
or
INTELLIGENCE SUMMARY.
(Erase heading not required.)

Place	Date	Hour	Summary of Events and Information	Remarks and references to Appendices
BÉCORDEL	Oct 1/1916		Tent Subdivision of 37th Field Ambulance arrives for duty at Main Dressing Station at 10 AM. A/Colonel A. Graham RAMC returns to their unit. (27 M.A.C.)	E.P.K.
	2nd		Capts Young & Hanby also return to their unit. 37 Field Ambulance moved in to take over Main Dressing Station in afternoon. 3 Officers & personnel attached to 64th F.A. returned to Day. Several casualties.	E.P.K.
	3rd		Transport under Capt. Brennan moved to BUIRE to join transport of 110th B.de en route for new area. Evacuated casualties. Handed over Capts. Main Dressing Station to 37th Field Ambulance at 6. P.M.	E.P.K.
	4th		Personnel left by motor lorries at 7 A.M. to entrain at MÉRICOURT station. Entrained at 2 P.M. & detrained at LONGPRÉ at 5.45 P.M. & marched to BOUCHON.	E.P.K.
BOUCHON	5th		Evacuated St. Egbert & New Zealand Stationary Hospital, AMIENS. Remained in billets. Submitted list of names for honours & despatches.	E.P.K.

Army Form C. 2118.

WAR DIARY
or
INTELLIGENCE SUMMARY.
(Erase heading not required.)

Instructions regarding War Diaries and Intelligence Summaries are contained in F. S. Regs., Part II. and the Staff Manual respectively. Title pages will be prepared in manuscript.

Place	Date October	Hour	Summary of Events and Information	Remarks and references to Appendices
BOUCHON	6th		Remained in billets	E.J.K.
"	7th		Remained in billets	E.J.K.
"	8th		Left BOUCHON at 6AM marched to LONGPRÉ where we entrained. Train left at 1:55 PM. Detrained at FOUQUEREUIL at 10PM & marched to LABEUVRIERE	E.J.K.
LABEUVRIERE 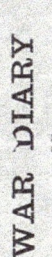	9th		Arrived at 1 A.M. Remained in billets. Visited M. Bressy 8r 9 26 Fues Ambulance at ECOLE JULES FERRY BETHUNE which they wish to take over.	E.J.K.
"	10th		Remained in billets.	E.J.K.
BETHUNE	11th		Marched off at 7:30 AM and reached ECOLE-JULES FERRY BETHUNE at 9:10 AM. Took over Main Dressing Station from 26th Field Ambulance. Capt. Greig & 16 OR marched to AUCHEL to take over Corps Scabies Station. Lent one motor ambulance & one motor cycle & from 90th FA. Lt. McCaughey & 13 OR marched to Mairie AUCHEL for duty three St. further reported for duty & A.D.M.S. 40th Division.	E.J.K.

WAR DIARY
or
INTELLIGENCE SUMMARY.

Army Form C. 2118.

(Erase heading not required.)

Place	Date	Hour	Summary of Events and Information	Remarks and references to Appendices
BETHUNE	October 11th		Took over 7 Motor Ambulances, 2 motor cycles & 1 G.O.R. & S.C. (M.T.) from 26th Field Ambce	J.J.K.
	12th		Visited A.D.S. & 91st Field Ambulance at CARRIN preparatory to taking it over. Sent 9 O.R. to C.R.S. & 2 Officers & 10 O.R. to No 1. C.C.S. & 4 O.R. to Corps Scabies Stn.	E.J.K.
"	13th		Admitted 17 O.R. Sent 4 O.R. to Aleut C.R.S. 7 O.R. to B Sect C.R.S. & 5 O.R. to C.C.S. (West Riding) Evacuates 5 O.R. to C.C.S. (West Riding) Capt Brennan & 25 O.R. proceeded to A.D.S. CARRIN & are working (6 Dressing Station before taking over)	J.J.K.
"	14th		Two N.C.O & 2 men proceeded to REUVRY to take over hutting/huts when 91st Field Ambulance proceeds out. Admits 3 Officers & 40 O.R. Sent 3 Officers to C.R.S. & evacuates 1 O.R. to 1. C.C.S. exchanges 1 Officer & 4 O.R. Proceeds 1 O.R. & 1 C.C.S. Visited A.D.S. & trench with A.D.M.S. 21st Div.	E.J.K.

WAR DIARY or INTELLIGENCE SUMMARY

Army Form C. 2118.

Place	Date	Hour	Summary of Events and Information	Remarks and references to Appendices
BETHUNE	Oct. 15		Admits 10 sick & 3 wounded. Sent 1 Officer to C.R.S. and evacuated 2 Officers sick, 2 O.R. sick & 7 O.R. wounded to W. Riding C.C.S. Visited AUCHEL.	E.J.R.
"	16th		Visited trenches (R.A.P.s) & A.D.S. Admits 2 Officers (1 S & 1 W) & 50 O.R. sick & wounded. Discharged 1 Officer & 4 O.R. to duty. Evacuates 2 O.R. sick, 10 O.R. wounded to 1 C.C.S. Sent 2 Officers & 1 O.R. wounded to W. Riding C.C.S. Rest Station & 12 O.R. to C.R.S.	J.J.R.
"	17th		Admits 9 O.R. sick & 20 O.R. wounded. Discharged 1 sick to duty. Evacuates 1 Officer sick & 1 wounded to W. Riding C.C.S. & 10 O.R. sick & 20 O.R. wounded to W. Riding C.C.S. 11 O.R. reinforcement arrives for the unit from base.	J.J.R.
"	18th		Visited A.D.S. Admits 1 Officer sick & 110 O.R. sick. Discharged 4 to duty. Sent 7 O.R. sick to Scottish Corps D.R. & wounded to C.R.S. & 2 O.R. to Scottish Corps D.R. Evacuates 1 sick & 7 wounded to 1 C.C.S.	E.J.R.

Army Form C. 2118.

WAR DIARY
or
INTELLIGENCE SUMMARY
(Erase heading not required.)

Instructions regarding War Diaries and Intelligence Summaries are contained in F. S. Regs., Part II. and the Staff Manual respectively. Title pages will be prepared in manuscript.

[Stamp: 63rd (WEST LANCS. T.F.) FIELD AMBCE. ROYAL ARMY MEDICAL CORPS]

Place	Date	Hour	Summary of Events and Information	Remarks and references to Appendices
BÉTHUNE	Oct 19th		D.D.M.S. I Corps inspects ambulance. Admitts Officers - on sick or wounded. O.R. 9 sick & wounded. Discharged 1 O.R. to duty. Sent 6 O.R. to C.C.S. & W. Riding C.C.S. Evact 4 O.R. to Corps Previously Officer wounded to W. Riding C.C.S. Scotch Stg.	E.J.K.
"	20th		Capt Brennan returns on A.D.L. by Lt. Penny. Admitts 1 sick & wounded. Discharged 1 Officer & duty. Sent 7 O.R. to C.R.S. Evacuates 4 O.R. sick & 2 O.R. wounded to C.C.S.	E.J.K.
"	21st		Lt. Egbert reported to command from hospital. Admitts 2 sick & 2 wounded. Discharged 5 to duty. Sent 5 sick & 2 wounded to C.R.S. Evacuates 2 O.R. to W. Riding C.C.S.T 2 O.R. sick case to 18.C.C.S.	E.J.K.
"	22nd		Admitts 1 Officer sick 9 O.R. sick & wounded. 1 O.R. & duty. Evacuates 1 O.R. sick & wounded to 33 C.C.S	E.J.K.
"	23rd		Admitts 1 Officer sick, 16 O.R. sick & 3 O.R. wounded. Sent 3 O.R. sick & 10 wounded to C.R.S. Evacuate 4 O.R. sick & wounded to W. Riding C.C.S. Visited A.D.S. & R.A.P.§.	E.J.K.

WAR DIARY
or
INTELLIGENCE SUMMARY.

Army Form C. 2118.

Place	Date	Hour	Summary of Events and Information	Remarks and references to Appendices
BETHUNE	October 24		Admitted sick Officer 3, OR 12. Discharged to duty 3 Officers & 2 OR. Evacuated 1 Officer to 1 C.C.S. & 6 OR. Sent 1 OR to Corps Scabies Station. Visited A.D.R. & R.A.P.s	E.J.K.
"	25th		Lt. Moore sent on temporary duty with 9th Rifles. Admitted 14 OR sick & wounded. Evacuated 4 OR to C.R.S. & R.S. Evacuated to C.R.S. & 1 to W.Riding C.C.S. Sent 4 to Corps Scabies Station	E.J.K.
"	26th		Admitted OR 11. Sub 6 OR sick & 2 wounded to C.R.S. & 1 OR to 1 C.C.S. Evacuated 1 OR to Corps Scabies Station	E.J.K.
"	27th		Capt. Winfield reported from leave. Admitted 9 sick & 1 wounded. Sent 5 to C.R.S. & 2 to Corps Scabies Station. Evacuated 1 to 33 C.C.S. & 3 to W.Riding C.C.S.	E.M.
"	28th		Visited A.D.S. & R.A.P. Admitted 9 sick & 3 wounded. Discharged 2 Officers & 1 OR to duty. Sent 9 to C.R.S. Evacuated 1 C.C.S. & wounded to 38 C.C.S. Sent 1 to Corps Scabies Station	E.J.K.
"	29th		Admitted 10 sick & 1 wounded. Sent 7 cases to D.R.S. Evacuated 1 sick & 1 wounded to W.Riding C.C.S. Sent 1 to Corps Scabies Station	E.J.K.

WAR DIARY
or
INTELLIGENCE SUMMARY

Army Form C. 2118.

Place	Date	Hour	Summary of Events and Information	Remarks and references to Appendices
BETHUNE	October 30th		Capt. Brennan attended lecture on Gas at 2 1/2 Kitchener Hospl on FR&S sick wounds. 1 CCS 2 sick to Remitts 4 sick + 1 wounded. Sent 8 to transferred 1 sick to 16th FA 18 CCS. Sent 4 to Corps Scabies.	E.J.K.
"	31st		Capt. Brennan made in attached out to 7th Leicester Regt. E.J.K. admits 10 sick discharged 2 to out sick 6 to C Rest Stn Evacuated 2 to 18 CCS. 1 to W. Riding CCS. 1 to Corps Scabies Station	

E J Kavanagh
Major RAMC
O.C. 63rd F. Amb.

140/1943.

21st Div.

63rd Field Ambulance.

Nov. 1916

COMMITTEE FOR THE
MEDICAL HISTORY OF THE WAR
Date 13 MAR. 1917

WAR DIARY or INTELLIGENCE SUMMARY

Army Form C. 2118.

VOL 15 MEDICAL

Place	Date	Hour	Summary of Events and Information	Remarks and references to Appendices
BETHUNE	November 6th		Admitted 7 OR sick & 3 wounded. Sent 2 to CRS. Evacuated 1 Officer, 20 R sick, 3 OR wounded to W. Riding C.C.S. & 1 self inflicted to Special Hospt Busnes	S.M.
"	7th		Admitted 6 sick. Sent 3 to C Rest Station. Evacuated 2 to 1 C.C.S. Lieut 1 self inflicted wound to Special Hospt Busnes + 16 Corps Scabies Stn	S.K.
"	8th		Admitted 5 OR sick. Discharged 15 duty. Evacuated 1 sick to 23 CCS 1 sick to 23 C.C.S. Sent 2 to Corps Scabies Station. Sent 3 Officers & to Rest station. Pts A.D.S. + R.A.P.s	E.J.K.
"	9th		Admitted 9 sick + 1 wounded. Discharged 11 out. Sent 4 to Corps Rest Stn and 1 to Corps Scabies Stn. 1 O.R. reported from Leper and sick Capt Stevenson RAMC gave demonstration on NOVITA apparatus	J.K.
"	10th		Admitted 8 OR sick, 1 OR wounded. Sent 2 to Corps Rest Stn + 1 to Corps Scabies Stn. Evacuated 1 OR sick to 23 CCS, 4 OR sick + 2 OR wounded to W. Riding CCS. Transferred 1 OR sick to 18th F.A. Visited A D S + new RAP being made in support line	E.J.K.
"	11th		Admitted 8 OR sick. Discharged 2 bands. Evacuated 1 Officer + 3 OR + 1 CCS + 1 self inflicted wound to Special Hosp Busnes + 15 to Stationary hospital. Sent to Corps Scabies Stn	

WAR DIARY
or
INTELLIGENCE SUMMARY.
(Erase heading not required.)

Army Form C. 2118.

Place	Date	Hour	Summary of Events and Information	Remarks and references to Appendices
BETHUNE	March 12		Admitted 1 Officer sick, 10 OR sick, 7 OR wounded. Sent 3 to Corps Rest Stn	J.M.
"	13th		Admitted 1 Officer sick, 2 OR sick, 9 OR sick & 1 wounded. 1 Officer sick & 2 OR sick to 1 C.C.S. 1 Officer sick & 1 OR wounded to 33 C.C.S. Visits R.A.P. & A.D.S	E.J.K.
	14th		Admitted 1 Officer sick, 7 OR sick & 3 wounded. Accounts (self inflicted wounds) to Special Hosp., Busnes. Sent 1 Officer to Rest Station. Sent 5 OR to Corps Rest Station & 2 to Corps Scabies Stn. Evacuated 3 to W. Riding C.C.S.	E.J.K.
	15th		Attended at 1 [Noon?] A.D.M.S. with reference to circular on "Shell Shock" Admitted 1 Officer sick, 13 OR sick 14 wounded. Sent 1 Officer to Rest Stn, 5 OR to Corps Rest Stn + 1 to Corps Scabies Stn. Evacuated 4 wounded to 33 CCS, + 3 sick & 1 wounded to 1 CCS.	E.J.K.
	16th		Admitted 2 Officers sick, 10 OR sick. Sent 2 to Corps Scabies Stn, 2 to C.R.S., + 1 Officer + 7 OR to W. Riding C.C.S. & 1 Officer to Officers Rest Stn. 7 OR to to General Hosp. Corps Commander with D.D.M.S. inspected our unit.	E.J.K.

Army Form C. 2118.

WAR DIARY
or
INTELLIGENCE SUMMARY.
(Erase heading not required.)

Instructions regarding War Diaries and Intelligence Summaries are contained in F.S. Regs., Part II. and the Staff Manual respectively. Title pages will be prepared in manuscript.

Place	Date	Hour	Summary of Events and Information	Remarks and references to Appendices
BETHUNE	November 17th		Admitted 1 Officer sick, 9 OR sick & 2 wounded. Sent 1 Officer & 1 Officer sick, 2 OR & 7 MT CCS. Visited A.D.S. & R.A.P. Also 1 R.E. Dressing men prepared for R.A.P. & A.D.S. Capt Starling relieved Lt. Penney at A.D.S.	J.M.
"	18th		Admitted 1 Officer sick, OR 9 sick, 2 wounded. Discharged to duty. 1 Officer sick (eye case) to 7 General. Evacuated 1 to 33 CCS (wounded) 1 to R.A.P. Sent 1 Officer sick, 2 wounded to W. Riding CCS. Hospital, 1, 6 sick to 28 CCS. 3 sick, 2 wounded 7th Leicesters (Bethune) Capt Brennan reported his arrival from temporary duty with 7th Leicesters.	E.J.K.
"	19th		Admitted 9 OR sick, RAP 10 OR sick to C.R.S. Sent and 2 to Capt Scabin. Stretcher 2 sick & wounded to C.C.S. Ambulance Capt. R.J. HEARN (T.C) reported for duty with this Ambulance. Admitted 6 sick & wounded. Discharged 2 Lieut, Park & C.R.S. W & Capt Scabin.	S.J.
"	20th		Evacuated 2 to W. Riding C.C.S. Attended T.J.C.M. as member of Court. Sent Capt Poulman & Lt. Penney for duty Day to 65th F.A. Lt. Splush proceeded for temporary duty with 96 Bat R.F.A. Lt. McCaughey proceeded to REMINGHELST as interpreter at Court Martial.	E.J.K.

Army Form C. 2118.

WAR DIARY
or
INTELLIGENCE SUMMARY.

(Erase heading not required.)

Instructions regarding War Diaries and Intelligence Summaries are contained in F.S. Regs., Part II. and the Staff Manual respectively. Title pages will be prepared in manuscript.

Place	Date November	Hour	Summary of Events and Information	Remarks and references to Appendices
BETHUNE	21st		Admitts 1/Muir sick 2, OR sick 8, wounded 1. Discharges 2 to duty. Sent 4 to C.R.S. Evacuates 2 sick + 2 wounded to 1 C.C.S. Dundas's Officer & duty. St. Moore moves to A.D.S. to relieve Capt Starling.	E.J.K.
	22nd		Capt Starling moves to 9th K.O.Y.L.I. in relief S.M. Malseed. Admitts 2 OR sick + wounded. Sent 3 to C.R.S. + 15 to C. Sealn P.M. Evacuates 3 to 16 F.A. Evacuates 1 Officer sick + 10 sick to W. Riding C.C.S. discharged 1 to duty. Visits A.D.S. + T.R.A.P.	E.J.K.
	23rd		Admitts 13 sick + 2 wounded, sent 4 to C.R.S. + 5 Capt Sealn P.M. discharged 1 to duty.	E.J.K.
	24th		Admitts 2 Officers sick + 50 OR sick. Sent 2 OR + 5 OR P.T. to Capt Sealn P.M. Evacuates 3 sick + 2 wounded to W. Riding C.C.S. Sent 1 inco. rect. Sept. Into Detailn Hospl. PARIS. Visits A.D.S. + T.R.A.P. + with A.D.M.S. 2/2/0.	J.J.K.
	25th		Admitts 1/Muir sick + 10 OR sick. Sent 3 G.C.R.S. Transfers 2 to 16th F.A. Evacuates 2 Officers to 1 C.C.S. 1 OR to 4 Stationary Hosp. + 2 OR (Pulpsum) to 7 General Hospital.	E.J.K.

Army Form C. 2118.

WAR DIARY
or
INTELLIGENCE SUMMARY.
(Erase heading not required.)

Instructions regarding War Diaries and Intelligence Summaries are contained in F. S. Regs., Part II. and the Staff Manual respectively. Title pages will be prepared in manuscript.

Place	Date	Hour	Summary of Events and Information	Remarks and references to Appendices
BETHUNE	26		Admits 1 Officer sick, 9 OR sick, 8 Officer wounded. Sent 3 to C.R.S. & 1 Officer & Officer Patient to Rly Stn. Evacuated 40 OR W. Riding C.C.S. M to Jeanne Hope. Bethune was shelled during the day. 	E.J.K
"	27th		Admits 2 Officer sick 50 OR sick & 10 R wounded. Sent 4 sick 1 wounded to C.R.S. & 3 to Corps Scabies Stn. Evacuates 1 C.C.S. 7 General Hosp. & 3 Officer & OR to 1 C.C.S. Lt + Bn. Price reported his arrival from leave.	E.J.K
	28th		Capt HEARN proceeded to 21 D.A.C. for permanent duty in relief of Lt. ROSS. Admits 6 OR sick + 10 R wounded. Sent 2 to Corps Scabies Stn. Evacuates 1 Officer sick, OR 3 sick + 2 wounded (W. Riding C.C.S., 10 R wounded) to 33 C.C.S. 1 OR (shell shock) to 32 C.C.S. 9. 1 self inflicted wound to Special Hosp. Busnes. Advance party of 16th Field Ambulance arrived at A.D.S. CORRINS learn working of evacuation. Capt Greig 2 NCO + 4 men proceeded to BREWERY, VERMELLES to learn method of evacuation of HOHENZOLLERN sector when we take over from 65th F.A. on 30th inst.	E.J.K. R.J.K.

WAR DIARY or INTELLIGENCE SUMMARY

Army Form C. 2118.

Place	Date	Hour	Summary of Events and Information	Remarks and references to Appendices
BETHUNE	November 29th		Handed over A.D.S. CHARING + to Fies Ambulance. Admitted 3 Officers sick, 70 OR sick, to C.R.S. + 15 Corpr Scabies St. Evacuated 3 Officers + 20 OR sick to C.C.S. Discharges (convales) Officers to duty.	S.J.K.
	30th		Took over A.D.S. + Ambulance posts of HOHENZOLLERN Sector from 65th F.A. Personnel rest 1 Officer + 33 O.R. Admitted 1 Officer sick + 80 OR sick. Sent 6 to Corpr R.St. 2 to Corpr Scabies St. Discharges 1 to duty. Evacuated 1 Officer sick, 73 OR sick to W. Riding C.C.S.	E.J.K.

E. J. Karasaf.
Major, RAMC
O.C. 63rd F.A.

140/1943

21st Division

63rd Field Ambulance

Dec. 1916

COMMITTEE FOR THE
MEDICAL HISTORY OF THE WAR
Date 13 MAR.1917

Army Form C. 2118.

MEDICAL

Vol 1

21

WAR DIARY
or
INTELLIGENCE SUMMARY.
(Erase heading not required.)

Place	Date	Hour	Summary of Events and Information	Remarks and references to Appendices
BETHUNE	DECEMBER 1st		Visited A.D.S. & R.A.P.s admitted 50R sick, sent 4 to C.R.S. Evacuated 2 to 1 C.C.S. Evacuated 1 Officer & out.	EM
	2nd		Visited A.D.S. & R.A.P.s. admitted 2 Officers sick, 9 OR sick & 3 OR wounded. Sent 4 C. Seabies & 1 m. & 4 to C.R.S. Evacuated 1 sick & 3 wounded to W. Riding C.C.S.	EVK
	3rd		Admitted 12 sick & 1 wounded. Sent 1 6 Scabies to 56 C.R.S. Evacuated 1 Officer sick, 20 R sick & 1 OR wounded to 1 C.C.S.	EVK
	4th		Admitted 21 OR sick & 10 OR sick. Sent 5 to C.R.S. Evacuated 1 OR to W. Riding C.C.S.	EVK
	5th		T.B board held by A.D.M.S. at A.D.S. and also at Headquarters. Admitted 1 Officer sick & 80 R sick. Sent 8 to C.R.S. 3 to C. Seabies S. Evacuated 2 Officers & 50 R to 33 C.C.S.	EVK
	6th		Admitted 2 Officers sick, 150 R sick & wounded. Evacuated 1 Sent 10 to C.R.S. & 3 to Corps Seabies S. Evacuated 2 sick & 17 wounded to 1 C.C.S. Visited A.D.S. & Ambulance pant.	EM
	7th		A.D.M.S. 2nd Div. inspected unit. Capt Ramsay reported from leave. St. Ramsay relieved Capt Greig (Att'd T.J.) who has been on leave on completion of 2 years service.	EM

Army Form C. 2118.

WAR DIARY
or
INTELLIGENCE SUMMARY.
(Erase heading not required.)

Place	Date	Hour	Summary of Events and Information	Remarks and references to Appendices
BETHUNE	DECEMBER 7th (cont)		Lt Moore proceeded to 96th Bde R.F.A. in relief of Capt. Gill reported sick. Admitted 2 Officers sick, 20 OR sick + 3 OR wounded. Evacuated 3 OR wounded to W. Riding C.C.S. + 2 sick to 33 C.C.S. Sent 1 Officer to Rest Stn + 6 OR to C.R.S.	E.J.K.
"	8th		Admitted OR 15 sick + 2 wounded. Evacuated 2 Officers sick, OR 3 sick + 1 wounded to 33 C.C.S. Sent 10 to C.R.S. + 1 to C. Leaties Stn.	E.J.K.
"	9th		Admitted OR 7 sick, 8 wounded. Sent 5 to A. ech- C.R.S. + 115 Bec- C.R.S. + E.R.S. + 115 Bec- C.R.S. + evacuated 1 wounded 2 sick to Corp Sealni Stn Stockings 3 tents, wounded 1 wounded to W. Riding C.C.S. + 2 to 4 Stat Hospl 1 C.C.S. + 1 wounded to W. Riding C.C.S. reported for duty with the unit Capt W. Miller (T.C.)	E.J.K.
"	10th		Admitted 1 Officer sick + 1 OR sick, evacuated 1 OR to W. Riding C.C.S. Sent 7 to Corp Rest Stn + 2 to C. Leaties Stn Visited A.D.S. T.R. A.P.s.	E.J.K.
"	11th		Admitted 3 OR sick. Sent 6 sick + 1 wounded to C.R.S. + evacuated to 33 C.C.S.	E.J.K.
"	12th		Admitted 1 Officer sick, OR 10 sick, 2 wounded. Discharged 1 Conf sent 1 Officer sick, 10 OR wounded, 1 Conf sent to C.R.S. Evacuated 1 Officer sick, 10 OR wounded to 1 C.C.S.	E.J.K.

WAR DIARY
or
INTELLIGENCE SUMMARY.

Army Form C. 2118.

Place	Date	Hour	Summary of Events and Information	Remarks and references to Appendices
BETHUNE	December 13th		Admitted 3 Officers sick + OR 3 sick. Evacuated 2 to W. Riding C.C.S. + 1 to 32 C.C.S. Sent 7 to C.R.S. + 1 to C. Seabies.  Capt Brennan went for temporary duty with 6th Lancers	S.P.K.
"	14th		Admitted 3 officers sick, 17 OR sick + 2 wounded. No change 1 officer + 17 OR to out. Sent 4 to C.R.S. + evacuated 1 officer sick, 3 OR sick to 2 wounded) to 33 C.C.S. Visited A.D.S. Y R.A.P.s with 96th Bde R.F.A. A. Moore reported from temporary duty with 13th Northumberland Fusiliers	S.P.K. E.J.K.
"	15th		Capt Miller went for temporary outpost duty (relief of Capt McKenzie) Admitted 1 officer (Lieut Stafford) OR 11 sick + 1 wounded. Sent 8 to C.R.S. + 1 to C. Seabies. Evacuated 2 sick + 1 wounded to 1 C.C.S. D.A.D.S. + 1 Corps inspected field ambulance	E.J.K.
"	16th		Admitted 1 officer sick, 16 OR sick. Discharged 2 Genl. Lak 1 to C. Seabies Sent 7 to C.R.S. + 1 officer to Rest Pm. Evacuated 2 to A.D.S. + 4 Stationary Hospt.	P.J.K.
"	17th		Mn Train inspector transport of this unit O.C. 2/1st Durham Train inspected. Sentry duty 2 to C. Seabies. Admitted 3 officers sick, 7 OR sick, discharged 1 sentry, sick to 33 C.C.S. Sent + 8 to C.R.S. Evacuated 10 officers + 3 OR to 33 C.C.S.	P.J.K.

Army Form C. 2118.

WAR DIARY
or
INTELLIGENCE SUMMARY.
(Erase heading not required.)

Place	Date	Hour	Summary of Events and Information	Remarks and references to Appendices
BETHUNE	December 18th		Corps Commander inspected the Field Ambulance & A.D.S. admitted 100 OR sick & wounded. Evacuated 1 to CCS. wounds 1 to 1 CCS & 33 C.C.S.	E.J.K.
"	19th		65th F.A. took over A.D.S. & Field Ambulance posts in trenches. Admitted 3 Officers sick, 9 OR sick, discharged 1 OR to duty, sent sick/officer to Officers Rest Stn, 1 to C. Labris Stn, 7 to C.R.S. Evacuated 2 Officers sick, 3 OR sick to M. Roig C.C.S.	E.J.K.
	20th		Lt Penny, 2 & OR proceeded to MINNIE AUCHEL to take over from 18th Field Ambulance.	E.J.K.
			Admitted 2 sick Officers, 17 OR sick. Sent 1 Officer to Officers R. Stn, 1 to Corps Lectr. Stn, 4 to C.R.S. Evacuated 2 to 23 C.C.S.	E.J.K.
			A.D.M.S. Division came to see hospital & billets.	
	21st		Admitted 1 Officer sick, 11 OR sick, sent 1 sick /nurses/ to C.R.S. Evacuated 1 Officer sick & 2 OR sick to 23 C.C.S.	E.J.K.
	22nd		Admitted 1 Officer sick, 7 OR sick, sent 2 Officers & 1 OR sick to Stn, 2 OR to C.R.S. Evacuated 1 to W.Riding C.C.S & 1 to 23 C.C.S.	E.J.K.
			Capt Greig reported from leave.	

WAR DIARY
or
INTELLIGENCE SUMMARY.

Army Form C. 2118.

(Erase heading not required.)

Place	Date	Hour	Summary of Events and Information	Remarks and references to Appendices
BETHUNE	DECEMBER 23rd		admitted 11 OR sick. Evacuated 4 to 23 CCS. Sent 4 to CRS & 2 to C Scabies Stn. Discharged 1 to Duty. Iron was intermittently bombarded.	E.J.K.
	24th		admitted 6 OR sick. Sent 1 Officer & Rest Station & 3 to C Scabies Stn. Evacuated 5 to 23 C.C.S.	E.J.K.
	25th		admitted 1 Officer sick & 3 OR sick. Evacuated 1 to W. Riding CCS & Sent 5 C.R.S. Discharged 1 to Duty.	E.J.K.
	26th		admitted 2 sick. Sent 1 Y.M.C.A worker & Officer Rest Station. Evacuated 1 Officer & 23 C.C.S. sent 1 to C. Scabies Stn. Advance party of 18th Field Ambulance arrives - We handed over 1 Officer & 1 OR & the F. Amb. & then all P.M.	E.J.K.
AUCHEL	27th	12 noon	Marched out at 8 A.M. & reached Mairie AUCHEL at 12 noon. Capt. Brennan reported from temporary duty with 6th Leicesters. Lt. McCaughey proceeds on temporary duty with 10th K.O.Y.L.I. admitted 4 Sick, Discharged 1 & evacuated 2 to C. Scabies.	E.J.K.

2353. Wt. W2544/1454 700,000 5/15 D, D & L. A.D.S.S/Forms/C. 2118.

Army Form C. 2118.

WAR DIARY
or
INTELLIGENCE SUMMARY.
(Erase heading not required.)

Instructions regarding War Diaries and Intelligence Summaries are contained in F. S. Regs., Part II. and the Staff Manual respectively. Title pages will be prepared in manuscript.

Place	Date	Hour	Summary of Events and Information	Remarks and references to Appendices
AUCHEL	DECEMBER 28th		Admitted 7 O.R. sick. Sent 5 to C.R.S. & 2 to C. Seubris Jn. Evacuated 2 to 23 C.C.S.	E.J.K.
"	29th		Sent 1 motor ambulance, 2 lorries + 1 touring car to 1st Corps Cavalry & Cyclists Detachment at THEROUANNE. Admitted 11 sick. Evacuated 5 to 23 C.C.S. Landrup. 1 sergt. Sent 2 to C.R.S. & 3 to C. Seubris Jn. Motor ambulance was returned from THEROUANNE — overnight was retained.	E.J.K.
"	30th		Admitted 4 sick. Sent 2 to C.R.S. 1 to C. Seubris Jn. + evacuated 1 to 23 C.C.S.	E.J.K.
"	31st		Admitted 7, sent 3 to C.R.S.	E.J.K.

E. J. Kavanah
Major R.A.M.C.
O.C. 63rd Field Ambulance

140/1943

21st Div.

63rd Field Ambulance

Jan 1917

COMMITTEE FOR THE
MEDICAL HISTORY OF THE WAR
Date 13 MAR. 1917

MEDICAL

Army Form C. 2118.

Vol 17

WAR DIARY
or
INTELLIGENCE SUMMARY.
(Erase heading not required.)

Instructions regarding War Diaries and Intelligence Summaries are contained in F.S. Regs., Part II. and the Staff Manual respectively. Title pages will be prepared in manuscript.

Place	Date	Hour	Summary of Events and Information	Remarks and references to Appendices
AUCHEL	JANUARY 1st		admitted 5 sick. Evacuated 2 to 23 C.C.S. Sent 6 to C.R.S. 7 & 15 C. Scabies Pt.	EJK
"	2nd		admitted 4 sick, sent 4 to C.R.S. & 1 & C Scabies Pt. DDMS I Corps visited Field Ambulance as DDMS Canadian Corps	EJK
"	3rd		admitted 10 Sick. Evacuated 1 to 23 CCS. Sent 3 to C.R.S. & 1 to C. Scabies. 1 French Civilian to BETHUNE HOSPITAL. Corps Commander visited unit. A.C.B.C. Anderson (S.R) reported for duty	EJK
"	4th		admitted 6 O.R. Evacuated 2 to 23 CCS & sent 5 to C.R.S.	EJK
"	5th			M.
"	6th		admitted 8 O.R. Evacuated 2 to 23 CCS sent 4 to C.R.S. & 1 to C.S.	
"			admitted 6 O.R. Evacuated 1 to 23 CCS. Sent 4 to C.R.S. & 1 to C.S. Scabies Ptn discharged 2 to duty. Lt Col C.B.C. Anderson (S.R) reported for duty with the unit	EJK
"	7th		admitted 5 O.R. Evacuated 3 to C.C.S. (No 23) sent 3 to C.R.S. & 1 & C. Scabies S.	EJK
"	8th		admitted 2 O.R. transferred to C.R.S. 2.O.R. Major Kenway & promoto on leave	ring
"	9th		admitted 8 O.R. Evacuated to CCS 10R transferred to CRS 3.O.R. & transferred 1 O.R to Corps Scabies Area & Staff.	Keng

WAR DIARY
or
INTELLIGENCE SUMMARY.
(Erase heading not required.)

Army Form C. 2118.

Place	Date	Hour	Summary of Events and Information	Remarks and references to Appendices
AUCHEL	JANUARY 10th		Admitted 13 O.R. Evacuated to C.C.S. 10 R. Transferred to C.R.S. S.O.R. Transferred to C.S.H. 1 O.R.	Nil
	11th		Admitted 6 O.R. Evacuated 1 Sick to CCS. Transferred 8 sick to CRS & 1 to CSH. ADMS at 11.30am Lt Col Caughey. Inspection of unit in full marching order. Reported from 10 KOYLI and Inspected on 14 days leave.	Nil
	12th		Admitted 6 O.R. Sick. Evacuated 1 O.R. sick Transferred to CRS & O.R. & to C.S.H. 1 O.R. Medical Board held at 10.30 am on 2/Lt R.G. Chadwell. D.A.D.M.S. acted as President. D.D.M.S. visited Hospital premises.	Nil
	13th		Admitted 11 O.R. Evacuated 5 O.R. sick to CCS & transferred 3 O.R. to CRS & 2 OR. to C.S.H. Discharged 1 O.R. to duty	Nil
	14th		Admitted 4 O.R. sick. Transferred to C.R.S. S.O.R. sick. Visited Bath at Raimbert. Capt. J.J. Shepherd R.A.M.C. reported for duty from No 3 Stat'y Hosp'l Rouen. Surgeon E.J. Knerupt Sug. 3 Mrs Lt Col whilst in Annual F. Amb form 22 Aug 1916.	Nil
	15th		Admitted 5 O.R. sick Transferred 4 O.R. to CRS Transferred 2 O.R. A.C.S.H. ADMS visited Hosp'l premises together with Portuguese medical officer. Visited Bath at AUCHEL. Capt. Penny reported from leave.	Nil
	16th		Admitted 5 O.R. sick. Evacuated to CCS 1 O.R. transferred to C.S.H. 1 O.R. Capt. Miller R.A.M.C. Proceeded to No 3 Stat'y Hosp. for duty in relief of Capt Shepherd. Capt Penny R.A.M.C. left for permanent duty as M.O. 10 KOYLI.	Nil

WAR DIARY
or
INTELLIGENCE SUMMARY.
(Erase heading not required.)

Army Form C. 2118.

Place	Date	Hour	Summary of Events and Information	Remarks and references to Appendices
AUCHEL	17th		admitted 9 O.R sick. Evacuated to 23 CCS 5 O.R sick. Transferred S.O.R. to CRS. Transferred 2 O.R. to C.S.H. Medical Board for P.B. men 62 m 110 & Inf Bde. 97 & 98 Field Co. R.E. RFA & 63rd 65th F.Amb. 265 O.R. Pte Standring Reed, y this unit was (a/as) P.B. Evacuation received instructions for 1902 Spelman B.A. ptn went to proceed forthwith for duty at HQ Lexington Base Authority DAG 3rd Echelon No 1999/3/C dated 11 inst. 63410 Pte McAteer ordered to join depot to town hypilleurs for duty with Vidange Apparatus.	Mh
	18th		admitted 6 O.R sick. Evacuated 3 O.R sick to No 23 CCS Transferred 2 O.R sick to CRS. & Discharged 1 O.R to duty.	Menes
	19th		admitted 8 O.R Evacuates 2 to 23 E.C.S. + Also 2 to C. Leahis S. Returned from leave.	E.J.K.
	20th		admitted 7 O.R sick. Sent 4 to CRS + St C.Leahis S. exchanges 2 R.Duty 1 to C Scabis S.	M
	21st		admitted 5 OR sick. Evacuates 1 to 23 CCS, sent 3 to CRS y to C Scabis S.	E.J.K.
	22nd		admitted 6 Officer sick, 16 O.R sick. Evacuates 1 Officer to 23 CCS + 7 OR. Sent 3 to CRS + 3 to C.Scabis. Pte. Capt Egbert went on 14 days leave to Paris. Visited 73rd Field Ambulance from whom we take over.	S.J.K.

Army Form C. 2118.

WAR DIARY
or
INTELLIGENCE SUMMARY.
(Erase heading not required.)

Instructions regarding War Diaries and Intelligence Summaries are contained in F. S. Regs., Part II. and the Staff Manual respectively. Title pages will be prepared in manuscript.

Place	Date	Hour	Summary of Events and Information	Remarks and references to Appendices
AUCHEL	Jan. 23rd		admitts 7 OR sick. Evacuated 3 & 23 CCS next 3 & C. Scales 8 pm	E.J.K.
"	24th		admitts 1 Officer sick, 1 OR. Evacuated 1 Officer to 23 CCS & 4 OR. Sent 2 to C.R.S. & discharged 1 to duty.	E.J.K.
"	25th		admitts 4 OR sent 3 to CRS M & C. Scales 8 pm discharged 1 went.	E.J.K.
"	26th		admitts 8 OR sick. Evacuated 7 to 23 CCS. Sent 4 to CRS. Sit. & discharged 1 to duty.	E.J.K.
"	27th		Admitts 5 OR & evacuated 5 OR to 23 CCS. Horse transport left for new area at 10 A.M. and marches to VIEUX BERQUIN under Capt. Brennan where it billetted for night. Personnel marched on to 4:30 PM & entrained at LILLER[?] at 8 PM. Detrained at PROVEN at mid-night and marched to billets. Motor ambulances accompanied main party. Went by road.	S.M.
PROVEN	28th		Personnel reached billets at PROGLAM DT at 4:30 AM. Horse transport arriving at 3:45 P.M. discharged 1 OR to duty.	E.J.K.

Army Form C. 2118.

WAR DIARY
or
INTELLIGENCE SUMMARY.
(Erase heading not required.)

Place	Date	Hour	Summary of Events and Information	Remarks and references to Appendices
DRAGOLAND	Jan 29th		Admitted 1 OR sick. Lt. McCaughey reported from Cowl. Capt Shepherd went to 9th Leicesters on temporary duty.	E.J.K.
"	30th		Admitted 50R. Evacuated 1 to 2nd C.C.S. Discharges to duty.	E.J.K.
"	31st		Admitted 20R. Evacuated 2 to 3 C.C.S. (Canadian)	

E.J. Kavanagh
Lt. Col. R.A.M.C.
O.C. 63rd Field Ambulance

14/6/04

21st Div.

63rd Field Ambulance.

Feb. 1917

COMMITTEE FOR THE
MEDICAL HISTORY OF THE WA..
Date 4 - APR. 1917

Army Form C. 2118.

MEDICAL

Vol 18

WAR DIARY
or
INTELLIGENCE SUMMARY.
(Erase heading not required.)

Instructions regarding War Diaries and Intelligence Summaries are contained in F. S. Regs., Part II. and the Staff Manual respectively. Title pages will be prepared in manuscript.

Place	Date	Hour	Summary of Events and Information	Remarks and references to Appendices
DROGLANDT	February 1st		Admitted 8 sick. Evacuated 4. Capt Shepherd appointed permanently to medical charge of 9th Leicesters	E.J.K.
"	2nd		Admitted 15 O.R. Evacuated 4 & 17 C.C.S. & 4 sent to cover to Northumbrian C.C.S. Sent 6 to 1st Army Rest Station	E.J.K.
"	3rd		Admitted 9 sick discharged 16 O/R evacuated 2 & 2 Canadian C.C.S.	E.J.K.
"	4th		Admitted 15 O.R. evacuated 2 & 3 Canadian C.C.S. Sent 5 to 1st Army	E.J.K.
"	5th		Nil Str. & discharged 16 O/R. Capt Greis went for temporary outpost of Leicesters Admitted 7. Sent 10 & D.R.S. discharged 1. 6 duty evacuated 2 to 10 Canadian C.C.S.	E.J.K.
"	6th		Admitted 14. Sent 6 & D.R.S. evacuated 4 & 17 Canadian C.C.S. Capt Eglen reported from leave. Lost ten out of unit owned by 110th B.o.C.	E.J.K.

WAR DIARY or INTELLIGENCE SUMMARY

Army Form C. 2118.

Place	Date	Hour	Summary of Events and Information	Remarks and references to Appendices
DROGLANDT	February 7th		Admitted 13 sick. Sent 10 to D.R.S. Evacuated 1 & 2 Canadian C.C.S.	EJK
"	8th		Admitted 13 sick, sent 14 to D.R.S. & Evacuated 1 & 3 Canadian C.C.S.	EJK
"	9th		Admitted 10. Evacuated 2 to 10 Canadian C.C.S., sent 4 to D.R.S., & 3 Scabies to Northumbrian C.C.S. Discharged 1 Scabies. St. Andrew went on leave.	EJK
"	10th		Admitted 18 sick. Evacuated 5 to 17 Canadian C.C.S., sent 4 to D.R.S. & 2 Scabies to Northumbrian C.C.S.	EJK
"	11th		Admitted 7. Evacuated 7 to 2 Canadian C.C.S. Sent 11 to D.R.S. Discharged 1 Scabies & 2 Scabies to Northumbrian C.C.S.	EJK
"			Unit marched out at 11:45 AM and billetted for the night at HAZEBROUCK.	EJK
"	12th			EJK
BETHUNE	13th		Marched out at 8:0 AM from billets and reached BETHUNE at 2:30 PM. Took over Ecole Jules Ferry as main dressing station from 18th Field Ambulance.	EJK

Army Form C. 2118.

WAR DIARY
or
INTELLIGENCE SUMMARY.
(Erase heading not required.)

Instructions regarding War Diaries and Intelligence Summaries are contained in F.S. Regs., Part II. and the Staff Manual respectively. Title pages will be prepared in manuscript.

Place	Date	Hour	Summary of Events and Information	Remarks and references to Appendices
BETHUNE	February 14th		Took over A.D.S. from 18th Field Ambulance at Cat BRIN. St Moore & 30 OR processes thus. Admitts 4 sick & 1 wounded. 2 OR transferred from 18th S.A. & 10 OR from 2/1 Wessex F.A.	E.J.K.
"	15th		Capt Greig & Brown on attend lecture at L&LE R.S on "administration arrangements made by a Division on the Somme". Sgt W.S.F. Lt Guarato medaille militaire. Wanted T.D.S. Admitto 18 sick & 4 wounded. Evacuates 2 sick & 2 wounded to no 1 C.C.S. & 1 car.R return to 4 Station Hope. Sent 8 to Corps Rest Stn & discharges 2 to Duty	E.J.K.
"	16th		Admitts 2 Officers & 13 OR sick & 2 OR wounded. Sent 11 sick & 1 wounded to C.C.S. Evacuates 1 sick & 2 wounded W. Riding C.C.S & 1 wounded to 33 C.C.S.	E.J.K.
"	17th		Admitts 1 Officer & 17 OR sick & 2 OR wounded. Sent 11 sick & 1 wounded to C.R. S. & 5 to C. Sealne S. Evacuates 2 sick & 1 wounded to 33 C.C.S. & 1 self inflicted wounded to Special H. BARNES	E.J.K.

Army Form C. 2118.

WAR DIARY
or
INTELLIGENCE SUMMARY.
(Erase heading not required.)

Place	Date	Hour	Summary of Events and Information	Remarks and references to Appendices
BETHUNE	February 18th		Admitted 2 Officers + 9 OR sick + 1 wounded (OR) Evacuated 2 Officers to 1 C.C.S. + 2 OR sick + 1 wounded. Sent 6 to C. Leslie St. Evacuated Officers sick + 1 wounded to 33 C.C.S. Visited A.D.S. + aid posts. Lt. McCaughey proceeded to A.D.S.	EJK
"	19th		Admitted 6 sick 14 wounded. Evacuated 2 wounded to 33 CCS + 2 sick to W. Riding C.C.S. + 1 self inflicted to Special Hosp Base. Sent 3 to C. Scarbro' St + 13 sick + 1 wounded to C.R.S. St. Moore reported from A.D.S.	EJK
"	20th		Admitted 1 Officer sick + 60 OR sick + 20 R wounded. Sent 4 to C.R.S. + 1 wounded to 33 C.C.S. Sent 1 Officer + 15 OR to reinforce A.D.S. + visited A.D.S. + R.A.P's. Sent Officer + 15 OR to reinforce A.D.S. + and cancelled later order by 64th Inf. Bde. It was proposed enterprise + 64th Inf. proposed enterprise discharged to duty	EJK
"	21		Admitted 2 Officers + 10 OR sick + 7 wounded. Sent 4 to 1 C.R.S. Evacuated 1 sick + 3 wounded to 1 C.C.S. + 2 wounded to 33 C.C.S. Sent with 1 other Officer + 20 OR to reinforce A.D.S. and put in view of possible raid by us. It did not come off	EJK

WAR DIARY or INTELLIGENCE SUMMARY

Army Form C. 2118.

Place	Date	Hour	Summary of Events and Information	Remarks and references to Appendices
BETHUNE	February 22		Admitted 20 sick & 4 wounded. Sent 8 to C.C.S. & 1 to C. Sebrin S. Evacuated 5 sick & 3 wounded to 33 C.C.S.; 1 sick & 1 wounded to W. Riding C.C.S. It 2 self inflicted to Special Hosp. Burnes. Some hand & feet cases were admitted.	E.J.R.
"	23rd		Admitted 1 Y.M.C.A. (Rev. Reynolds) with measles & evacuated him to 7 General Hospital. Admitted 27 sick & 3 wounded. Several trench feet cases. Discharged 1 officer & 10 O.R. sent to C.R.S. & evacuated 4 sick & 4 wounded to 33 C.C.S. Saw Gillies reported from leave St. Anderson reported from leave.	E.J.R.
	24th		Admitted 3 officers sick; 2 O.R. sick & 2 wounded. Discharged 16 O.R. Sent 2 to C. Sebrin S. & 13 sick & 1 wounded to C.R.S. & 1 sick & 1 wounded to 1 C.C.S. 11 sick & 1 wounded to 18 C.C.S. Evacuated 1 to 33 C.C.S. 4 to 18 C.C.S. Cases of trench feet are still being admitted. Sent 2 officer to Queen Rest Station. Visited A.D.S. & R.A.P.	E.J.R.
	25th		Lieuts Anderson & Gillies went to A.D.S. & visited Lt. McCaughey. Admitted 7 sick, Evacuated 10 to W. Riding C.C.S. Sent 2 to Sebrin S. & 16 to C.R.S.	P.J.K.

2353 Wt W2344/1454 700,000 5/15 D.D.&L. A.D.S.S./Forms/C. 2118.

WAR DIARY or INTELLIGENCE SUMMARY

Army Form C. 2118.

Place	Date	Hour	Summary of Events and Information	Remarks and references to Appendices
BETHUNE	February 26th		Admitted 15 sick + 12 wounded. Sent 5 to C.R.S. 2 & C. Leave S. and 1 Officer to Officers Rest Station. Evacuated 12 to 33 C.C.S.	EJK
"	27th		Admitted 1 Officer sick, 13 O.R. sick 14 wounded. Sent 5 C.R.S, 15 to C. Leaves Sp. ten days. 1 B.off. sent Officer to Officers Rest Stn. Evacuated 4 sick 14 wounded to 1 C.C.S. 14 Officer sick + 30 R wounded to 33 C.C.S.	EJK
"	28th		A.D.M.S. Lees P.B. board on A.D.S. Visited aid posts. Admitted 11 sick, 2 wounded. Sent to C.R.S 1 & 3 & C. Leave S. 1 Officer to W. Riding C.C.S. Evacuated 1 sick + 2 wounded	EJK

E. J. Kavanagh
Lt. Col. R.A.M.C.
O.C. 63rd Field Amb

140/2042

21st Div.

63rd Field Ambulance.

COMMITTEE FOR THE
MEDICAL HISTORY OF THE WAR
Date 11 MAY 1917

Army Form C. 2118.

MEDICAL

Vol 19

WAR DIARY
or
INTELLIGENCE SUMMARY.
(Erase heading not required.)

Place	Date	Hour	Summary of Events and Information	Remarks and references to Appendices
BETHUNE	March 1st		admits 1 Officer sick, 15 OR sick & 2 OR wounded. Sent to C.R.S. 3 & (Serious S. enlarged) 1 Lieut. wounded, 1/Officer to 1 C.C.S. & 3 OR sick & 2 wounded to 33 C.C.S.	E.J.K.
"	2nd		admits 1 Officer sick, 23 OR sick and 1 OR wounded. Sent to C.R.S. & 3 to Corps Section, 1 Officer sick, 11 OR sick & 1 wounded to 1 C.C.S. Ampt admission with six (6) cases of trench foot	S.J.K.
	3rd		Capt McCurphy & Moore went to lecture, marched to ROBECQ and took over billets & 16th Field Amb. admits 20 OR sick, sent 15 to C.R.S. Discharged 1 to duty & evacuates 1 to 18 C.C.S. 50th Field Ambulance billetted for night with us.	S.J.K.
"	4th		admits 2 Officers sick, 30 OR sick (2 trench feet) 4 OR wounded. Sent 8 to C.R.S. 5 to C. Section S. discharged 2 to duty. Evacuates 6 sick, 17 wounded to 33 C.C.S. & 2 (one measles & one (? diphtheria) to 7 General Hospl. Visited "C" Sect at ROBECQ.	E.J.K.

Army Form C. 2118.

WAR DIARY
or
INTELLIGENCE SUMMARY.
(Erase heading not required.)

Instructions regarding War Diaries and Intelligence Summaries are contained in F. S. Regs., Part II. and the Staff Manual respectively. Title pages will be prepared in manuscript.

Place	Date	Hour	Summary of Events and Information	Remarks and references to Appendices
BETHUNE	March 5th		Handed over A.D.S. CAMBRIN to 13th Field Ambulance, also aid posts in trenches. Discharged 1 Officer & 8 sergeant admitted 6 sick & 5 wounded. Sent 20 sick & 5 wounded to C.R.S. 1 Officer & Rest Station. 1 Officer & 8 sick, 2 O.R. sick prior to evacuation. L 4 to C. Scales Str. evacuated to 33 C.C.S. wounded to 1 C.C.S. 1 O.R. wounded to ECOLE JULES FERRY.	E.J.K.
ROBECQ	6th		Handed over Main Dressing Station at 10:15 A.M. to 18th Field Ambulance. Unit marched out at 1 P.M. reached ROBECQ at 4 P.M. Sent 2 to C. Scales Str. & evacuated 7 to W. Riding C.C.S. admitted 9 sick. Sent 2 to C. Scales Str. & evacuated 7 to W. Riding C.C.S. & 1 to C. Scales S.	E.J.K.
"	7th		admitted 17 O.R. sick. Sent 7 to C.R.S. & 7 to C. Scales S. evacuated 4 to W. Riding C.C.S.	E.J.K.
"	8th		admitted 22 sick. Sent 23 to C.R.S. 1 to C. Scales S. & evacuates 6 to W. Riding C.C.S.	E.J.K.
ST. HILAIRE	9th		Unit marched out from billets at 2:45 P.M. and reached ST HILAIRE per at 6 P.M. 1 to C. Scales S. Discharged 1 transft and admitted 18 O.R. sent 8 to C.R.S. 1 to C. Scales S. Discharged 1 transft and evacuated 2 to W. Riding C.C.S.	E.J.K.

WAR DIARY or INTELLIGENCE SUMMARY

Army Form C. 2118.

(Erase heading not required.)

Place	Date	Hour	Summary of Events and Information	Remarks and references to Appendices
ST. HILAIRE	March 10th		Admitted 1 Officer + 8 O.R. Evacuates 1 Officer + 3 O.R. to W. Riding C.C.S. Transfers 14 to 4th Stat: & Discharged 2 to duty	E.J.K.
PERNES	11th		Marched out at 1:15 P.M. and rec'd PERNES at 4:30 P.M. Admits 33 O.R. Discharged 1 to duty. Evacuates 6 to W. Riding C.C.S. + 4 to 23 C.C.S. O.R. & Composite Co. reported to march with unit.	E.J.K.
HONVAL	12th		Marched out at 10:15 A.M. + rec'd HONVAL at 6:10 P.M. Admits 5 to 23 C.C.S. Evacuates 5 to 23 C.C.S. Sent 20 to T. Corps Rest St. 37 Sick.	E.J.K.
BREVILLERS	13th		Marched out at 3:0 P.M. + reached BREVILLERS at 5:15 P.M. Transport marched by different route + arrived at 6:45 P.M. Took over hospital at LE SOUICH. Admits 12 O.R. Evacuates 9 to 43 C.C.S.	E.J.K.
"	14th		Composite Co. left to report to 940 Bn. Admits 11 O.R. Evacuates 6 to 20 C.C.S. + 1 case of German measles to 12 Stationary Hosp'l.	E.J.K.
"	15th		One French Civilian (diphtheria) evacuated to Civil Hosp. ST. POL. Capt J.P. O'Connor (T.C.) reported for duty from 25th Amb.Tr.s to replace Capt. Egbert who is to report to A.D.M.S. Ambulance Trains (H.Q. L. of C.) for duty.	E.J.K.

WAR DIARY
or
INTELLIGENCE SUMMARY.
(Erase heading not required.)

Army Form C. 2118.

Place	Date	Hour	Summary of Events and Information	Remarks and references to Appendices
BREUILERS	March 15th		admits 5 O.R. Discharged 23 & Duty & evacuated 3 to 43 C.C.S.	E.J.K.
"	16th		Capt Egbert reports his departure and is struck off the strength of the unit. Admits 1 Officer (measles) also one evacuated to 12 Stationary Hospl. admits 10 O.R. Discharged 1 to Duty & evacuated 7 to 20 C.C.S.	E.J.K.
"	17th		admits 2 Officers & 16 O.R. Evacuates 2 Officers & 3 O.R. & 43 C.C.S. Evacuates 1 case Diphtheria (?) to 12 Stationary Hospl (On bacteriological examination case was not diphtheria.) Discharged 3 to Duty.	E.J.K.
"	18th		admits 10 O.R. Discharged 5 to Duty & evacuated 3 to 20 C.C.S. Details motor ambulance to follow 1st E. Yorks Regt on march	E.J.K.
"	19th		admits 9 O.R. Discharged 1 to duty, evacuated 1 to 12 Stationary Hospl (German measles) + 2 to 43 C.C.S.	E.J.K.
"	20th		admits 6 O.R. Discharged 5 to Duty & evacuated 5 to 20 C.C.S. 2 (1 German measles + measles) to	E.J.K.
"	21st		admits 14 O.R. Evacuates 1 to 43 C.C.S. 2 (1 German measles + measles) to 12 Stationary Hospl + discharged 2 to duty	E.J.K.

Army Form C. 2118.

WAR DIARY
or
INTELLIGENCE SUMMARY.
(Erase heading not required.)

Instructions regarding War Diaries and Intelligence Summaries are contained in F. S. Regs., Part II. and the Staff Manual respectively. Title pages will be prepared in manuscript.

Place	Date	Hour	Summary of Events and Information	Remarks and references to Appendices
BAENILLERS	March 22		Admitted 15 OR. Discharged 6 OR's. Evacuated 6 & 20 C.C.S. + 2 & 12 Stationary Hosp. (one invalid, one german invalid.)	E.P.K
GRENAS	23rd		Marched over to billets at 10 AM + reached GRENAS at 3:30 PM. Admitted 18 B.R. Discharged 1 Buts, evacuated 2 & 43 C.C.S.	E.P.K
GRENAS	24th		Admitted 1 Officer + 7 OR Discharged 17 Buts, evacuated 1 Officer 46 OR to 20 C.C.S.	E.P.K
"	25th		Admitted 16 OR Evacuated 5 to 43 C.C.S.	E.P.K
"	26th		Admitted 10 OR. Evacuated 8 to 20 C.C.S. transferred 1 to 2/2 Home Counties F.A. Discharged 8 Buts.	E.P.K
"	27th		Capt Moore, Lt. Anderson + 20 OR proceeded as advance party to take over from 65th FA at LA CAUCHIE. Admitted 12 OR Discharged 7 Buts. Evacuated 13 & 32 CCS	E.M
LA CAUCHIE	28th		Marched out at 9:30 AM + reached LACAUCHIE at 1:0 PM Admitted 3. Evacuated 1 to 6 Stationary Hosp. Discharged 1 Buts. We took over Field Ambulance billets and hospital from 65th Field Ambulance who transferred 31 cases to us	E.M

2353 Wt. W2514/1454 700,000 5/15 D. D. & L. A.D.S.S./Forms/C. 2118.

WAR DIARY
INTELLIGENCE SUMMARY

Army Form C. 2118.

Place	Date	Hour	Summary of Events and Information	Remarks and references to Appendices
LA CAUCHIE	March 29th		Admitted 1 Officer + 23 OR. Discharged 3 to duty. Evacuated 1 Officer + 10 OR. to 23 C.C.S. + 1 car of wounded to 12 Stationary Hospital	SPR
"	30th		Admitted 12 OR. 25 OR transferred from 65th F.A. when we sent lorry + cars. 1 NCO + 5 OR to HUMBERCAMP. We got all cases out here. Discharged 13 to duty. Evacuated 3 to 32 CCS. I went round front Bearers and wrote RAPs + prepared collecting posts.	SPR
"	31st		Admitted 1 Officer + 7 OR. Evacuated 1 self inflicted to 37 CCS. 1 Officer + 20 OR to 43 CCS. Discharged 31 to duty. Capts Grey and Brennan, St Andrews and two wagons + auto-ambulances proceeded to O.C. 65th Field Ambce	SPR

E. J. Kavanagh
Lt Col RAMC
O.C. 63rd Field Ambce

140/2020

U

21st Div.

63rd (N.R.) Y.A.

COMMITTEE FOR THE
MEDICAL HISTORY OF THE WAR
Date -6 JUN. 1917

Army Form C. 2118.

MEDICAL
Vol-2

WAR DIARY
or
INTELLIGENCE SUMMARY.
(Erase heading not required.)

Place	Date	Hour	Summary of Events and Information	Remarks and references to Appendices
LA CAUCHIE	April 1st		admits 11 sick. Evacuats 6 to 20 CCS + discharges 1 to duty	E.J.K.
"	2nd		St Gilles and 9 O.R. proceeds for temporary duty to 20. C.C.S. admits 6. 19 Transferred from 65th F.A. Evacuates 5 to 32 C.C.S.	F.J.K.
"	3rd		admits 7 O.R. 200 O.R. transferred from 65th F.A. Evacuats 15 to 43 C.C.S, 1 to 37 C.C.S. + 1 to 12 Stationary Hosp. discharged 4 to duty	E.J.K.
"	4th		Transferred all our cases to 64th Field Ambulance	E.O.K.
"	5th		Unit left LA CAUCHIE at 9 A.M. + reached BOIRY ST RICTRUDE at 2:45 P.M. I went to BOYELLES to reconnoitre advanced front to form collecting post for all wounded.	89X
BOIRY ST RICTRUDE	6th		I from H'dr all bearer division to BOYELLES also Capt Moore then leaving 3 tent Sub-division and Capt McCaughey behind.	
"	7th		2 Bearer Sub-division to 65th Field Ambulance to me for duty. I was placed in command of advance bearer division and made reconnaissance of advance front	E.J.K.

2353 Wt. W2544/1454 700,000 5/15 D.D. & L. A.D.S.S./Forms/C. 2118.

WAR DIARY
or
INTELLIGENCE SUMMARY.

Army Form C. 2118.

Place	Date	Hour	Summary of Events and Information	Remarks and references to Appendices
BOIRY ST. RIETRUDE	April 8th		Lt Anderson + 1 OR clerk proceeded to 9 B Field Amb for temporary duty. Sanapier to have an advanced collecting post at T.2 D.73 composed of 1 Officer and 2 Bearer Subdivisions to collect wounded from left flank of Division (Map Ref France Sheet 51b 1-40,000) Reserve can be reinforced from BOYELLES as occasion calls. Also arranged to have an advanced collecting post at ST LEGER composed of 1 Officer + 2 Bearer Sub-Divisions (Map ref T.2.g.a.5.5) the line to be reinforced w 10 Bearers when attacks take place.	F.J.K.
	9th		Capt Menzies & Bearer Division B & 4 Field Amb were reported as out and sent with 9 such them to stuff ST LEGER advanced post. Active operations known. Wounded were collected.	F.J.K.
	10th		In view of Casualties I sent up 2 OR from tent sub-division. Evacuation.	F.J.K.
	11th		Casualties evacuated. As with sector was comparatively quiet and ready fighting was taking place in left of Division I withdrew 2 OR Bearers from ST LEGER	F.J.K.
	12th		Evacuation of Casualties proceeds smoothly. As Division had moved forward I made a relay post of Bearers between regimental and posts and advanced collecting post on left of Division. This consequently relieves work of Bearers	F.J.K.

Army Form C. 2118.

WAR DIARY
or
INTELLIGENCE SUMMARY.
(Erase heading not required.)

Instructions regarding War Diaries and Intelligence Summaries are contained in F. S. Regs., Part II. and the Staff Manual respectively. Title pages will be prepared in manuscript.

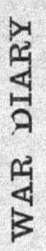

Place	Date	Hour	Summary of Events and Information	Remarks and references to Appendices
BOYELLES	April 13th		Whole unit moved up to BOYELLES. Evacuation of Casualties proceeded normally. Capt. O'Connor reported from leave for duty.	E.J.K.
	14th		Evacuation of Casualties proceeded.	E.J.K.
BASSEUX	15th		Handed over collection of wounded in left sector to 19th Field Ambulance and right sector to 101st Field Ambulance as Divisions was relieved by 33rd Divn. Unit marched out at 2:15 P.M. & reached BASSEUX at 9:30 P.M. Personnel 1/64+ 70 5th Field Ambulance (billeting unit).	E.J.K.
"	16th		Admitts 37 sick & 1 wounded. Transferred to 64th F.A. 34 sick & 1 wounded.	E.J.K.
"	17th		Admitts 26 sick. Transferred 29 to 64th F.A. One death, but respiration & pulse taken by all ranks were inspected.	E.J.K.
"	18th		Admitts 110 R. Transferred 7 to 64 F.A.	E.J.K.
"	19th		Admitts 26 Recruits 16, 12 Station Hospl, Sent 3 to VII Corps. M.D.S. Transferred 26 to 64th F.A.	E.J.K.
"	20th		Admitts 2 Officers + 80 OR sick & 1 wounded. Transferred 2 Officers + 80 R to 64 F.A. Staff-Sergeant W. Brooke awarded Military Medal.	E.J.K.

WAR DIARY
or
INTELLIGENCE SUMMARY.
(Erase heading not required.)

Army Form C. 2118.

Place	Date	Hour	Summary of Events and Information	Remarks and references to Appendices
BASSEUX	April 21st		Capt McCaughey & 10 OR proceeded for temporary duty at Corps Rest Station, GOUY. Admitted 1 Officer & 16 OR. Transferred 1 Officer & 15 OR to 64 F.A. Sent 16 recruits 1 Officer <u>& Kit Cpl</u> to D.R. <u>Kit Cpl</u> to D.R.	E.M.
"	22nd		Capt O'Connor & 20 OR proceeded for temporary duty at VII Corps M.D.S. Admitted 15 OR. Transferred 16 OR to 64 FA. Lt. F.W. Cleeve (T.C) reported to assume his duties for out-patients.  Staff of unit:	E.J.K.
"	23rd		Admitted 1 Officer & 13 OR. Sent 1 Officer to Observation Rest Station & 2 OR to Corps M.D.S. Transferred 11 OR to 64 FA.	80K
BOISLEUX AU MONT	24th		Left billets at 9 AM & reached Boisleux-au-Montal 1 PM. Admitted 18 OR & transferred them to 64 FA	59K
"	25th		Admitted 1 OR & transferred him to 64 FA. Capt Brennan & 72 OR proceeded to report to OC 65th FA for Stretcher party in trenches.	79K

Army Form C. 2118.

Instructions regarding War Diaries and Intelligence
Summaries are contained in F.S. Regs., Part II
and the Staff Manual respectively. Title pages
will be prepared in manuscript.

WAR DIARY
or
INTELLIGENCE SUMMARY.
(Erase heading not required.)

Place	Date	Hour	Summary of Events and Information	Remarks and references to Appendices
HENIN	April 26th		Marched out at 7 A.M. & reached HENIN where we took over A.D.S. from 99th F.A at 8.20 A.M. Capt O'Connor posted to relieve charge 21st D.A.C. Evacuated casualties.	F.J.K.
"	27th		Evacuated Casualties.	E.J.K
"	28th		Evacuated casualties. S/r Gillies having reported his departure report for duty to D.D.M.S ETAPLES is struck off strength from hour.	E.J.K
"	29th		D.D.M.S. VIIth Corps Inspected Dressing Station RAMC 21st Divn routine seen state that Capt. R.C. Irvine & T.H. Roberts have reported to Division and are posted to this unit. Evacuated casualties.	E.J.K
"	30th		Sgt F. King, Cpl E. Sheel & Pte F.M. Clark awarded Military Medal	

E. J. Kavanagh R.A.M.C
O.C. 63 F Ambce

B.E.F.

SUMMARY OF MEDICAL WAR DIARIES FOR 63rd F.A., 21st Divn., 7th Corps., 3rd Army

----

WESTERN FRONT April- May. '17.

O.C. Lt. Col. E.J. Kavanagh.

SUMMARISED UNDER THE FOLLOWING HEADINGS.

Phase "B" Battle of Arras- April- May. '17.

1st Period Attack on Vimy Ridge April.

2nd Period Capture of Siegfried Line May.

B.E.F.

63rd F.A. 21st Divn. 7th Corps.   WESTERN FRONT.
O.C. Lt. Col. E.J. Kavanagh.   April '17.
3rd Army.

Phase "B" Battle of Arras- April_ May. '17.
1st Period Attack on Vimy Ridge April.

1917.	Headquarters. At La Cauchie.
April- 1st.	Moves Detachment: 1 and 9 to 20th Casualty Clearing Station.
4th.	Evacuation: All cases transferred to 64th Field Ambulance.
5th.	Moves: To Boiry St Rictrude.
6th.	Medical Arrangements: Coll. P. formed at Boyelles by Br. Divn.
7th.	2 Br. S.Ds. of 65th Field Ambulance attached for collection of wounded in front line.
	O.C. placed in command of Br. Divns. of Divn. for evacuation of wounded from front line.
8th.	Adv. Coll. P. formed at T.2.d.7.3 (Sheet 51B) — personnel 1 and 2 Br. S.D.Ss. to collect wounded from L. Sector.
9th.	Adv. Coll. P. formed at St.Leger T.28.0.5.5. by Br. D. of 64th Field Ambulance.
	Operations. Active operations commenced in evening.
10th.	Operations R.A.M.C. wounded collected and evacuated.
	Medical Arrangements: 20 Brs. obtained from T.S.D. at Boiry St. Rictrude.
11th.	20 Brs. transferred from Adv. Coll. P. St. Leger to Adv. coll. Post. T.2.d.7.3. as Casualties heavy.
12th.	Casualties: Evacuation: Collection and evacuation of wounded proceeded smoothly.
13th.	Moves: To Boyelles.

B.E.F.

63rd F.A. 21st Divn. 7th Corps.   WESTERN FRONT.
O.C. Lt. Col. E.J. Kavanagh.   April. '17.
3rd Army.

Phase "B" cont.

1st Period cont.

1917.

April. 15th.	**Military Situation:** 21st Divn. relieved by 33rd Divn.
	Medical Arrangements: Collection of wounded handed over to 19th Field Ambulance on L. Sector and 101st F.A. on Right Sector.
	Brs. of 64th and 65th F.As. returned to their Headquarters.
	Moves: To Basseux- Rest Area.
20th.	**Decoration:** Staff. Sgt. Brooke W. awarded M.M.
21st.	**Moves Detachment:** 1 and 10 to C.R.S.
22nd.	1 and 20 to 7th C.M.D.S.
	Casualties Sick. 16th- 23rd 4 and 170.
24th.	**Moves:** To Boisleux-Au- Mont.
25th.	**Moves Detachment:** 1 and 72 to 65th Field Ambulance as brs. in front line.
26th.	**Moves: Medical Arrangements:** To Henin and took over A.D.S. from 99th Field Ambulance.
27th- 30th.	**Operations R.A.M.C.** Casualties evacuated.
30th.	**Decorations:-** Sgt. King F.)
	Pte. Clark F.M.) awarded M.M.
	Cpl. Sheel E.)

B.E.F.

63rd F.A. 21st Divn. 7th Corps.   WESTERN FRONT.

O.C. Lt. Col. E.J. Kavanagh.   April '17.

3rd Army.

Phase "B" Battle of Arras- April_ May. '17.
1st Period Attack on Vimy Ridge April.

1917.	Headquarters. At La Cauchie.
April- 1st.	Moves Detachment: 1 and 9 to 20th Casualty Clearing Station.
4th.	Evacuation: All cases transferred to 64th Field Ambulance.
5th.	Moves: To Boiry St. Rictrude.
6th.	Medical Arrangements: Coll. P. formed at Boyelles by Br. Divn.
7th.	2 Br. S.Ds. of 65th Field Ambulance attached for collection of wounded in front line.
	O.C. placed in command of Br. Divns. of Divn. for evacuation of wounded from front line.
8th.	Adv. Coll. P. formed at T.2.d.7.3 (Sheet 51B) personnel 1 and 2 Br. S.D.Ss. to collect wounded from L. Sector.
9th.	Adv. Coll. P. formed at St Leger T.28.0.5.5. by Br. D. of 64th Field Ambulance.
	Operations. Active operations commenced in evening.
10th.	Operations R.A.M.C. wounded collected and evacuated.
	Medical Arrangements: 20 Brs. obtained from T.S.D. at Boiry St. Rictrude.
11th.	20 Brs. transferred from Adv. Coll. P. St. Leger to Adv. coll. Post. T.2.d.7.3. as Casualties heavy.
12th.	Casualties: Evacuation: Collection and evacuation of wounded proceeded smoothly.
13th.	Moves: To Boyelles.

B.E.F.

<u>63rd F.A. 21st Divn. 7th Corps.</u>   <u>WESTERN FRONT.</u>
<u>O.C. Lt. Col. E.J. Kavanagh.</u>   <u>April. '17.</u>
<u>3rd Army.</u>

<u>Phase "B" cont.</u>
<u>1st Period cont.</u>

1917.

April. 15th.   <u>Military Situation:</u> 21st Divn. relieved by 33rd Divn.

<u>Medical Arrangements:</u> Collection of wounded handed over to 19th Field Ambulance on L. Sector and 101st F.A. on Right Sector.

Brs. of 64th and 65th F.As. returned to their Headquarters.

<u>Moves:</u> To Basseux- Rest Area.

20th.   <u>Decoration:</u> Staff. Sgt. Brooke W. awarded. M.M.

21st.   <u>Moves Detachment:</u> 1 and 10 to C.R.S.

22nd.   1 and 20 to 7th C.M.D.S.

Casualties Sick. 16th- 23rd 4 and 170.

24th.   <u>Moves:</u> To Boisleux-Au- Mont.

25th.   <u>Moves Detachment:</u> 1 and 72 to 65th Field Ambulance as brs. in front line.

26th.   <u>Moves: Medical Arrangements:</u> To Henin and took over A.D.S. from 90th Field Ambulance.

27th- 30th.   Operations R.A.M.C. Casualties evacuated.

30th.   <u>Decorations:-</u>   Sgt. King F.   )
                                     Pte. Clark F.M.) awarded M.M.
                                     Cpl. Sheel E.   )

140/2/01

21st Div.

No. 63. 7.a.

COMMITTEE FOR THE
MEDICAL HISTORY OF THE WAR
Date   10 JUL. 1917

Army Form C. 2118.

WAR DIARY
or
INTELLIGENCE SUMMARY.
(Erase heading not required.)

Place	Date	Hour	Summary of Events and Information	Remarks and references to Appendices
HENIN	May 1st		Evacuate casualties.	J.M.
"	2nd		Receive Casualties	J.M.
"	3rd		Division attacked. Casualties evacuated. O.D.M.S. III Corps on sheets	J.M. E.P.K.
"	4th		Receive Casualties	E.P.K.
"	5th		Receive Casualties	E.P.K.
"	6th		Receive Casualties	J.M.
"	7th		Evacuate.	J.M.
"	8th		Evacuate Casualties	E.P.K.
"	9th		Evacuate Casualties	J.M.
"	10th		Evacuate Casualties	
RAMPART	11th		Unit marched out at 2:15 PM (having handed over A.D.S. to 99th Field Amb) & reached RAMPART at 6 PM. Capt Brennan & 72 OR reported arrival from temporary outpost 65th Field Amb.s. One reinforcement (cook) reported from leave.	E.P.K.
"	12th		2 casualties & 2 sick.	E.P.K.

Army Form C. 2118.

WAR DIARY
or
INTELLIGENCE SUMMARY.
(Erase heading not required.)

Instructions regarding War Diaries and Intelligence Summaries are contained in F.S. Regs., Part II. and the Staff Manual respectively. Title pages will be prepared in manuscript.

Place	Date	Hour	Summary of Events and Information	Remarks and references to Appendices
RAMPART	May 13th		admitted 7 sick + 1 wounded. Sent on number to Capt M.D.S. Sea 4 to C. Rail Stn r & t Capt Deulin Stn	F.J.K.
"	14th		admitted 3 sick. Sent to VII Corps R.S. Evacuated 1 to 43 CCS	F.J.K.
"	15th		admitted 1 officer sick + 2 O.R. Evacuated 1 officer (minor) & 12 stretcher Hoshs. Sent 1 to Capt Sealin S. Capt T.H. Roberts reported his arrival for duty	F.J.K.
"	16th		admitted 5 O.R. Sent 3 to 21st Div Rest Stn Officer & 3 to 4 CCS, 8 OR & 21 D.R.S.	F.J.K.
"	17th		admitted 9 O.R. 1 officer + 8 O.R. Evacuated 1 officer to C. Sealin Hospt.	F.J.K.
"	18th		admitted 1 officer + 8 O.R. transferred 1 officer to 2 NOR.S. Sent 7 OR to 21st D.R.S. & 1 O.R. to 43 CCS.	F.J.K.
"	19th		Capt T.H. Roberts reported his departure to 33 Labour Group, ARRAS + 4 taken off strength. Capt Redding reported his arrival from 33 Labour Group. Admitted 7 OR Evacuated 7 OR to 21st D.R.S. 2 to Capt Sealin S.	F.J.K.
"	20th		admitted 11 O.R. transferred 4 O.R. to 21st D.R.S. + evacuated 1 to 43 CCS.	F.J.K.

2353 Wt. W2544/1454 700,000 5/15 D. D. & L. A.D.S.S./Forms/C. 2118.

Army Form C. 2118.

WAR DIARY
or
INTELLIGENCE SUMMARY.
(Erase heading not required.)

Instructions regarding War Diaries and Intelligence Summaries are contained in F. S. Regs., Part II. and the Staff Manual respectively. Title pages will be prepared in manuscript.

Place	Date	Hour	Summary of Events and Information	Remarks and references to Appendices
RANSART	May 21st		Admitted 10 Sick, Sent 11 to 21st D.R.S. Evacuates 1 to 43 C.C.S.	E.M.
"	22nd		Admitted 7 O.R. Evacuates 1 O.R. to 32 C.C.S. Sent 2 to 21st D.R.S. Sent 10th K.O.Y.L.I.	E.M.
			Capt H.S. Moore reported out from duty temporary outpost an Capt Penny on return.	P.M.
"	23rd		Admitted 7 O.R. Discharged 3 O.R. to duty. Sent 8 O.R. to 21st D.R.S. Sent 1 to 12 Stationary Hosp.	
"	24th		Inspector of and drill in Box respirators, P.H. helmets + goggles. This drill to take place daily when a thorough inspection to be made weekly in future. Sent 4 to 21st D.R.S. + evacuates 2 to 32 C.C.S. Admitted 7 O.R. Sent 6 to 21 D.R.S. + 3 were evacuates to 43 C.C.S.	E.M.
"	25th		Admitted 7 O.R.	
"	26th		A.D.M.S. 21st Div inspected Field Ambulance. Admitted 8 O.R. Evacuated 5 to 21st D.R.S. Capt R.C. Irvine reported from duty temporary out at 20 C.C.S. who was relieved by Lt. Cheese. 9 O.R. sent for temporary duty at 20 C.C.S. in relief of men of the unit who were there.	

2353 Wt. W2544/1454 700,000 5/15 D. D. & L. A.D.S.S./Forms/C. 2118.

WAR DIARY
or
INTELLIGENCE SUMMARY.

Army Form C. 2118.

Place	Date	Hour	Summary of Events and Information	Remarks and references to Appendices
RAMPART	May 27th		Admitted 13 OR Sick Etc 21 D R I – 3 OR + O.C. Sudan Hosp – 1 OR Evacuated 4 to 43 CCS	JJK
"	28th		Reorganisation of unit into 4 Sec in Bn Light Chambers. Admitted 10 OR. Sent 6 to 21 DRS. Evacuated 1 to 32 C.C.S. O.C. 21st Div train inspected transport & Field Ambulance.	JJK
"	29th		7 ORk Admitted 8 OR. Sick 21st D.R.C. Evacuated 2 to 32 CCS	JJK
"	30th		Admitted 7 OR Sent 7 to 21 D.R.S. Evacuated 16 to 32 CCS & 1 ORk & 12 Rofs Hope. Endings 3 Evant	JJK
HENIN	31st		Unit marched out at 6 AM arrived at 10 AM. we relieve Boyelles No. took over from 19th Field Ambulance 3 Officers and N.M.S r 360 R moved to HENIN the war Esl. Conv. & staff Et. Henri Quarter A.D.S. North in. A.D.S. Trino 99S Field Ambulance and arrived at 11th D. post in A.D.S. This in & S. R remain also the Ambulance post in Ecurie. 9 Writer & supplies to Ecurie. Aoft. 1 Office 2 4 8 OR Staff the support post in Ecurie. Wandern r 200 R reported from Corps M. DS. admits 1 Office evaced r 1 2 OR r 20 OR sick. Evacuated OR 2 sick & 9 wounded to 20 CCP 15 OR sick and 6 21st D.R.S., r 2 OR E.C. Sudan St5	JJK

E.J. Kennedy
Major & Officer
O.C. 63rd Fd Ambu

B.E.F.

SUMMARY OF MEDICAL WAR DIARIES FOR 63rd F.A., 21st Divn., 7th Corps., 3rd Army.

WESTERN FRONT April- May. '17.

O.C. Lt. Col. E.J. Kavanagh.

SUMMARISED UNDER THE FOLLOWING HEADINGS.

Phase "B" Battle of Arras- April- May. '17.

1st Period Attack on Vimy Ridge April.

2nd Period Capture of Siegfried Line May.

B.E.F.   1.

63rd F.A. 21st Divn. 7th Corps.   WESTERN FRONT
O.C. Lt. Col. E.J. Kavanagh.   May. '17.
3rd Army.

Phase "B" Battle of Arras- April- May. '17.
2nd Period Capture of Siegfried Line May.

1917.
May. 3rd.   Operations: 21st Divn. attacked.
4th- 10th.   Operations R.A.M.C. Casualties. evacuated.
11th.   Medical Arrangements: A.D.S. handed over to 99th Field Ambulance.
                 Moves Detachment: 1 and 72 returned to Headquarters.
                 Moves: To Ransart. Rest Area.
12th - 30th.   Operations R.A.M.C. Routine. Collection of local sick.
                 Casualties Sick. From 12th - 30th. 3 and 130.
31st.   Moves: Medical Arrangements: To Henin and took over A.D.S. and Adv. Posts from 99th Field Ambulance.
                 Casualties. 1 and 12 wounded admitted.

B.E.F.

63rd F.A. 21st Divn. 7th Corps.   WESTERN FRONT
O.C. Lt. Col. E.J. Kavanagh.   May. '17.
3rd Army.

Phase "B" Battle of Arras- April- May. '17.
2nd Period Capture of Siegfried Line May.

1917.

May. 3rd.   Operations: 21st Divn. attacked.
4th- 10th.   Operations R.A.M.C. Casualties. evacuated.
11th.   Medical Arrangements: A.D.S. handed over to 99th Field Ambulance.
               Moves Detachment: 1 and 72 returned to Headquarters.
               Moves: To Ransart. Rest Area.
12th - 30th.   Operations R.A.M.C. Routine. Collection of local sick.
               Casualties Sick. From 12th - 30th   3 and 130.
31st.   Moves: Medical Arrangements: To Henin and took over A.D.S. and Adv. Posts from 99th Field Ambulance.
               Casualties. 1 and 12 wounded admitted.

146/22.30

No. 63. F.A.

June 19?

COMMITTEE FOR THE
MEDICAL HISTORY OF THE WAR
Date -7 AUG. 1917

WAR DIARY or INTELLIGENCE SUMMARY

Army Form C. 2118.

Place	Date	Hour	Summary of Events and Information	Remarks and references to Appendices
HEMIN	June 1st		Admits Officer 1 sick & 2 wounded, OR 18 sick & 9 wounded. Sent 21st D.R.S. 8 OR sick. Cwent to 20 C.C.S. 1 Officer sick, 2 wounded), OR 2 sick & 9 wounded. Evacuated to C.R.S. 1 Officer wounded 12 OR wounded. Sent to Corps Sickies Pt. Visited R.A.Ps & Ambulance aid posts in trenches	MK
"	2nd		Visited R.A.Ps & ambulance aid posts. Admits 1 Officer sick, 28 OR sick & 11 OR wounded. Sent 19th 21st D.R.S. 11 OR sick, 1 OR wounded to C.R.S. 1 Officer & Officer sent Pt. Evacuated 20 C.C.S. Sent 1 to C Scales 16 Passingers, wounded sent	MK
"	3rd		Visited R.A.Ps & ambulance aid posts. Admits 1 Officer sick, 98 OR sick, 74 wounded. Evacuated 40 & wounded. to 20 C.C.S. 4 wounded & 49 C.C.S. sent 2 sick & 7 wounded to C.R.S. & 9 sick & wounded to 21 D.R.O. & 1 C. Scales Sgt wounded to 21 D.R.O. & 15 D.R. 1 to relieve Lieut. Capt Irvine went on leave, out 6. 15 D.R. 1 to relieve Lieut. Watkins who reports sick.	8DX
BOYELLES	4th		Admits 41 OR sick & 13 wounded. Sent 20 sick to 21 D.R.S. 9 & C.R.S. 1 Officer (sick) 1 Officer sent Pt. Evacuates 3 sick wounded to 49 C.C.S. Our Transport & Tees Ambu transferred to BOYELLES. Under orders B. ADM 1. 21st Four reinforcements arrived	MK

WAR DIARY or INTELLIGENCE SUMMARY

Army Form C. 2118.

Place	Date	Hour	Summary of Events and Information	Remarks and references to Appendices
BOYELLES	June 5th		Admitted 2 Officers wounded, 24 OR sick + 17 OR wounded. Sent 7 to C.R.S. + 10 sick + 1 wounded to D.R.S. + 1 to Copr. Leave S. 1 Officer + 20R wounded recd at A.D.S. Discharged 1 sick + 3 wounded to duty. Evacuated 4 OR sick to 2 C.C.S. 1 sick to 12 Stationary Hospl (German measles) + 14 OR wounded – 6 to 2 Canadian Hospl + 8 to 49 C.C.S. + 1 Officer wounded to 49 C.C.S. + 5 OR sick to 45 C.C.S.	S.J.K.
"	6th		Capt. Brennan went on leave. Admitted 1 Officer sick, OR 23 sick + 3 wounded. Evacuated 1 Officer + 1 Officer sick, OR 23 sick + 3 wounded. 5 OR to 49 C.C.S. + 1 OR to 37 C.C.S. Sent 5 to C.R.S. 2 to Leave S. 7 to 21 D.R.S. Discharged 5 to duty. Visited R.A.P.s + Field Ambulance posts in trenches.	G.J.R.
"	7th		Admitted 1 Officer sick, 2 5 OR sick + 2 OR wounded. Evacuated 3 OR wounded to 45 CCS + 1 OR sick to 9 C.C.S. Sent 6 OR sick to C.R.S. + 1 Officer + 2 3 OR to 21 D.R.S.	G.J.R.
"	8th	pm	Admitted 2 Officers sick, 50 OR sick + 3 wounded. Evacuated 1 Officer to 45 CCS, OR 3 sick 1 wounded to 45 CCS + 7 to 49 CCS, 1 to 9 C.C.S. Evacuated OR 1 to C.C.S. Sent 22 to 21st D.R.S., 6 to C.R.S. + 3 to Copr Scabs. 1 V9 C.C.S. Discharged 9 OR. Reports from army temporary out at 20 CCS. St Cheese and 9 OR reports from army temporary out at 20 CCS. Visited R.A.P.s + Ambulance aid posts	S.J.K.

Army Form C. 2118.

WAR DIARY
or
INTELLIGENCE SUMMARY.
(Erase heading not required.)

Instructions regarding War Diaries and Intelligence Summaries are contained in F.S. Regs., Part II. and the Staff Manual respectively. Title pages will be prepared in manuscript.

Place	Date	Hour	Summary of Events and Information	Remarks and references to Appendices
BOYELLES	JUNE 9th		Admitted 2 Officers sick, 2 OR sick & 7 OR wounded. Evacuated 1 Officer sick, 9 OR sick, 16 OR wounded to 4 9 C.C.S. Sent 1 Officer to D.R.S. 76 OR Sick wounded to D.R.S. & 4 OR to C. Scabies & 8 OR to C.R.S. Visited R.A.P.s & advance posts in trucks.	SJK
"	10th		Admitted 2 Officers & 38 OR sick. Evacuated 10 OR & 45 C.C.R. & 1 OR to 9 C.C.S. Sent 1 Officer & 14 OR to D.R.S. 7 OR to C.R.S. Evacuated 1 Officer to 9 CCS. Visited R.A.P.s & Field Ambulance for C.	SJK
"	11th		Lt. Anderson detailed for duty with 13th Northumberland Fus. 1st & replace Capt Mackenzie evacuated sick. Admitted 1 Officer sick, 35 OR sick & 10 OR wounded. Evacuated 40 R & 4 9 C.C.S. Sent 16 OR sick & 10 R wounded to D.R.S. Sent 1 & Corps Scabies St. 14 OR sick & 120R wounded Discharged 2 OR to duty 1 Officer sent to D.R.S. Visited R.A.P.s & Ambulance and posts in trucks.	SJK

Army Form C. 2118.

WAR DIARY
or
INTELLIGENCE SUMMARY.
(Erase heading not required.)

Place	Date	Hour	Summary of Events and Information	Remarks and references to Appendices
BOYELLES	June 12th		Sgt Kay awarded the Military Medal. Admitted 5 Officers sick & 3 wounded, OR 30 sick & 14 wounded. Evacuates 1 Officer sick & 3 wounded, OR 6 sick & 14 wounded to 45 CCS. Sent 3 Officers to Officers Corps Rest Stn & 1 Officer to D.R.S. Sent OR 5 sick & wounded to C.R.S., 16 sick & 2 wounded to D.R.S. and 3 to C. Sealvis S. Visited R.A.P.s & ambulance aid posts.	G.J.K.
	13th		Admitted 1 Officer sick, OR 32 sick & 7 wounded. Evacuates OR 3 sick & 3 wounded to 49 C.C.S. & 1 sick to 9 C.C.S. 7 to C.R.S. & 1 to C. Sealvis Sn. Sent 1 Officer sick, OR 17 sick, 12 wounded to D.R.S.	G.J.K.
	14th		Admitted OR 40 sick & 7 wounded. Evacuates 1 to 9 CCS, 7 sick & 5 wounded to 45 CCS. Sent 10 sick to C.R.S. 17 sick & 1 wounded to D.R.S, 2 to C. Sealvis S & discharges 2 to duty. Visited R.A.P.s & ambulance aid posts.	G.J.K.
	15th		Admitted 1 Officer sick, 40 OR sick & 19 wounded. Sent 1 Officer sick,14 OR sick & 6 wounded to 9th D.R.S. & 14 to C.R.S. 12 sick & 10 wounded to 49 CCS. Evacuates 1 OR to 9 C.C.S. Visited R.A.P.s and posts	G.J.K.

Army Form C. 2118.

WAR DIARY
or
INTELLIGENCE SUMMARY.
(Erase heading not required.)

Place	Date	Hour	Summary of Events and Information	Remarks and references to Appendices
BOYELLES	JUNE 16th		Admits 3 Officers sick, 146 OR sick + 26 wounded. Sent 2 Officers to D.R.S. + 1 to C.C.S. Offrs Ret S. Evacuates OR 5 sick + 5 wounded to 45 CCS, 3 sick to 49 CCS, 5 to 9 CCS Sent 16 sick + 7 wounded to D.R.S. 12 sick + 4 wounded to R.P. 2 to C Sadus + On days 1 sick + 2 wounded died. Visits R.A.P. + Ambulance posts.	J.R.
"	17th		Admits Officers 2 sick, OR 38 sick + 4 wounded. Sent 2 Officers to Officer Ret S. 19 OR to C.R.S. 11 OR to D.R.S. Mulcahey 1 to out S. Evacuates OR 7 sick + 1 wounded to 45 CCS, 2 sick to 9 CCS. Visits R.A.P. + Ambulance posts	F.J.R.
"	18		Admits Officers 3 sick, OR 34 sick + 8 wounded. Sent 3 Officers, OR 17 sick + 6 wounded to D.R.S. 2 to Chester S + 13 OR sick + 1 wounded to C.R.S. discharged 18 duty. Evacuates OR 6 sick + 1 wounded to 49 CCS. 1 sick to 9 CCS Visits R.A.P. + Ambulance and posts. Capt Breen on reports from leave. Advance party of 99th F.A. arrived to take over from us.	S.J.R.

2353 Wt. W2544/1454 700,000 5/15 D. D. & L. A.D.S.S./Forms/C. 2118.

WAR DIARY or INTELLIGENCE SUMMARY

Army Form C. 2118.

Place	Date	Hour	Summary of Events and Information	Remarks and references to Appendices
BOYELLES	JUNE 19th		Admitted OR 26 sick & 1 wounded. Evacuated 1 K45C&S discharged 26 duty. Sent 1 sick & 1 wounded to CRS & Struck & 1 wounded to DRS. Evacuated 4 sick to 33 D.R.S. Moved our ADS at HENIN & tents in trenches 699th Field Ambulance. Personnel at these places reported headquarters.	E.J.K.
RANGART	20th		Moved over at BOYELLES & 99th Field Ambulance. Unit marched in at 5:40 A.M. reached RANSART at 9:30 A.M. Discharged 1 duty. Sent 1 to CRS, 2 to DRI & evacuated 3 to 12 Stationary Hospital.	E.J.K.
	21st		Admitted 1 Nurs. sick & 1 to Rouen. Sent 1 Officer & 10 OR to D.R.S. & 2 OR to C.R.S. & 2 to C. Section. Field Ambulance. D.D.M.S. XIII Corps visited.	E.J.K.
"	22nd		Admitted OR 12. Sent 4 to DRS & movements 4 to 3 Canadian Stationary H.	E.J.K.
"	23rd		Admitted 1 Nurs. (Capt. Greig[?] the unit) and sent him to D.R.S. No 3 Canadian S.H. Sent 1 to CRS 7 to DRS & 1 to C. Section. Admitted 9 O.R. Evacuated 3 to E. Capt. Brennan sent for temporary duty with 21st Divisional Train.	E.J.K.

Army Form C. 2118.

WAR DIARY
or
INTELLIGENCE SUMMARY.
(Erase heading not required.)

Place	Date	Hour	Summary of Events and Information	Remarks and references to Appendices
RANSART	JUNE 24th		Admitted 1 Officer sick + 4 OR sick, 1 wounded, 1 to 3 Canadian S.H. + 1 wounded Officer + 4 OR to 21 D.R.S. Cpl Lumley (Cook) reported for duty from leave	E.J.K.
"	25th		Admitted 16 wounds 3 to No 3 Canadian S.H. Sent 7 to D.R.S., 11 to Leeds St. Discharged 1 to duty. S/S Price went on leave.	E.J.K.
"	26th		Admitted 8. Discharged 1 & out. Sent 5 to D.R.S. 1 to C. Scotia S + wounds 1 to 12 Stationary H.	E.J.K.
"	27th		Admitted 12 sick + 1 wounded. Evacuated 2 to 3 Canadian S.H. + 1 to 6 Stationary H. Sent 10 to D.R.S. + Discharged 2 to duty	E.J.K.
"	28th		Lt. A.F. Cowan reported for duty from 39 General Hospl. Capt Irvine reported from temporary duty with 15th Division L.J. Sent 1 Officer (Lt. Cheese of this unit) to D.R.S. Admitted 9 OR wounds 1 to 3 Canadian S.H. + sent 8 to D.R.S.	E.J.K.
"	29th		C section met Capt Robey + Moore went on advanced party to take over from 99th Field Amb. Admitted 2 Officers, Sent 1 to D.R. [illegible] + one to 3 CC. & Capt Leake 1 Officer. 1 OR Sent 7 to D.R.S. 1 to CRS 2 & Capt Leake 2 & 3 Canadian S.H. 1 wounds	E.J.K.

Army Form C. 2118.

WAR DIARY
or
INTELLIGENCE SUMMARY.
(Erase heading not required.)

Instructions regarding War Diaries and Intelligence Summaries are contained in F. S. Regs., Part II. and the Staff Manual respectively. Title pages will be prepared in manuscript.

Place	Date	Hour	Summary of Events and Information	Remarks and references to Appendices
BOYELLES	Jul 30th	9:20 AM	Remainder of unit left RIVINART at 6:30 AM & reached BOYELLES at 9:20 AM.	BK
		20 OR	20 OR sent as Corps Working Party under instructions of A.D.M.S.—	
			COLIN	
			Took over A.D.S. at HENIN and relay posts to HINDENBURG Support line from 99th Field Ambulance.	
			Took over at BOYELLES from 99th Field Amb centre.	
			Evacuated 2 officers sick to D.R.S. 1 O/R wounded to 9 CCS	
			Sent 1 officer & 4 OR to D.R.S.	
			Sent 5 OR to C.R.S. Conveyances 40R & 45 C.C.S.	

E. J. Kavanagh
N. Cd. R.A.M.C.
O.C. 63rd Field Amb

COMMITTEE FOR THE
MEDICAL HISTORY OF THE WAR
Date   10 SEP. 1917

No. 63. 7.a.

WAR DIARY
or
INTELLIGENCE SUMMARY.

Army Form C. 2118.

Vol 2 MEDICAL

Place	Date	Hour	Summary of Events and Information	Remarks and references to Appendices
BOYELLES	July 1st		Visited ADS & ambulance aid posts in trenches. Admitted 1 officer sick, OR 22 sick & 1 wounded. Evacuated 1 officer, 1 OR to 49 CCS. Sent OR 6 sick & 1 wounded to CRS, 14 to DRS & 1 to C. Leulie S. Bandaged 15 out	P.J.K.
"	2nd		Admitted 8 officer sick, OR 28 sick & 3 wounded. Evacuated officer sick to 45 CCS. OR 6 sick, 2 wounded to 45 CCS. Sent 4 to CRS, 17 to DRS, 15 C Leulie S. Bandaged 15 out. Visited ADS & ambulance posts in trenches.	G.P.K.
"	3rd		Admitted 1 officer sick, OR 38 sick & 1 wounded. Evacuated 1 officer sick & 1 wounded to 49 CCS, 2 OR 9 CCS. Sent 15 to DRS, 9 sick & 1 wounded to CRS, 6 to C Leulie S & bandaged 15 out. Visited ADS & ambulance posts in trenches.	G.P.K.
"	4th		Admitted OR 13 sick & 6 wounded. Evacuated 7 to 45 CCS. 16 to DRS, 3 to C.C.S. Sent 5 to CRS, 7 to DRS. Bandaged 15 out. Visited ADS & aid posts	P.J.K.
"	5th		Admitted 17 sick & 8 wounded. Evacuated 3 to 49 CCS. 16 to 45 CCS. One man died on A.D.S. Evacuated 1 to 12 Stationary Hosp. Sent 5 sick & 2 wounded to CRS. 6 sick & 4 wounded to DRS. Visited ADS & aid posts in trenches.	P.J.K.

WAR DIARY
INTELLIGENCE SUMMARY

Army Form C. 2118.

Place	Date	Hour	Summary of Events and Information	Remarks and references to Appendices
BOYEFFLES	July 6th		Admitts 2 Officer sick, OR 18 sick & 5 wounded. Evacuated 1 Officer & 1 OR to 49 CCS, 1 OR & 3 Canadian St H. sent 1 Officer to Rest Station, 6 OR to CRS., 17 OR to 21st DRS. Visited ADS.	SJK.
"	7th		Admitts OR 12 sick & 2 wounded. Evacuated 1545 CCS. Sent 6 to CRS & 5 to DRS. 2 O.R. sent to COWIN reports arrival for rest with F.A. Visited ADS. & field ambulance post in trenches.	EJK.
"	8th		Admitts OR 11 sick & 6 wounded. Evacuated 2 & 45 CCS, 18 49 CCS sent 4 to CRS & 5 to DRS. Visited ADS & aid posts in trenches.	JK.
"	9th		Admitts OR 22 sick & 13 wounded. Evacuated 169 CCS, 16 45 CCS, 14 to 49 CCS. 16 3 Canadian St H, 16 12 Stat H. Sent 3 to CRS 5 to DRS. & discharged 1 Conf. Visited ADS & aid posts in trenches. St Clause evacuates from DRS to 3 Canadian F.M.	PJK.

WAR DIARY
or
INTELLIGENCE SUMMARY.

Army Form C. 2118.

Place	Date	Hour	Summary of Events and Information	Remarks and references to Appendices
BOYELLES	July 10th		Admitted Officers 1 sick OR 21 sick & 2 wounded. Evacuated 3 sick & 2 wounded to 45 CCS. 5 to CRS. 3 to C Sectn H & 1 & 2 to 21st D.R.S. Visited ADS & aid posts in trenches	SPK
"	11th		Admitted Officers 3 sick, OR 11 sick, 4 wounded. Evacuated 4 & 49 CCS. 1 to 12 Stationary H. 2 to 6 Stationary H.S.t.M. to CRS. 2 Officers to 10CR to D.R.S. 1 Officer to Officers R.S. Discharged 2 to dut. Visited A.D.S. & aid posts in trenches	SPK
"	12th		Admitted 1 Officer sick, OR 23 sick & 4 wounded. Evacuated 1 Officer 10R to 49 CCS. 1 OR to 9 CCS, 2 OR to 45 CCS. Sent 10 to DRS. 1 to CRS & Discharged 1 to dut. Visited ADS & aid posts in trenches	SPK
"	13th		Admitted 12 sick & 12 wounded. Evacuated 8 to 43 CCS, 2 to 3 Canadian SH. Sent 1 to CRS, 5 to D.R.S. 1 to C. Sectn H + discharged 3 to dut. Visited A.D.S.	SPK
"	14th		Admitted 12 sick & 3 wounded. Evacuated 2 sick & 2 wounded to 43 CCS. Sent 6 sick to CR S, 4 sick & 4 wounded to D.R.S. Visited ADS & aid posts in trenches. Capt Greif evacuated to England sick and is struck off strength of unit	SPK

Army Form C. 2118.

WAR DIARY
or
INTELLIGENCE SUMMARY.
(Erase heading not required.)

Instructions regarding War Diaries and Intelligence Summaries are contained in F. S. Regs., Part II and the Staff Manual respectively. Title pages will be prepared in manuscript.

63rd (WEST LANCS. T.F.) FIELD AMBCE
ROYAL ARMY MEDICAL CORPS
No. ....
Date ....

Place	Date	Hour	Summary of Events and Information	Remarks and references to Appendices
BOYELLES	JULY 15th		admitted OR 15 sick & 2 wounded. Evacuated 4 sick & 1 wounded to 43 CCS, 1 & 12 Stationary. Sent 5 to C.R.S. 4 & to DRS 1 & C. Leslie. Discharged 2 to duty. Visited A.D.S. and ambulance posts. Capt Ridley went on temp. duty to C.R.S. until Capt McCrumpsey to return	J.McK
"	16th		admitted 1 Offr sick, OR 17 sick & 14 wounded. Evacuated 2 sick & 2 wounded to 43 CCS. Sent 9 to CRS 2 & to DRS 1 & C. Leslie & and 1 Offr to Officer Rest S. Visited A.D.S. and posts.	E.McK
"	17th		admitted 1 Offr sick. 2 sick, OR 22 sick & 4 wounded. Evacuated 4 wounded to 40 CCS, 9 sick to 43 CCS, 7 sick & 9 wounded sent to C.R.S. 2 Officers 5 OR to DRS 1 & C. Leslie # & wounded 1 OR to 3 Canadian S. H. Discharged 1 duty. Visited A.D.S.	J.McK
"	18th		admitted OR 15 sick & 2 wounded. Evacuated 3 sick to 43 C.C.S. & 2 to 12 Stationary Hosp. Sent 7 to C.R.S. 4 & to DRS g. D.C. Runcon inspected ambulance.	E.McK
"	19th		admitted OR 12 sick & 3 wounded. Evacuated 1 sick to 43 CCS. 2 wounded to 49 CCS. Sent 5 to CRS 4 & to DRS 1 & to Cps Leslie S. Evacuated 1 sick to 40 CCS. Visited ADS & ambulance and fort intended Lt/Col Price proceeded on course in III Army School of Cookery.	J.McK

WAR DIARY
or
INTELLIGENCE SUMMARY.

Army Form C. 2118.

Place	Date	Hour	Summary of Events and Information	Remarks and references to Appendices
BOYELLES	July 20th		Admits 1 Officer 2 sick, OR 9 sick & 9 wounded. Evacuats 1 Officer sick OR & 43 C.C.S. 1 OR to wound to 45 C.C.S. Sent 3 to C.R.S. 9 to D.R.S. 1 Officer to Officers rest. Evacuats 1 to 9 C.C.S. Ventes A.D.S & Field ambulance and posts in trenches.	S.M.
	21st		Admits 15 sick & 2 wounded. Evacuats 2 & 3 C.C.S. Sent 1 & D.R.S. 1 to C.R.S. Ventes A.D.S. & and posts.	S.M.
	22nd		Admits 1 Officer sick. OR 11 sick & 3 wounded. Evacuats 1 Officer & OR & 43 C.C.S. Sent 7 to C.R.S. 4 to D.R.S. 2 to C. Rein. H. wounded. 2 OR to 45 C.C.S. and posts in trenches (wounded) Ventes A.D.S. & ambulance and posts in trenches.	S.M.
	23rd		Admits 1 Officer sick, OR 2 sick & 5 wounded. Evacuats 1 Officer & C.R.S 6 to D.R.S. Discharged 1 sent. C.C.S 2 sick & 43 C.C.S. Sent 7 to C.R.S. 6 to D.R.S. Sent 1 Officer to Officers Rest pts. A.D.S & ambulance and posts. Ventes A.D.S & ambulance and posts.	S.M.
	24th		Admits 1 Officer wounded, OR 8 sick & 6 wounded. Evacuats 1 wounded to 45 C.C.S. 1 OR wounded & 49 43 C.C.S. 1 Officer wounded & 1 sick to 45 C.C.S. 1 OR wounded & 43 C.C.S. Sent 2 to C.R.S & 5 to D.R.S. Discharged 1 Bat. Ventes A.D.S. C.C.S.	S.M.

WAR DIARY
or
INTELLIGENCE SUMMARY.
(Erase heading not required.)

Army Form C. 2118.

Place	Date	Hour	Summary of Events and Information	Remarks and references to Appendices
BOYELLES	July 25		Admitts 1 Officer sick & sent him to Officers Hospt LUCHEUX. Admitts OR 15 sick & 3 wounded. Evacuates 1 & 43 CCS, 1 & 6 Stationary H 1 & 49 CCS, 1 & 12 Stationary H. Sent 3 to C.R.S. 6 to D.R.S. & 3 to C. Sealen H. Capt Rayner (T.C.) & St. Moore United States Medical Corps reported for duty and retaken on strength of unit. Lt & Dr Price reported for duty from course at III Army School of Cookery	S.J.K.
"	26th		Lt. Thompson reported for duty and is taken on strength. Admitts 1 Officer + 20 OR sick. Evacuates 1 & 43 CCS. 1 & 49 CCS. Sent 10 Officers & 10 OR to D.R.S. + 3 to C.R.S. Capt Brennan proceeds to 21st Aux Train for duty and is struck off strength of unit. Visits ADS & ambulance posts in trenches.	S.J.K.
"	27th		Capt Rayner proceeded to take over charge of VII Corps Nature Hospt. Admitts OR 15 sick & 1 wounded. Evacuates 2 to 20 CCS. 1 wounded to 49 CCS. 1 to 3 Canadian S.H. Sent 4 to C.R.S. 6 to D.R.S. + 3 to C. Sealen H. Visited ADS & field ambulance aid posts in trenches	S.J.K.
"	28th		Admits 1 Officer sick 17 OR sick. Evacuates 3 & 43 C.C.S. Sent 8 to CRS 4 to D.R.S. 1 to C. Sealen H. & 1 Nurse to Officers Rest Pts	S.J.K.

WAR DIARY
or
INTELLIGENCE SUMMARY.
(Erase heading not required.)

Army Form C. 2118.

Place	Date	Hour	Summary of Events and Information	Remarks and references to Appendices
Boyelles	29/7/17		Admitted 8 O.R. Sick. Evacuated 1 to No 20 C.C.S. Transferred 2 to C.R.S. and 7 to D.R.S. and 1 to F.C.S.H. and discharged 1 to Duty. Admitted 1 Officer & evacuated 1 Officer to No 49 C.C.S. The A.D.M.S. 7th Corps visited Camp & saw the O.C.. Capt E.J. Kavanagh went on leave.	RCJ
"	30/7/17		Admitted 12. Other Ranks Sick. Evacuated 2 to No 9 C.C.S. Transferred 1 to C.R.S. 7th Corps. & 2 to D.R.S (65th Field) Major Macdonald A. Visited Horse lines & considered animals in excellent condition. Lieut Conan detailed for duty in relief of M.O. 9th K.O.Y.L.I. (Sick)	RCJ
"	31/7/17		Admitted 14. O.R. Sick. Evacuated to No 20 C.C.S. 2 Officers transferred 4 to C.R.S. & 8 to D.R.S. Admitted 3 wounded & evacuated 2 to 49 C.C.S. RCJ	RCJ

R.J. Irvine Capt RAMC.
for
O.C. 63 Field Ambulance.

140/2264.

No. 63. F.A.

Aug 1917

COMMITTEE FOR THE
MEDICAL HISTORY OF THE WAR
Date -1 OCT. 1917

WAR DIARY
or
INTELLIGENCE SUMMARY.

Army Form C. 2118.

MEDICAL Vol 24

Place	Date	Hour	Summary of Events and Information	Remarks and references to Appendices
BOYELLES	1/8/17		Admitted 1 Officer (sick) & Transferred 1 Officer to D.R.S. Admitted 15 O.R. sick. Evacuated 2 O.R. to no 6 Stationary Hospital. Transferred 3 O.R. to C.R.S. & 8 O.R. to D.R.S. & Discharged 3 to Duty. Admitted 2 O.R. (wounded) & Evacuated 1 to No 45 C.C.S. & Transferred 1 to D.R.S.	R.b.t.
"	2/8/17		Admitted 19 O.R. (sick) Evacuated 3 to no 20 C.C.S. 1 to No 3. Canadian Stat'y Hospl. Transferred 3 to C.R.S. & 10 to D.R.S. & 3 to C.S.H. 1 O.R. died before arrival at R.D.S. (Gunshot wds 146 R.F.A) Capt Rayner reported for Duty from VII Corps Rest Hospital. Visited HENIN & Trenches. Continuous rain for 48 hours prevented outside work.	R.b.t.
"	3/8/17		Sent 7 Horses for Dipping in mange Dipping Bath MONDICOURT. Admitted 16. O.R. (Sick). Evacuated 4 to 43. C.C.S. Transferred 6 to C.R.S. Transferred 6 to D.R.S. Admitted 1 Other Rank wounded. Evacuated 1 O.R. (wounded) to No 45 C.C.S. 7 Horses & 2 Mules returned from being Dipped in Mange Dipping Bath. Second lot of Animals Proceeded to MONDICOURT for Dipping.	R.B.S.

WAR DIARY or INTELLIGENCE SUMMARY.

Army Form C. 2118.

Place	Date	Hour	Summary of Events and Information	Remarks and references to Appendices
BOYELLES	4/8/17		Admitted 11 O.R. (Sick). 3 O.R.(Wounded). Transferred 2 O.R. (Sick) to C.R.S. & 1 2 O.R. (Sick) to D.R.S. Evacuated 2 O.R.(Wounded) to No 20 C.C.S. Accompanied D.A.D.M.S. to ERVILLERS + interviewed Officer present with regard to but taking over Main Dressing Station. Visited HENIN + relay posts. Second lot of animals reported 9-30 P.m. from Mange Sopping Bath.	Ref. 
"	5/8/17		Admitted 15 O.R.(Sick) 6 O.R. wounded. Evacuated to 49 C.C.S. 1 O.R. Sick, 2 O.R. wounded. Transferred 7 O.R. Sick to C.R.S. Transferred 6. O.R. Sick to D.R.S. & Transferred 3. O.R. Sick & C.S.H. + Discharged 1.O.R Sick to Duty. + 2 O.R. Wounded to Duty. + 1 O.R Died at A.D.S HENIN. (Pte. C. W. HORNER. 10th yorks.)	
		10AM	Visited HENIN to meet O.C. 2/2 Northumbrian Field Amb. by appointment re his taking over Material at A.D.S. D.A.D.M.S present. Visited Bearer posts + arranged about Trench Stores to be handed over. Arranged with M.O. 12th N.F.'s about 4 O.R. Stretcher Bearers to be at two Advanced Whilst holding the line to connect up with the 1st 5.D.th Durhams. Relay first 60 for Operation Order No 53 para 6. Dated 4/8/17. He arranged that Bearers should remain at Shaft 13.2.	Ref.

WAR DIARY or INTELLIGENCE SUMMARY.

Army Form C. 2118.

Place	Date	Hour	Summary of Events and Information	Remarks and references to Appendices
BOYELLES	4/5/17		Admitted 17 O.R. Sick + 1 O.R. Wounded. Evacuated 1 O.R. Sick to No 20 C.C.S. + 1 O.R. Sick to No 3 Canadian Stationary Hospital + 1. O.R. Sick to No 6 Stationary Hospital PREVENT. Transferred 5 O.R. Sick to C.R.S. + 8 O.R. to D.R.S. + 1 wounded to C.R.S.  Handed over A.D.S. HENIN + Bearer Posts No 47. 68. 91 + 105 to 2/2nd Northumbrian Field Ambulance. Places + Stretcher Bearers at No 132 Shaft. Got Accepted of M.O. 12th Northumberland Fus to Connect up with its 1st S.B. Dump + Relay Post. Party of 31 Men (including 1 N.C.O. + Cook) left in Trenches for work at new Regimental Aid Post. Visited H.Q. ERVILLERS. (22nd Field Amb.) + Proceeded to A.D.S. St LEGER + Relay Posts St LEGER-CROISILLES, Sect. + made arrangements for taking over, Visited A.D.M.S. to obtain arrangements + accommodations + relieving 2/Party of 31 (in Trench). Issued orders to ration + accommodate the men. Visited HENIN + Trenches to Conclude the arrangements Lieut MOORE U.S. M.C. + 18 O.R. returned to Field Amb H.Q. from Trenches Capt RAYNE R.A.M.C. Personnel from A.D.S. Returned for Duty to H.Q. 3rd Lot of Animals went for Dipping in Mange Bath + 2 Peelers brought back for Transfer	R.E.I.

WAR DIARY or INTELLIGENCE SUMMARY

Army Form C. 2118.

Place	Date	Hour	Summary of Events and Information	Remarks and references to Appendices
BOYELLES	7/8/17		Admitted 13 O.R. Sick. Evacuated 1 & 43 C.C.S. T.1 & No 6 Stationary Hospital. Transferred 7 to C.R.S. & 6 to D.R.S. & Discharged 1 to Duty. Staff Sgt Brooke & 22 O.R. proceeded to A.D.S. St LEGER & Relay Posts ST LEGER – CROISILLES Sector to take over from 22nd Field Amb. Sent for inspection to No 1 Coy. Train Re reduction of Horse Establishment. 5 Horses returned from Mange Dipping Bath.	RES
			3rd Lot of Horses returned from Mange Dipping Bath. Admitted 13. O.R. Sick. Transferred 10. O.R. to 7th Corps R.S. Transferred 1 to D.S.H. & 3 to D.R.S. & Discharged one to Duty.	
	8/8/17		Visited A.D.S. & Relay posts. Arranged for Transfer of same to 64th Field Ambulance. A.D.M.S. was present. Made arrangement for returning of 35 personnel of this unit & 4 Sappers of Div 184 Tunnelling Coy (at Miss Regimental Aid-Post). Received permission from Town Major BECQUERELLE & Stable Horses in Buildings on Side of Road.	DDS

Army Form C. 2118.

WAR DIARY
or
INTELLIGENCE SUMMARY.

(Erase heading not required.)

Place	Date	Hour	Summary of Events and Information	Remarks and references to Appendices
BOYELLES	9/8/17	10-15 A.M	Marched from BOYELLES & arrived at ERVILLERS. 10-15 A.M (Advanced Party consisting of 2 Officers & 15 O.R. took over from 22nd Field Ambulance.) Left Personnel of Capt Redding & Capt Rayner & 90 O.R. on Duty at BOYELLES. D.D.M.S. visit. A.D.M.S. visited ERVILLERS @ 11-30 A.M. Staff Sgt Brook & 22 O.R. returned to Field Amb. H.Q. from A.D.S. & Relay posts St LEGER-CROISILLES, Sector at 1-30 P.M. Admitted 16 O.R. Sick Evacuated 1 O.R. to C.C.S. & 1.543 C.C.S. & Transferred to C.R.S. & 1 to C.S.H.	
ERVILLERS	10/8/17		Visited BOYELLES & the Transport of material & ERVILLERS. Went to ACHIET-LE-GRAND Stn to make arrangements for testing of B Section VII Corps Scabies Station. Detailed 3 Officers & 35 O.R. on Duty at 9 A.M on 11/8/17. 1 G.S. 1 Limber, 1 water cart & 2 motor Ambulances to accompany party.	P.K.V.

WAR DIARY
INTELLIGENCE SUMMARY.
(Erase heading not required.)

Army Form C. 2118.

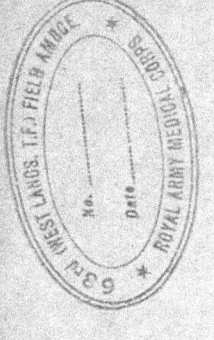

Place	Date	Hour	Summary of Events and Information	Remarks and references to Appendices
FRVILLERS	10/8/17		Capt C.B.C. Anderson R.A.M.C. reported for duty from 13th Northumberland Fusiliers vice 4. Craquato 4 & 20 CCS. Lieut 3 & 21 ORS 13 & III CRS returning from leave	S.M.
	11/8/17		Capt Moore, Anderson & Rayner with 35 OR proceeded at 9 A.M. to Corps Scabies Station (B Section) at ACHIET-LE-GRAND.	E.J.K.
			Take over Corps Scabies Station. Admitted 18 OR. Recruits 4 & 43 CCS. 1 & 3 Canadian S.H. Sent 4 & C.R.S (A sect) & 1 & CRS (B Sect) Visited Scabies Stn	
	12/8/17		Visited officers attached to unit. Lt Thompson proceeded to England on expiry of his contract. Admits 1 officer & 150 OR Recruits 20 CCS and 1 OR 420 CCS. Sent 2 & ORS 6 6 CRS & 5 4 OR & 49 CCS. Sent 2 & ORS 6 6 CRS & 5 & C. Scabies H.	EJK.
	13/8/17		Admits 1 officer & 150 OR Recruits 2 OR & 43 CCS Sent 1 officer & ORS 3 OR & CRS. DMS 3rd Army inspects unit. Capt Irvine III at or leave	SJK.

Army Form C. 2118.

WAR DIARY
or
INTELLIGENCE SUMMARY.
(Erase heading not required.)

Instructions regarding War Diaries and Intelligence Summaries are contained in F. S. Regs., Part II. and the Staff Manual respectively. Title pages will be prepared in manuscript.

Place	Date August	Hour	Summary of Events and Information	Remarks and references to Appendices
ERVILLERS	14th		Admitts 1 Officer + 250 R. Evacuates 4 & 49 CCS, 1 & 52 CCS 3 & 20 CCS discharges 5 & duty. Sent 4 & 21 DRS 13 & CRS 1 & C. Leavis S.	GJK
"	15th		Admitts 1 Officer + 160 R out + 15 R wounded (Evacuates 8 R 18 & 5 CCS, 8 & 43 CCS, 18 & 20 CCS n 2 & Stationary Hospl 16 & 12 Stationary Hospl Inr 1 Officer & Officer Rest Wn and 8 & CRS.	JK
"	16th		Admitts 1 Officer + 140 R. Evacuates 2 & 49 CCS. Sent 1 Officer + 40 R to DRS. 3 & CRS. Transferred 1 & 211 W. Riding to Conv. + Discharges 2 & duty.	SJK
"	17th		Admitts 24 OR. Sent 8 & DRS 11 & CRS. 3 & C. Leavis S. Evacuates 1 & 20 CCS 2 & 43 CCS 4 & 45 CCS discharges 1 & duty.	EJK
"	18th		Capt Rayner reports him defective for duty with 4th Cavalry Divsn. Admitts 11 OR. Evacuates 1 & 49 CCS. 4 & 28 CCS 1 & 3 Canadian Sh Sent 2 & CRS. 4 & DRS 1 & C. Leavis S. Capt Peddin attended for lecture at third Army HQ Div. St Gard 64 FA reported for temporary duty.	PJK

A.D.S.S./Forms/C. 2118.   3353 Wt. W2544/1454 700,000 5/15 D. D. & L.

Army Form C. 2118.

WAR DIARY
or
INTELLIGENCE SUMMARY.
(Erase heading not required.)

Place	Date	Hour	Summary of Events and Information	Remarks and references to Appendices
ERVILLERS	August 19th		Lieut Moore U.S.M.C. proceeds on four days leave to Paris. Admitted 1 Officer & 13 OR. Evacuated 1 & 45 CCS 3 & 43 CCS 1 & 9 CCS. Sent 1 Officer & 4 OR to D.R.S. & 4 OR to C.R.S.	EJK
"	20th		Capt Robbin proceeds on leave. Admitted 1 Officer sick OR 13 sick & 2 wounded. Evacuated 2 & 9 CCS. Sent 4 to C.R.S. 1 Officer & C Seaties S, 1 Officer & 3 OR to D.R.S.	EJK
"	21st		Withdrew 2 S OR from trench on completing an R.A.P. CCS 1 & 45 CCS 1 & 43 CCS. Admitted 10 sick. Discharged 2 & Evacuated 1 & 45 CCS. 26 C Seatie H 76 to D.R.S. 1 & 20 CCS 1 & 9 CCS. Sent 6 & C.R.S. 26 C Seatie. Buried W 3 Bent.	EJK
"	22nd		Admitted 1 Officer 2 sick, OR 23 sick & 7 wounded. 1 wounded to CCS. Evacuated 1 & Station on Hope, 5 & Corp Seatie S. 3 & C.R.S. Sent 2 Officers & 8 OR to D.R.S. & 64th Flotch Split. Evacuates 5 sick to OCS.	EJK
"	23rd		Lieut Moore reports from leave. St. 500 returned. Admitted 1 Officer sick, 150 R sick & 1 wounded. Evacuated 1 & 45 CCS 16 & 9 CCS 1 & 20 CCS Discharged 2 & Evacuated 1 Officer 8 OR & 43 CCS (nyo punt case). Sent 5 & C.M.S. & 2 & Corp Seatie Offre	EJK

Army Form C. 2118.

WAR DIARY
or
INTELLIGENCE SUMMARY.
(Erase heading not required.)

Instructions regarding War Diaries and Intelligence Summaries are contained in F. S. Regs., Part II and the Staff Manual respectively. Title pages will be prepared in manuscript.

Place	Date	Hour	Summary of Events and Information	Remarks and references to Appendices
ERVILLERS	April 24th		Handed over Corps Scabies Sqn (south) to 112th Field Ambulance. Handed over aid posts in trenches, and rain bearing station at ERVILLERS to 112th Field Ambulance. Personnel at 49 C.C.S. rejoined unit. Capt. McCauley rejoined from Corps Rest Station. admits 12 Offr + 5 O.R. wounded transferred 9 to 1/12 FA, Remainder OR rcvs 58 + 3 CCS + 69 CCS. Sent 4 to CRS.	G.M.
BARLY	25th		Unit marched out at 7 A.h. and reached BARLY at 3 P.M. Personnel from Corps Rest Station rejoined unit at BARLY	F.D.S. G.M.
IZEL-LES-HAMEAU	26th		Unit marched out at 10:30 A.h. and reached IZEL-LES-HAMEAU at 2 P.M. Capt Irvine reported from leave. Lt Conran rejoined from temporary duty with 10th K.O.Y.L.I.	
"	27th		admits 6 O.R. wounded 1 case (suspects enteric) to 12 Stationary H. P.M.	F.P.S.
"	28th		admits 1 Officer + 9 O.R. wounded 1 Officer to 42 C.C.S. Sent 12 to D.R.S.	F.D.S.
"	29th		admits 7 O.R. wounded 16 to 42 C.C.S. Sent 4 to D.R.S.	F.D.S.
"	30th		admits 13 OR. wounded 5 cases (gonorrhea) to 42 Stationary Hosp. Sent 7 to D.R.S.	F.D.S.

WAR DIARY
or
INTELLIGENCE SUMMARY.

Army Form C. 2118.

Place	Date	Hour	Summary of Events and Information	Remarks and references to Appendices
IZEL-LES-HAMEAU	August 31st		Admitted 5 O.R. sent 5 to D.R.S. Box respirators of entire unit tested in Gas Chamber.	E.M.
	September			

E. J. Kavanagh
Lt Col R.A.M.C
O.C. 63rd Field Ambce
August 31, 1917

14.0/2438

No. 63. F.A.

COMMITTEE FOR THE
MEDICAL HISTORY OF THE WAR
Date -5 NOV. 1917

Army Form C. 2118.

WAR DIARY
or
INTELLIGENCE SUMMARY.
(Erase heading not required.)

VOL 25 MEDICAL

63rd (WEST LANCS. T.F.) FIELD AMBCE · ROYAL ARMY MEDICAL CORPS

Place	Date	Hour	Summary of Events and Information	Remarks and references to Appendices
IEL-LES-HAMEAU Map Ref Sheet 51c J 2. a 8.4	September 1st		Admitted 6 O.R. & Lt-B. Price of the unit. Evacuated & 27 O.Rs also 5 O.R.	FM
"	2nd		Lt Moore W.O.M.C. proceeded to 95th Bde R.F.A. for temporary duty. Capt. Redding reported from leave. Admitted 3 O.R. Sent 2 to DRS, evacuated 1 & 42 CCS & 2 to Etaponnyth. Discharged 3 to duty	FM FM
"	3rd		Admitted 7 O.R. Evacuated 1 to 30 CCS and sent 6 to DRS	E.J.K.
"	4th		St Curran and one tent subdivision proceeded to No 8 CCS for temporary duty. 4 O.R. proceeded to 33 Armoured D. Motor Flow Coy temporary duty. Admitted, sent 10 DRS and 1 to VI CRS (Arrah)	EJK E.J.K. E.J.K.
"	5th		Admitted 5 O.R. Sent 5 OR to D.R.S.	
"	6th		Admitted 9 O.R. Discharged 2 to duty. Sent 6 to D.R.S. Evacuated 1 to 30 CCS.	

Army Form C. 2118.

WAR DIARY
or
INTELLIGENCE SUMMARY.
(Erase heading not required.)

Instructions regarding War Diaries and Intelligence Summaries are contained in F. S. Regs., Part II and the Staff Manual respectively. Title pages will be prepared in manuscript.

Place	Date	Hour	Summary of Events and Information	Remarks and references to Appendices
12 EL-LES-HAMEAU	September 7th		10 P.B. men reported from base to replace 10 A.S.C. between Blettery A. recruits 7. Died 46 D.R.S.	S.J.K.
"	8th		9 A.S.E. bearers sent to H.T.T.S. Base depot Havre. One bearer on leave who will be sent on arrival. recruits 16 & 2 CCS & sent 6 to D.R.S.	E.J.K.
"	9th		recruits 4. recruits 16 & 2 CCS and recruits 2 & 30 C.C.S. died 11. died 8 to D.R.S.	S.J.K.
"	10th		Capt. Andrews reported from leave recruits 50 R recruits 4 & 42 C.C.S. Sent 1 & D.R.S.	E.J.K.
"	11th		recruits 5. Sent 4 to 2 R.S. 1 to IV C.R.S (N) recruits 16 & 42 CCS	S.J.K.
"	12th		16-12 Stationary Hospital recruits – nil. Sent 1 to IV C.R.S (N)	S.J.K.
"	13th		A men transferred at 8. C.C.S. returns for duty as one removal 33 A. D. Medical Store recruits 15. recruits 1 & 42 CCS & sent 11 & D.R.S.	S.J.K.

WAR DIARY
or
INTELLIGENCE SUMMARY.

Army Form C. 2118.

Place	Date	Hour	Summary of Events and Information	Remarks and references to Appendices
MEL-LES-HANEAU	September 14th		Admitted 10 O.R. Sent 10 to D.R.S.	E.J.K.
"	15th		Admitted 9 O.R. Evacuated 1 to 6 Stationary # Sent 8 to D.R.S. Discharged 2 to duty. Capt Anderson proceeded to CAESTRE to report to Staff Captain 110th Inf. Bde with one motor ambulance	E.J.K.
"	16th		Left MEL-LES-HANEAU at 9.18 A.M with personnel R.A.M.C. Transport left at 7.38 P.M. under Capt Irvine. Entrained at AUBIGNY and detrained at BAVINCHOVE (CASSEL) at 5.30 A.M. Marched on 17th inst. Motor ambulance proceeded by road under Capt Ridding. Admitted 2 to 42 C.C.S.	E.J.K.
CAESTRE Map Refce Sheet 27 Q.33 C.2.4.	17th		Marched from BAVINCHOVE to CAESTRE. Admitted 5. St Moore reports from temporary duty with 95th Bde R.F.A.	E.J.K.
"	18th		Capt Irvine and St Cowan with a section of the ambulance proceed to take over Hospice, WESTOUTRE – this is advanced operating Centre for urgent cases. Three taken over from 140th Field Ambulance. Admitted 12. Evacuated 4 to 37.C.C.S.	E.J.K.

WAR DIARY or INTELLIGENCE SUMMARY

Army Form C. 2118.

Place	Date Hour September	Summary of Events and Information	Remarks and references to Appendices
CAESTRE	19th	Sent 22 OR to WEST OUTRE. Admitted 7. Evacuats 9 to 41 CCS 2 to 50 CCS & 2 sent to RPN	F.M.
"	20th	Admitted 7. Sent 6 to 41 C.C.S.	F.M.
"	21st	Admitted 12. Evacuats 8 to 2 C.C.S. Discharged 3 to duty (Evacuats 12 to 43 C.C.S)	F.M.
"	22nd	Admitted 5. Evacuats 4 to 2 CCS. Discharged 1 to duty	F.M.
"	23rd	Unit marched out at 8:20 AM and reached METEREN at 10:45 AM Discharged 2 to duty.	F.M.
METEREN (Map Reference Sheet 27. X.16.D.8.9.)	24th	Admitted 9 sick & 2 wounded. Evacuats. 6 sick & 2 wounded to 2 CCS	F.M.
"	25th	Lt. Moore U.S.M.C. proceeded for duty with R.E. 2nd Div in relief 8 Capt. Davies. Admitted 19. Evacuats 19 to 2 C.C.S. & 4 to 50 CCS.	F.M.
MIC MAC Camp. OULDERDOM Map Ref Sheet 28 H31.C.9.9.	26th	Unit marched out at 7AM and reached MIC MAC Camp at 11:5 AM Admitted 1. Discharged 1 to duty & evacuats 5 to D.R.S.	F.M.

Army Form C. 2118.

WAR DIARY
or
INTELLIGENCE SUMMARY.
(Erase heading not required.)

Instructions regarding War Diaries and Intelligence Summaries are contained in F. S. Regs., Part II. and the Staff Manual respectively. Title pages will be prepared in manuscript.

Place	Date	Hour	Summary of Events and Information	Remarks and references to Appendices
MICMAC Camp.	September 27th		Admitts 9. Evacuats 1 to 53 C.C.S. and sent 2 to D.R.S.	FM
"	28th		Admitts 5. Evacuats 1 to 2 CCS. 1 to 57 CCS and sent 2 to D.R.S.	FM
"	29th		Admitts 1 Officer + 19 O.R. Evacuats 2 O.R.'s. Sent 1 Officer + 17 O.R. to D.R.S.	E.O.K.
(Map Ref Mt a B.5 Sheet 28 (1-40000)			Unit marched out at 10 AM and reached Camp at 10.30 AM at map reference Sheet 28. 1-40000 M6a8.5	FM
DICKEBUSCH	30th		Unit marched out at 2:0 PM and reached DICKEBUSCH (Sheet 28 H34.a.4.9) at 3:0 PM and took over M.D.S. from 69th Field Ambce. Cpt Irvine, St Cowen and detachment at WESTOUTRE were relieved by 69th Field Ambce and rejoined unit. Admitts. Officers 1 sick, 2 wounded, OR 22 sick + 53 wounded Evacuats 2 Officers wounded, OR 14 sick + 53 wounded to RENY SIDING Sent 1 Officer sick 1 + 8 OR sick to D.R.S.	FM FM

E.J.Maranah
Lt.Col RAMC
O/c 63rd F.Ambce

COMMITTEE FOR THE
MEDICAL HISTORY OF THE WAR
Date −8 DEC. 1917

No. 63. F. A.

Army Form C. 2118.

MEDICAL
Vol 26

WAR DIARY
or
INTELLIGENCE SUMMARY.
(Erase heading not required.)

Place	Date	Hour	Summary of Events and Information	Remarks and references to Appendices
DICKEBUSCH	Oct 1st		Capt. Redding, Lt Erwin & 90 O.R. proceed to 64 FA for duty in the line. Capt Redding was transferred to C.C.S. 4 Motor Ambulances detailed for duty with 64 F.A. Evacuate Casualties.	E.J.K.
"	2nd		Capt Irvine detailed for temporary duty on 37. C.C.S. 1 NCO & 4 O.R. proceed to "Central Bureau" II Corps. Evacuate Casualties.	E.J.K.
"	3rd		Evacuate Casualties. 3 G.S. wagons with ambulance team proceed to 64 F.A. for duty.	S.M.
"	4th		Capt Anderson & 16 O.R. went to ECOLE BIEN FAISANCE, YPRES for Capt Moore proceeded for duty at Dressing Station 64th F.A. Evacuate Casualties	E.J.K.
"	5th		Capt Anderson detailed for medical charge 7th Leics & Rep to replace Capt Wallace proceeding home & expiry of 2 yrs service. G.S wagon returns from 64th Field Ambce. Evacuate Casualties.	E.M.

Army Form C. 2118.

WAR DIARY
or
INTELLIGENCE SUMMARY.

(Erase heading not required.)

Instructions regarding War Diaries and Intelligence Summaries are contained in F. S. Regs., Part II. and the Staff Manual respectively. Title pages will be prepared in manuscript.

Place	Date	Hour	Summary of Events and Information	Remarks and references to Appendices
DUKEBUSCH	Oct 6th		Evacuated Casualties	BJK
"	7th		Capt S.S. Meighan (T.) reports for out return Evacuates Casualties	BJK
"	8th		IOR Doig out at Ecole BIEN FAISANCE reported unit	BJK
"	9th		Evacuates Casualties	BJK
"			Transport Union left to meet unit at 1:15 PM unit marched out at 5:0 PM to OUDERDOM where it entrained Headquarters opened Station 6:23 Field Ambs at 10.4 M. between at EBBLINGHEM at 12:30 AM and moved to BLARINGHEM	BJK
BLARINGHEN	10th		where we arrived 2:30 AM Transport Arrived at 4:0 PM	BJK
"	11th		Capt O. Heath (T.C.) reports for duty	SJK
"			Capt Meighan reports for duty. Opened Rest Station for Division admits 33 Am Wounds 3 to 15 C.C.S.	SJK
"	12th		admits 10. Evacuates 3 to 15 C.C.S. Cpl Moore & Facam Drivers attached to 7th Div returned	SJK

WAR DIARY or INTELLIGENCE SUMMARY

Army Form C. 2118.

Place	Date	Hour	Summary of Events and Information	Remarks and references to Appendices
BLARINGHEM	October 13th		Admits 15. Evacuates 3 & 6 15 C.C.S. Discharged 3 & duty. Capt Heath detailed to medical charge 95th Hvy R.F.A. Brigade vice Lt Cowan evacuated sick	F.D.K.
"	14th		Admits 2. Officers to 9 O.R. Evacuates 2 Officers to 7 O.R. & 15 C.C.S.	E.O.K.
"	15th		Admits 1 Officer to 6 O.R. Evacuates 1 Officer to 5 O.R. & 15 C.C.S.	F.M.
"	16th		Admits 3. Discharged to duty. Evacuates 15 C.C.S.	E.O.K.
"	17th		Admits 8. Evacuates 4 & 15 C.C.S.	F.M.
"	18th		Admits 1 Officer & 10 O.R. Evacuates 1 Officer & 6 O.R. & 15 C.C.S. Discharged 1 duty. 3 Motor ambulances proceeded to 21st Div Supply Column in exchange for Cars from 8th Div Supply Column.	F.M.
"	19th		3 Mtor ambulances and cyclist orderlies arrived from 8th D.S.C.	F.O.K.
"	20th		Remainder of motor ambulances arrived. Transport left at 9th H and billets for night at STRAZEELE. Personnel marched on at 4:20 P.M. and entrained at EBBLINGHEM at 8 P.M.	F.M.

WAR DIARY
or
INTELLIGENCE SUMMARY.

Army Form C. 2118.

Place	Date	Hour	Summary of Events and Information	Remarks and references to Appendices
YPRES I9c6.2 (Map Sh 28)	October 2/1st		Detrained at DICKLEBUSCH at 4 A.M and marched to ECOLE BIEN FAISANCE YPRES. Took over A.D.S. there from 70th Field Ambulance. Relieved detachments of that ambulance in and posts in trenches. and posts were situated at CRICHTON POST J10.c.5.5., SCOTT POST J9.2.9.9 NEW POST J15.a.9.9 McKAY POST J14.2.24 BLACK WATCH CORNER J15.a.9.9 CLAPHAM JUNCTION J13.d.7.9 HOOGE TUNNEL J13.a.4.4 HOOGE CRATER I18.9.0.5 Capt Graham and Weaver division ½ 64th Field Ambulance reported for duty. Capt Raine and Weaver division ½ 65th Field Ambulance for duty. Capt Duncan & Lt Burton reported for duty and are taken on duty.	S/M
"		9.20	Strength of unit 84 other ranks. Capt Ralan 64th F.A. reports for duty at A.D.S. Proceeded to McKAY POST to supervise evacuation of wounded. Casualties evacuated. St. GLADDEN U.S.M.C. reports for duty and is taken on strength.	S.P.K.
"		2/3	Casualties evacuated. 6 men from Devon Brunel Myer reported at A.D.S.	S/K

WAR DIARY
or
INTELLIGENCE SUMMARY.

Army Form C. 2118.

Place	Date	Hour	Summary of Events and Information	Remarks and references to Appendices
YPRES	October 24th		Evacuate casualties. Capt Irvine returned from temporary duty at 37 C.C.S.	SJK
	25th		Casualties evacuated. Cases from Scott Post 7 Bomb Post called HALF WAY HOUSE. CRICHTON Post was blown in. All M.O.s evacuated with 1 N.C.O + 5 men at J9c 1.5.40	E.J.K 5JK
	26th		Casualties evacuated	SJK
	27th		Casualties evacuated. Capt Paton returned to 64th F. Ambce	SJK
	28th		Casualties evacuated	JK
	29th		Lt Cameron from 65th F.A. reported for duty at A.D.S.	JK
	30th		Casualties evacuated. W.S.M.C. reported for duty and is taken on strength.	SJK
	31st		Returned to A.D.S. Casualties evacuated	SJK

E.J. Barrall
Major RAMC
O/C 63rd Fd Ambce
31/10/17

44.0/2578.

No. 63. J.A.

COMMITTEE FOR THE
MEDICAL HISTORY OF THE WAR
Date   17 JAN. 1918

Army Form C. 2118.

MEDICAL

WAR DIARY
or
INTELLIGENCE SUMMARY.
(Erase heading not required.)

Place	Date	Hour	Summary of Events and Information	Remarks and references to Appendices
YPRES 19C.6.2 (MAP REF SHEET 28)	November 1st		Casualties evacuated. Capt Meighen reports departure to 57th Divn and is struck off strength. Lt. Bennett detailed for duty at 21st Divn Reinforcement Camp, nr BERTHEN. A.D.S. shelled at night.	SJK
	2nd		Casualties evacuated. A.D.S. was shelled at night.	MK
	3rd		Casualties evacuated	MK
	4th		Capt J CHALMERS reports for duty from 57th Divn to replace Capt Meighen. Capt. Moore proceeded on leave.	MK
	5th		Casualties evacuated Lt Connor returned to 65th F.A.	MK
	6th		Casualties evacuated	MK
	7th		Casualties evacuated	MK

WAR DIARY
or
INTELLIGENCE SUMMARY.

(Erase heading not required.)

Army Form C. 2118.

Place	Date	Hour	Summary of Events and Information	Remarks and references to Appendices
YPRES	November			
	8th		Casualties evacuated	AM
	9th		Casualties evacuated	AM
	10th		Casualties evacuated	AM
	11th		Casualties evacuated	AM
	12th		40 O.R. from 65th F.A. returned to this Unit. Casualties evacuated.	AM
	13th		Remainder of heavier Division of 65th F.A. returned to New Zealand. 40 O.R. & 3 New Zealand Officers & 40 O.R. of 3 N.Z. F.A. arrived as entrance party & take over this Unit.	SPM
	14th		Handed over Scott Post - BLACK WATCH CORNER, HALF WAY HOUSE to 3rd N.Z. F.A. We still hold other posts so as to ensure showing relieving unit the method of evacuation. One Officer & 3 N.Z. F.A. relieved our Officer at McKAY Post. Casualties evacuated.	SPM

WAR DIARY
or
INTELLIGENCE SUMMARY.

(Erase heading not required.)

Army Form C. 2118.

Instructions regarding War Diaries and Intelligence Summaries are contained in F. S. Regs., Part II and the Staff Manual respectively. Title pages will be prepared in manuscript.

Place	Date	Hour	Summary of Events and Information	Remarks and references to Appendices
YPRES.	November 15th		Handed over mowning duty Ports and A.D.S. to 3rd N. Zealand F.A. Capt. Raine returned to his unit. Capt. Graham returned to the unit. Personnel at A.D.S. marched to DOMINION CAMP OUDERDOM at 8 AM	S.J.K.
OUDERDOM DOMINION CAMP	16th		Beevor Brewer & 64th F.A. were loaned to their unit. Beevor Brewer & this unit turned to 4 Pm and arrived at 11 AM. We are attached to 64th Bde group till further orders.	S.J.K. S.J.K.
DOULIEU	17th		Marched out at 11:30 AM and reached DOULIEU at 6 PM.	P.J.K.
LA COURONNE	18th		Unit marched out at 9 AM and reached LA COURONNE at 11:15 AM Capt. Irvine proceeded on leave	P.J.K.
ANNEZIN	19th		Unit marches out at 9 AM and reached ANNEZIN at 2:30 PM	S.J.K.
BARLIN	20th		Marched out at 9 AM and reached BARLIN at 12 noon. 2 Officers and 200 OR moved to MAROEUIL to take over from 4th Lond - Field Ambce	S.J.K.
BARLIN	21st		Marched out at 11 AM and reached MAROEUIL at 3:30 PM and	
MAROEUIL Raffles Sheet 51C L.4.2.9			took over Field Ambulance premises from 4th London on 11 gased cases taken out. Admits 4 to 42 C.C.S. + 2 Chinese to & Stationary Hosp. Sent 5 to 1 C.R.S.	P.J.K.

WAR DIARY
INTELLIGENCE SUMMARY

Army Form C. 2118.

Place	Date	Hour	Summary of Events and Information	Remarks and references to Appendices
MARŒUIL	November 22nd		St Pearse + 10R proceed for Emergency duty to XIII Corps Rest Stn. Transferred 21 to C.R.S. Amounts 2 Chinese & 4 Stationary people	E.J.K.
"	23rd		St Ruston proceeded to 7th Warwick. Regt in relief of Capt. English who reports for duty with this F.A. Amounts 1 Officer + 20R & 2 CCS discharged 2 OR to our XIII C.R.S. Amounts 1 Chinaman & 4 Stat. Hop. Sent 1 Officer + 12 OR to XIII C.R.S. Amounts & 4 Stationary H	E.J.K. F.M.
"	24th		Amounts 3 & 42 CCS, 2 Chinese & 4 Stationary H Sent 1 Officer + 10 OR to CRS	F.M.
"	25th		Amounts 4 & 42 CCS, 1 Chinese & 4 Stat H. discharged 1 to duty Sent 14 to C.R.S.	F.M.
"	26th		Recalled all ranks from leave. Amounts 5 & 42 CCS, 3 Chinese & 4 Stat H Sent 9 & C.R.S.	F.M.
"	27th		Amounts 1 Officer + 3 OR & 42 CCS, 2 Chinese & 4 Stationary H. Sent 10 & C.R.S.	F.M.

WAR DIARY
or
INTELLIGENCE SUMMARY.

Army Form C. 2118.

Place	Date	Hour	Summary of Events and Information	Remarks and references to Appendices
MARDEUIL	November 28th		Evacuated 1 Officer to B.O.R. 642 2 CCS. And 9 to C.R.S. Boot reparation work & fitter out in continues.	E.M
"	29th		Evacuated 3 to 4 CCS. And 11 to CRS. Capt Mc Caughey resigned contract	E.M.
"	30th		Evacuated 2 Officers to OR & 42 CCS. And 9 to CRS & discharged 3 to duty. Unit marched out at 7:30 PM to entrain at SAVY where we arrived at 10:30 PM. Transport left by road at 7:0 PM to meet unit at 64th Inf Base. St Gladden T1 OR reported from C.R.S.	E.M

E.J.Kavanagh
Lt/Col R.A.M.C
OC 63rd F.A.

COMMITTEE FOR THE
MEDICAL HISTORY OF THE WAR
Date -1 FEB. 1918

No. 63. F.A.

Army Form C. 2118.

MEDICAL

WAR DIARY
or
INTELLIGENCE SUMMARY.
(Erase heading not required.)

Instructions regarding War Diaries and Intelligence Summaries are contained in F. S. Regs., Part II and the Staff Manual respectively. Title pages will be prepared in manuscript.

Place	Date	Hour	Summary of Events and Information	Remarks and references to Appendices
TINCOURT	December 1st		Arrived at SAVY at 2 A.M. and arrived at TINCOURT at 1 P.M. Evacuated 4 to 5 C.C.S.	EJK
"	2nd		Admitted 9 and sent them to 55th Div. R.S. Retained 2 — moved to 64th 110th 237th Transport under Capt Chalmer arrived at 3 P.M. 62nd Machine Gun Co.	EJK
LONGAVESNES	3rd		Unit marched out at 12.45 P.M. and reached LONGAVESNES at 2:0 P.M. We took over rest station from 2/1 West Lancs Field Ambce 55th Divn who transferred two 2 Officers + 187 OR sick, + 350R wounded	EJK
Sheet 62c E.9.6.1.3	4th		Discharged 44 OR to duty Evacuated 2 Officers + 40R to 5 CCS Capt. Irwin reports from leave. DSONS VII Corps visits B.R.S. Admits 41 sick + 1 wounded. Evacuates 3 to 55CCS, 115 to 41 Stat Hospl Sent 2 to C Sectn S. Winchcape 13 tents. Capt Engfeld proceeded to England on expiry of contract	EJK
"	5th		Admits 102. Evacuates 40 to 5CCS, 113 to 41 Stat Hospl Sent 1 to C Sectn S. Winchcape 37 tents	EJK

Army Form C. 2118.

WAR DIARY
or
INTELLIGENCE SUMMARY.

(Erase heading not required.)

Instructions regarding War Diaries and Intelligence Summaries are contained in F.S. Regs., Part II. and the Staff Manual respectively. Title pages will be prepared in manuscript.

Place	Date	Hour	Summary of Events and Information	Remarks and references to Appendices
LONGUENESSE	December 6th		Admits 114 N/K and 1 wounded. Discharged 20 & duty. Evacuates 34 to 41 Stat'y Hosp', 83 & 55 C.C.S. Sent 6 to C. Sentin 1.	88X
"	7th		Admits 55. Discharged 32 & duty. Evacuates 30 to 41 Stat'y Hosp 4 & 5 CCS & Sent 5 to C. Sentin S/n	89X
"	8th		Admits 24 offic'rs & 39 O.R. Discharged 24 to duty. Evacuates 31 to 41 Stat'y Hosp, 2 offic'rs & 30 R & 55 CCS. Sent 3 to C. Sentin S/n	80X
"	9th		Admits 57 O.R. Discharged 12 to duty. Sent 3 to C. Sentin S. Evacuates 13 to 41 Stat'y Hosp & 8 to 5 CCS.	81X
"	10th		Admits 1 offic'r & 43 O.R. Discharged 20 to duty. Evacuates 11 to 41 Stat'y Hosp & 10 offic'r & 8 OR & 5 CCS. Sent 7 to C. Sentin S.	82X
"	11th		Admits 3 offic'rs & 68 O.R. Discharged 11 to duty. Evacuates 26 to 41 Stat'y Hosp, 8 offic'rs & 9 OR & 55 CCS. and 1 cur'd to theatre. 6 to 56 CCS. Sent 3 to C. Sentin S/n	83X
"	12th		Admits 56. Discharged 1 to duty. Evacuates 30 to 41 Stat Hosp & 11 to 55 CCS. Sent 2 to C. Sentin S/n	84X

2353 Wt. W2544/1454 700,000 5/15 D. D. & L.   A.D.S.S./Forms/C. 2118.

WAR DIARY
or
INTELLIGENCE SUMMARY.

Army Form C. 2118.

Place	Date	Hour	Summary of Events and Information	Remarks and references to Appendices
LONGAVESNES	Dec 13th		Admits 1 Officer & 65 O.R. Discharged 20 & diff. Evacuates 48 & 41 Stat Hosp.	E.J.K.
"	14th		+ 1 Officer + 100 O.R. & 5 C.C.S. Capt Chainier proceeded to 95th Div RFA for pronouncement and is struck off strength of unit.	
"	14th		Admits 1 Officer + 17 O.R. Discharged 4 & diff. Evacuates 3 & 41 Stat Hosp, 1 Officer + 15 O.R. & 55 C.C.S., Serv 3 to C. Leatris Stn	E.J.K.
"	15th		Admits 2 Officers + 41 O.R. Discharged 14 & diff. Evacuates 2 Officers & 55 C.C.S. + 26 O.R. & 41 Stat Hosp. Sent 2 to C. Leatris Str	E.J.K.
"	16th		Admits 3 Officers + 610 O.R. Discharged 19 & diff. Evacuates 3 Officers + 24 O.R. to 41 Stat Hosp, 3 O.R. to 55 C.C.S. Sent 4 to C. Leatris S.	E.J.K.
"	17th		Admits 1 Officer + 48 O.R. Discharged 10 & diff. Evacuates 26 & 41 Stat Hosp + 1 Officer + 4 O.R. & 5 C.C.S. Sent 3 to C. Leatris Str	E.J.K.
"	18th		Admits 49. Discharged 22 & diff. Evacuates 17 to 41 Stat Hosp, 2 & 55 CCS + 1 ing case to 3 C.C.S. Sent 20 to C. Rest Str	E.J.K.
"	19th		Admits 1 Officer + 57 O.R. Discharged 5 & diff. Evacuates 1 case (Ruptern) & 58 CCS 1 Officer + 14 O.R. to 55 C.C.S. Sent 30 to C.R.S. and 1 to C. Leatris Str	E.J.K.

Army Form C. 2118.

WAR DIARY
or
INTELLIGENCE SUMMARY.
(Erase heading not required.)

Place	Date	Hour	Summary of Events and Information	Remarks and references to Appendices
LONGUENESSE	DECEMBER 20th		Admitted 5 Officers & 55 OR. Discharged 17 Sentry Commands 5 Officers & 17 OR & 55 CCS and sent 36 to C.R.S.	JM
"	21st		Capt McCaufery went in temporary charge of 15th Durham & I Ouvey Care's Capt Walters. Admitted 2 Officers & 52 OR. Discharged 65 Sentry Commands 1 Officers & 7 OR & 5 CCS Sent 11 Officers & 30 OR to CRS and 2 OR to C. Section Stn. Capt Irvine detailed to daily visit 7th Corps Siege Artillery Park.	JM JM
"	22nd		Admitted 53. Discharged 8 Sentry Sent 31 to CRS. & 4 to C. Section Stn. Commands 8 to T.C.S. Capt Irvine detailed to daily visit 4 Cos A.S.C. (21st Divn)	JM
"	23rd		Admitted 1 Officer and 44 OR. Discharged 13 Sentry Commands 11 to 5 CCS. Sent 1 Officer & 38 OR to C.R.S. 41 Stat. Hosp., 5 to 5 CCS 4 to C. Sections Stn. Detailed 2 orderlies for duty at water front X Road E14 & 9.4 Capt Duncan instructed them as to their duties. (Ref 62 C)	JM
"	24th		Admitted 1 Officer & 55 OR. Discharged 1 Sentry Sent 36 to CRS & 1 Officer Commands 6 to 5 CCS.	JM

Army Form C. 2118.

WAR DIARY
or
INTELLIGENCE SUMMARY.
(Erase heading not required.)

Instructions regarding War Diaries and Intelligence Summaries are contained in F.S. Regs., Part II. and the Staff Manual respectively. Title pages will be prepared in manuscript.

Place	Date	Hour	Summary of Events and Information	Remarks and references to Appendices
LONGAVESNES	December 25th		Capt Moore proceeded for temporary duty with 8th Leicester Regt. Admitted 22 OR sent 11 to C.R.S. 3 to C Leader H. Evacuated 6 to 5 C.C.S. & sick case to 3 C.C.S.	E.J.K.
"	26th		Admitted 1 Officer & 43 OR. discharged 13 to duty. Evacuated 1 Officer & 9 OR to 5 C.C.S. & sent 2 to C Sealie Pm	E.J.K.
	27th		Admitted 3 Officers & 33 OR. discharged 31 to duty. Sent 1 Officer & 1 OR to C Sealie H. 1 Officer & 20 OR to 5 C.C.S. Evacuated 1 Officer & 9 OR to 5 C.C.S.	E.J.K.
	28th		1 MCO & 12 men proceeded to 9th Leventie Regt. to [unclear] an R.A.P. Casualties. Admitted 1 Officer & 53 OR. discharged 11 to duty. Evacuated 1 Officer & 7 OR to 5 C.C.S. & 1 OR to 4 Stationary Hospe. Sent 9 to C.R.S.	E.J.K.
	29th		[unclear] 9 Officers & 38 OR. Sent 1 Officer & 8 OR to C.R.S. & 1 Officer & [unclear] to E.R.S. [unclear] duty [unclear] Evacuated 1 Officer & 8 OR to 5 C.C.S. & 1 Off. Stat. Hosp. px Admitted 3 Officers & 32 OR. discharged 6 to duty. Sent 2 Officers & 3 OR to C.R.S. Evacuated 1 Officer & 2 OR to 5 C.C.S.	E.J.K.

Army Form C. 2118.

WAR DIARY
or
INTELLIGENCE SUMMARY.
(Erase heading not required.)

Instructions regarding War Diaries and Intelligence Summaries are contained in F. S. Regs., Part II. and the Staff Manual respectively. Title pages will be prepared in manuscript.

Place	Date	Hour	Summary of Events and Information	Remarks and references to Appendices
LONGUESSES	December 3	9 am	Admits 2 Officers & 38 OR Sent 1 Officer & 25 OR to CRS. Evacuates 1 Officer & 8 OR to 5 CCS & 15 to Stat Hosp. Discharged 3 to unit	S.9.K.
	31st	3 pm	St Glasgow injuries temporary outst 9th K.O.Y.L.I. Admits 2 Officers & 45 OR Discharges 2 to duty. Evacuates 1 Officer & 18 OR to CCS Sent 1 Officer & 14 OR to CRS.	S.9.K.
	31/12/17			

E. J. Kavanagh
Lt Col RAMC
O.C. 63rd Field Ambulance

COMMITTEE FOR THE
MEDICAL HISTORY OF THE WAR
Date -4 MAR. 1918

No. 63. T. C.

WAR DIARY or INTELLIGENCE SUMMARY

Army Form C. 2118.

1918

Place	Date	Hour	Summary of Events and Information	Remarks and references to Appendices
LONGUENESSE E.28 6 1.3.	1/1/18		Admitted 33 O.R. Evacuated 65. No 41 Stationary Hospital. Transferred 10 to C.C.R.S. Discharged 3 to duty.	RA1
			Lt Col Kavanagh R.A.M.C. proceeded on leave. Capt McCausland (65th Field Ambulance) reported for duty temporarily	
	2/1/18		Admitted 1 Officer & 28 O.R. Transferred 1 Officer to C.C.R.S. & 7 O.R. Evacuated 20 O.R. 5 CCS & Discharged 18 O.R. to duty	RL1
	3/1/18		Admissions 1 Officer & 29 O.R. Evacuated to No 5. C.C.S. 1 Officer & 3 O.R. Transferred 15 O.R. & 7 C.R.S. & Discharged 7 O.R. to duty	RA1
	4/1/18		Admitted 48 O.R. Evacuated 7 O.R. to 5 C.C.S. & Discharged 24 O.R. to duty. Lieut Gladden R.A.M.C. returned leave from 9th K O Y L I Lieut Col Kavanagh. M.C. M.B R.A.M.C. awarded D.S.O. Received orders from A.D.M.S. to detail whole N.C.O. to see slight cases. No Horse Amb/ys etc at Transport lines A 63.n.62.d. R.A.M.F. detailed for this duty	RA1

WAR DIARY or INTELLIGENCE SUMMARY.

Army Form C. 2118.

Place	Date	Hour	Summary of Events and Information	Remarks and references to Appendices
	5th		Admitted 1 Officer & 33 O.R. Evacuated 1 Officer & 4 O.R. to 5 C.C.S. & 6 O.R. to 41 Stationary Hospital. Transferred 25 O.R. to 7th Corps C.R.S. & Discharged 7 to Duty.	12A
	6th		Admitted 41 O.R. Evacuated 4 O.R. to 5 C.C.S. Transferred 18 O.R. to VII Corps Rest Station & Discharged 15 O.R. to Duty	A.A.
	7th		Admitted 3 Officers & 33 O.R. Evacuated 3 Officers & 3 O.R. to No 5 C.C.S. Transferred 18 O.R. to VII C.R.S. Discharged 15 O.R. to Duty. Capt McCausland joined to Field Ambulance	A.A.
	8th		Admitted 3 Officers & 33 O.R. Evacuated 3 Officers & 3 O.R. to 5 C.C.S. Transferred 18 O.R. to VII C.R.S. & Discharged 15 to Duty (O.R.)	A.A.
	9th		Admitted 3 Officers & 31 O.R. Evacuated 1 Officer & 6 O.R. to 5 C.C.S. Transferred 2 Officers to VII Corps C.R.S. & Transferred 2 O.R. to 113 Field Ambulance. Capt. McCaughy rejoins Unit from 15 D.I.)	A.A.

WAR DIARY
or
INTELLIGENCE SUMMARY.
(Erase heading not required.)

Army Form C. 2118.

Place	Date	Hour	Summary of Events and Information	Remarks and references to Appendices
	10th		Admitted 1 Officer & 42 O.R. Evacuated 1 Officer & 11 O.R to 5 C.C.S. Evacuated 30 O.R to VII Corps C.R.S. Discharged 20 O.R to Duty. Capt. F. Bayly rejoined unit from 1/3 D.L.I.	R.A.1
	11th		Admitted 3 Officers & 45 O.R. Evacuated 3 Officers & 8 O.R. to No 5 C.C.S. Transferred 17 O.R. to VII Corps C.R.S. Discharged 9 O.R to Duty	R.A.1
	12th		Admitted 48 O.R. Evacuated 14 O.R. to No. 5 C.C.S. Transferred 24 O.R to VII Corps C.R.S. & Discharged 17 O.R to Duty. Capt Moore rejoined unit from 6th Leicesters	R.A.1
	13th		Admitted 4 Officers Sick & 1 Officer wounded & 34 O.R. Sick. Discharged 8 O.R. to Duty. Transferred 5 O.R to VII Corps C.R.S. Evacuated 4 Officers Sick & 1 Officer Wounded & No 5 C.C.S. & 9 O.R Sick to 5 C.C.S.	R.A.1
	14th		Admitted Officers Sick 1 O.R. Sick 38. Evacuated 10 O.R. Sick to C.C.S. Transferred 1 Officer Sick & 27 O.R. Sick to VII Corps C.R.S. Discharged 8 O.R. to Duty	R.A.1
	15th		Admitted 39 O.R Sick Evacuated 8 O.R Sick to No 5 C.C.S Transferred 32 O.R Sick to VII Corps C.R.S. and 6 Googook D.V.E. Discharged 12 O.R. to Duty	R.A.1

WAR DIARY
or
INTELLIGENCE SUMMARY.

Army Form C. 2118.

Place	Date JANUARY	Hour	Summary of Events and Information	Remarks and references to Appendices
LONGNESNES	16th		Admitted 49 Discharged 12 to duty Sick 18 to CRS and evacuated 9 to 55 CCS	
"	17th		Returned from leave. Admitted 4 Officers and 37 OR Discharged 14 to duty Sent 2 Officers + 22 OR to CRS and evacuated 2 Officers + 8 OR to 5 CCS	
"	18th		DDMS corps inspects rest station. Admitted 2 Officers and 46 OR Discharged 14 to duty. Sent 1 Officer + 17 OR to CRS. Evacuated 1 Officer + 7 OR to 55 CCS	
"	19th		Admitted 3 Officers + 39 OR Discharged 11 to duty. Sent 1 Officer + 26 OR to CRS. Evacuated 2 Officers + 8 OR to 5 CCS + 187 tunnelling Co to work in reserve	
"	20th		17 OR + 16 men proceeded on leave. Admitted 2 Officers + 40 OR Discharged 4 to duty. Sent 1 Officer + 27 OR to CRS. Evacuated 2 Officers + 18 OR to 55 CCS Hospe + 1 Officer + 8 OR to 55 CCS + 41 Stationary. Sent 1 Officer + 3 OR GERS.	
"	21st		Admitted 1 Officer + 20 OR Discharged 14 to duty. Evacuated 4 to 5 CCS.	
"	22nd		Admitted 1 Officer + 42 OR Discharged 25 to duty. Sent 21 OR + 1 Officer to CRS evacuated 4 to 55 C.C.S.	

Army Form C. 2118.

WAR DIARY
or
INTELLIGENCE SUMMARY.
(Erase heading not required.)

Instructions regarding War Diaries and Intelligence Summaries are contained in F. S. Regs., Part II. and the Staff Manual respectively. Title pages will be prepared in manuscript.

Place	Date	Hour	Summary of Events and Information	Remarks and references to Appendices
LONGAVESNES	Jan-y 23rd		Admits 34 OR. Discharged 23 & duty. Sent 23 to CRS & evacuated 4 to 5 CCS Class 1 Chiropody commenced for men of different units in the division under Capt Irvine.	E.J.K.
"	24th		Capt McCauley proceeded on leave – his duties being done by Capt Moore. Admits 1 officer + 31 OR. Discharged 10 & duty. Sent 18 to CRS & evacuated 1 officer + 2 OR to 5 CCS	J.M.
"	25th		Admits 33 OR. Discharged 25 to duty. Sent 13 to CRS & evacuated 5 to 41 Stationary Hosp	E.J.K.
"	26th		Admits 19 OR. Discharged 8 to duty. Sent 16 to CRS & evacuated 5 to 5 CCS.	E.J.K.
"	27th		Admits 2 officers + 39 OR. Less 1st CRS. Discharged 10 to duty. Evacuated 8 to 5 CCS + 2 to 41 Stationary Hosp	E.J.K.
"	28th		Admits 1 officer + 25 OR. Discharged 5 to duty. Sent 1 officer + 13 OR to CRS Evacuated 2 to 34 CCS & 41 Stationary Hosp + 1 to 55 CCS.	J.M.
"	29th		Admits 1 officer + 25 OR. Discharged 2 officers + 14 OR to duty. Sent 11 to CRS Evacuated 1 officer + 5 OR to 5 CCS	J.M.
"	30th		Admits 24. Discharged 20 to duty. Sent 6 to CRS. Evacuated 1 officer + 11 OR to CRS. Sent 1 officer + 11 OR & CRS. Evacuated 4 to 5 CCS & 1 to 34 CCS.	E.J.K.
"	31st		Admits 1 officer + 24 OR. Discharged 46 to duty. Sent 1 officer + 11 OR to CRS. Evacuated 4 to 55 CCS.	

E. Waranof
Lt Col RAMC
O.C. 63rd Field Ambce

140/284

No. 63. 7. A.

COMMITTEE FOR THE
MEDICAL HISTORY OF THE WAR
Date -8 APR 1918

WAR DIARY or INTELLIGENCE SUMMARY

Army Form C. 2118.

Place	Date	Hour	Summary of Events and Information	Remarks and references to Appendices
LONGAVESNES SE 25.B.1.3 Sheet 62c	February 1st		Admitted 30 O.R. Discharged 8 O.R. to duty. Sent 5 to C.R.S. and evacuated 5 to 5 CCS. G.O.C. Division inspected Rest Station and transport.	EGK
"	2nd		Admitted 13. Discharged 8 to duty. Sent 19 CCS. Evacuated 16 to 5 CCS. To 5 CCS.	EGK
"	3rd		Sent 2 officers & 120 O.R. ADS EPEHY as advance party to take over from 65th Field Ambce. 9 men per mr. from 65th Field Ambce. Took over ADS EPEHY (Sheet 62c F.1. (6.5)) and dresser post at F.1.d.8.6 and X 25.a.4.2 (Sheet 57c) from 65th Field Ambce. (Sheet 62c) Admitted 20. Discharged 9 to duty. Sent 9 to C.R.S. & 9 mtrs. Evacuated 3 to 5 CCS.	EGK
"	4th		Sr O/Nr J. Flavell arrived from 1/1 W. Lancs. field amb to take over duties of Quartermaster. Admitted 1 Officer + 30 O.R. Evacuated 16 to 5 CCS. Sent 1 Officer + 13 OR 6 CNS Discharged 9 to duty.	EGK
"	5th		Visited ADS & dresser posts. Admitted 22 OR. Discharged 10 to duty. Sent 33 to C.R.S. Evacuated 16 to 5 CCS, 1 to 34 CCS.	EGK
"	6th		Admitted 1 officer + 31 OR. Discharged 11 O.R. to duty. Sent 1 Sub 6 to R/B. Evacuated to 6 5 CCS and 5 Officers.	PGK
"	7th		Visited ADS & dresser posts. Admitted 22. Discharged 11 to duty. Sent 3 to CNS Evacuated 3 to 34 CCS.	EGK

WAR DIARY or INTELLIGENCE SUMMARY.

Army Form C. 2118.

63rd (WEST LANCS. T.F.) FIELD AMBCE.
ROYAL ARMY MEDICAL CORPS

Place	Date February	Hour	Summary of Events and Information	Remarks and references to Appendices
LONGAVESNES	8th		admitts 14 O.R. discharged 9 R & T. Sent 12 to C.R.S. wounds 1 & 34 C.C.S. 2 to 5 C.C.S. Visits H.Q & advanced posts	G.J.R.
"	9th		admitts 19 O.R. discharged 13 & wounds to 4 C.C.S. wounds 2 & 34 CCS Visits H.Q & advanced posts	S.D.Y.
"	10th		Capt R.C. Carss returned from leave. admitts 28 OR. discharged 4 & Lieut St. Plazen relieved Capt Denver at H.Q. wounds 3 to 5 CCS, 2 & 34 CCS 7 18	G.J.R. T.R.
"	11th		admitts 8. discharged 8. 2 Sent wounds to 4 CRS 3 evacuated 41 Stationary Hospital.	S.D.Y.
"	12th		admitts 16. sick 7 15 OR. discharged 2 & sent sick 14 & CRS evac. hosp. 1 & 34 CCS & 3 to 5 CCS. Lieut on leave Visits A.D.S & advance posts. Capt Denver proceeded on leave Pelusal	G.J.R.
"	13th		Sgt J. Hancock proceeded on far course to VII corps from school admitts 20. evacuates 2 to 55 CCS 1 & 34 CCS. 3 & 41 Statty Hosp. Sent 2 to CRS Discharged 13 & sick	
"	14th		admitted 1 officer 16 OR. evacuates 1 officer 5 O.R. 55 CCS Lieut B.E.R.I. discharged 7 & sick D.D.M.S. Corps inspects Rest Station and A.D.S. Hauled over A.D.S & Reserve Posts to 113th L. Ambce. 16th Divn	G.J.R.
"	15th		Capt McCaughey proceeded to 14 Northumberland Fusir for temporary duty. Capt R.M. Greig returns sick out from 36th Div. discharged 9 & Sent lost 7 & CRS. evacuates 1 & 55 CCS. 2 & 34 CCS. admitts 11 O.R.	S.D.Y.

Army Form C. 2118.

WAR DIARY
or
INTELLIGENCE SUMMARY.
(Erase heading not required.)

Instructions regarding War Diaries and Intelligence Summaries are contained in F.S. Regs., Part II and the Staff Manual respectively. Title pages will be prepared in manuscript.

Place	Date February	Hour	Summary of Events and Information	Remarks and references to Appendices
LONGAVESNES	16th		Admitted 11. Discharged 2 to duty. Sent 3 to CCS. Evacuated 3 & 34 CCS.	EgR
"	17th		Admitted 18. Discharged 1 to duty. Evacuated 2 & 34 CCS 6 & 55 CCS sent 5 to CRS	EgR
"	18th		Admitted 9 OR r 14 OR. Discharged 2 to duty. Sent 2 to CRS. Evacuated 1 & 55 CCS	EgR
"			2 & 55 CCS r 1 & 34 CCS. Capt Moore, Diphtheria + Dewell went 5 Army School Sanitation for instruction personnel in Sanitary appliances	EgR
"	19th		Admitted 13 OR. Evacuated 16&34 CCS, 1 & 55 CCS, sent 5 to CRS. Discharged 3 to duty.	EgR
			Capt Moore, myself + one nursing orderly attended lecture at V Army RAMC	
			School of Instruction (N 61 CCS) on "Treatment of Fractures"	
"	20th		Admitted 3 OR. Evacuated 1 & 41 Staff Hosp, 1 & 55 CCS, and 3 to CRS	EgR
			Discharged 6 to duty	
"	21st		Admitted 5 OR. Discharged 10 to duty. Sent 2 to CRS.	EgR
"	22nd		Admitted 10 OR r 2 10 OR. Evacuated 2 & 55 CCS 3 & 34 CCS. Sent 1 officer + 7 OR to	
			CCS.	
			Col— (Commander) inspected RAP Station	
"	23rd		Admitted 9 OR. Evacuated 2 & 55 CCS 2 & 34 CCS sent 3 to CRS Evacuated	EgR
			4 to duty	BgT
"	24th		Admitted 9 OR Discharged 2 to duty. Sent 6 to CRS Evacuated 16 & 55 CCS r 1	
			& 34 CCS	

WAR DIARY or INTELLIGENCE SUMMARY

Army Form C. 2118.

Place	Date	Hour	Summary of Events and Information	Remarks and references to Appendices
LONGAVESNES	February 25th		admitted 15 OR. Evacuated 16 to 5CCS, 16 & 34CCS discharged 2 to duty	FJK
"	26th		admitted 1 Officer + 10 OR. Evacuated 1 Officer to 5CCS, 20R to 34CCS, 3 OR to 55CCS. discharged 3 to duty	FJK
			Capt. McCririck R. reported for duty from 65th Field Ambulance	FJK
"	27th		admitted 10 OR. Evacuated 16 to 55CCS, 3 & 34 CCS. Sent 6 FCPS discharged	FJK
			7 to duty	
"	28th		admitted 2 Officers + 11 OR. Evacuated 6 to 5CCS, 2 Officers + 4 OR to	FJK
			34CCS. Sent 2 to CCS & discharged 2 to duty	
			Capts Grey + Moore + 3 OR proceeded to EPEHY + took over	
			F.I.C. 65 (Sheet 62c) and twenty hrs at	
			A.D.S. at X.25 a 4.2 (Sheet 57.c) from 113th Field	
			F.I & 6 (Sheet 62c) and at X.25 a 4.2 (Sheet 57.c)	
			Ambce 16th Divn.	

F. J. Kavanagh.
Lt Col. RAMC
O.C. 63rd Field Ambce

14C/2849

No. 63. F.A.

COMMITTEE FOR THE
MEDICAL HISTORY OF THE WAR
Date 12 MAY 1918

Army Form C. 2118.

WAR DIARY
or
INTELLIGENCE SUMMARY.
(Erase heading not required.)

Place	Date	Hour	Summary of Events and Information	Remarks and references to Appendices
LONGAHESNES (Sh.62C) (E25 d 1.3)	March 1st		Aonette 1 Officer, 25 OR. Evacuate 1 Officer 1 OR to 5 CCS, sent 10 OR.s on duty. 1 party look over relay post at W18 a 3 & 14 a 65c) and X13 a 2.7 (Sh.57c) from 13 & Field Amb. 39 Div. as our division took over this piece of front of 39th Div. Sent 1 NCO & 19 men to these relay pts. Video 4 O.S. & ploy. post	P.K.
"	2nd		Aonette 21 Officers 180 OR. Evacuate 4 & 5 CCS. 1 Officer 40 OR & 34 CCS	P.K.
"	3rd		Sent 1 Officer 7 OR to C.R.S. Discharged 2 to duty. Visited ADS & relay posts. Aonette 19 OR wounded 5 & 5 CCS, 36 34 CCS. Sent 29 OR.s to discharges 1 duty.	P.K.
			Visits A.D.S. & relay posts.	E.R.
"	4th		Aonette 18. wounded 26 5 CCS, 36 34 CCS, 3 & 42 Stat. Hosp.	
			Int 36 CCS. Discharges 7 duty. Visits ADS & relay posts.	
"	5th		Aonette 23 wounded 11 duty. Sent 5 CCS wounded 4 5 CCS 1 & 2 & 34 CCS. Capt Duncan took medical charge of medicine been hitt received visit.	P.K.
"	6th		Aonette 24 OR. Discharges 4 duty. Sent 10 GCRS wounded 5 5 CCS 1 r 5 r 34 CCS. Planned our relay posts on our left Bos front & 65 F.A.	T.K.
"	7th		Aonette 1 Officer r 16 OR. Discharges 7 to duty. Sent 6 OR.s wounded 3 6 5 CCS 4 & 34 CCS. DDMS XV Corps r Country Insp. left army inspected Station and A.D.S.	P.K.

Army Form C. 2118.

WAR DIARY
or
INTELLIGENCE SUMMARY.
(Erase heading not required.)

Instructions regarding War Diaries and Intelligence Summaries are contained in F. S. Regs., Part II. and the Staff Manual respectively. Title pages will be prepared in manuscript.

Place	Date	Hour	Summary of Events and Information	Remarks and references to Appendices
LONGAVESNES	March 8th		Admitted 32. Discharged 2. 6 cont. wounds. 2 to CCS, 16 to 32CCS, 16 to 34CCS.	SJR.
"	9th		Capt. Irvine attres leave at 7AM. Capt. Ian Schage in. Enemy fire. Admitted 21. Discharged 5. 24 cnty. wounds, 1 Sgt. Stationary Hosp. 2 to B 34CCS, 5 to 5CCS.	JM JM
"	10th		Admitted 18. Discharged 5 cnty. wounds. 4 to 54CCS, 5 to CCS. Visited ADS & relay posts.	PX
"	11th		Admitted 25. Discharged 4 6 cnty. Sent 15 to CRS, 3 to C Section S. cnty wounds 48-34 CCS, 1 to 42 Stationary Hosp. 16 to 55CCS. Visited ADS & relay posts.	JSX
"	12th		Admitted 32. Discharged 6 6 cnty. Sent 15 to CRS, 8 to C Section S cnty wounds To 34CCS & 8 to 5CCS. Visited ADS & relay posts.	SJR
"	13th		A. Stuben proceeded on 14 days leave. Lt. Bennett A.S.M.C. reports on out from 21st Div Rly. Discharged 16 cnty. Sent 10 to CRS, 6 to Admitted 28. Nous to 37 OR. Discharged 16 cnty. Sent to 34CCS. Seeking St. Nourners 1 officer & 10 OR & 4 Stat Hosp. 5 to 34CCS. 1 Sir & 14 OR to 5 Stat CCS.	JM
"	14th		Relayed post at X25a42 & N29d.9.9 (Place 57c) Admitted 1 officer & 26 OR sick, 11 O. wound. Count 164 Stat Hosp. 13 to 5CCS. Sent 10R to 34CCS, Sent 20 to CRS. Discharged 1 ont. One wounded acc). Enemy 12 60 & 19 OR to relay posts. RAP for 1/9 Leicesters Regt Sumb ADS Fair Way Country for 1/9 Leicesters Regt.	SJR

WAR DIARY or INTELLIGENCE SUMMARY

Army Form C. 2118.

Place	Date	Hour	Summary of Events and Information	Remarks and references to Appendices
LD GRAVESNES	Dec 15th		Admitts 2 Offrs r 13 OR. Discharged 1 Out. Sent 2 t 14 CCS. Evacuated 2 Offrs r 20 R t 55 CCS r 5 OR t 34 CCS. Vents ADS and relay post	17 X
"	16th		Admits 1 Offr r 30 OR. Evacuated 6 t 5 CCS, 1 Offr r 20 R t 14 CCS. Sent 14 t CRS r exchanged staff; Sent Capt McCormick and 20 OR to ADS to reinforce staff for evac by 62 Divn to tpt. Vents ADS r relay posts	1 X
"	17th		Capt Duncan r extra personnel returned from tpt. Admits 2 Offrs r 21 OR. Discharged 5 Out. Sent 15 t CRS. Lent 2 t O.R. r 2 OR t 55 CCS	2 X
"	18th		Capt Scobie H. evacuated by Motor Amb Convoy 4 CCS, 1 Offr r 2 OR t 55 CCL St Bennet was removed 2 t out. Discharged 28. Ent 10 t CRS r t C Scobie Mr Crauvets Admits 28, Discharged 26 out. Vents ADS r relay posts 11 t 5 CCS. r 5 t 34 CCS.	8 X
"	19th		Admits 29. Sent 11 t CRS 3 t C Scobie L Crauvets 16-42 Stat Hosp , 3 t 55 CCS. 2 t 34 CCS.	9 X
"	20th		Capt Duncan detailed for duty with 21st M.G. Bn struck off strength of Unit. Admits 1 Offr and 27 OR. Evacuated 1 t 5 CCS 16 t 55 CCS 6 t 34 CCS 16.55 CCS r Offrs r 20 R r 42 Stat Hosp. Sent 9 t CRS r 2 t C Scobie Mr Crauvets 3 Sous	80 X
"	21st		66 OR remain Admits for Gunner Offrs wounded 62 OR were evacuated t 34 CCS and 4 discharged duty	

Army Form C. 2118.

WAR DIARY
or
INTELLIGENCE SUMMARY.
(Erase heading not required.)

Instructions regarding War Diaries and Intelligence Summaries are contained in F. S. Regs., Part II. and the Staff Manual respectively. Title pages will be prepared in manuscript.

Place	Date	Hour	Summary of Events and Information	Remarks and references to Appendices
LONGAVESNES	May 21st	9	Capt. Grey and Moore proceed to St EMILIE with Driver Duncan & recruits. Wounded from Right side of Division. LONGAVESNES Becomes a Walking Wounded Dressing Station. Capt. Duncan. Skeers reported for duty. Nine Evacuments Casualties.	8 PM
"			Beacon Driver fell back to VILLERS FAUCON about 7 PM and took to LONGAVESNES. Party at EPEHY with exception of 6 men reported 4TH Dr. Capt McCRIRICK and nursing section reported to 113th F.A. Dr. acts	8 PM
PERONNE	22nd		Evacuments Casualties. We now became ADS Dr. Division. Capt McCRIRICK & nursing section reported from 113 F.A. Fell back from LONGAVESNES to BUSSU at 11 A.M. Late fell back to SUGAR FACTORY PERONNE. Left 2 officers and 10 men at BUSSU to collect wounded. Capt BENNET reported from 2/65 Army RAMC School	PDK
MARICOURT	23rd		Left PERONNE at 10:30 A.M. Personnel from BUSSU rejoined unit. Marched to MARICOURT & Corps Rest Stn 64 F.A. Becoming main station. Capt Duncan & Skeen attached for duty with 64 F.A.	7 PM
BRAY-S-SOMME	24th		Marched to BRAY. Became division unit & 64 F.A. Became main unit rejoined unit about 2 P.M.	6 PM
SAILLY LE SEC	25th		Marched to SAILLY LE SEC. Sent 6 nursing orderlies and 2 cars for duty at Hospice BRAY	6 PM

Army Form C. 2118.

WAR DIARY
or
INTELLIGENCE SUMMARY.

(Erase heading not required.)

Instructions regarding War Diaries and Intelligence Summaries are contained in F. S. Regs., Part II. and the Staff Manual respectively. Title pages will be prepared in manuscript.

Place	Date	Hour	Summary of Events and Information	Remarks and references to Appendices
CONTAY	March 26		Marched to BAISIEUX. Reveille at 6:30 am, left at 5:45 pm and marched to CONTAY	APX
"	27th		Remained at CONTAY	APX
"	28th		Remained at CONTAY	APX
"	29th		Marched to MOLLIENS-au-BOIS and reveille at 10 AM	APX
MOLLIENS au BOIS	30th		Remained in billets	
	31st		Reveille. Personnel marched to POULAINVILLE and entrained there for BOURDON arriving 6:30 PM. Transport marched and arrived BOURDON at 2 PM	APX
BOURDON				

E. J. Kavanagh
Lt.Col. R.A.M.C.
OC 65th Field Ambce

63rd. Field Ambulance.

COMMITTEE FOR THE
MEDICAL HISTORY OF THE WAR
Date 6 JUN 1918

63rd Field Ambulance

Army Form C. 2118.

WAR DIARY
or
INTELLIGENCE SUMMARY.
(Erase heading not required.)

Instructions regarding War Diaries and Intelligence Summaries are contained in F.S. Regs. Part II. and the Staff Manual respectively. Title pages will be prepared in manuscript.

Place	Date	Hour	Summary of Events and Information	Remarks and references to Appendices
BOURDON	April 1st		Marched out at 7:0 PM and entrained at HANGEST-SUR-SOMME and detrained on April 2nd at 1:15 PM at PESELHOEK	S.V.K
KENNEL	2nd		Annex KENNEL - personnel by bus, transport by route march	M.K.
"	3rd		Sent 1 Officer + 40 O.R. on advance party & took over from 3rd Australian Field Ambulance. Remainder to 64th F.A. auxilts. S.R.	
YONCE ST (nr KENNEL) Map Ref (N.29 & 3.9 Sht 28)	4th		Marched out at 9:0 AM and took over MDS at YONCE ST, ADS at WYTSCHAETE (Map ref O.19.d.3.9) and relay posts at ONRAET Wood (O.14.c.5.8) CABARET FARM (O.15.c.6.9) RAVINE Wood (O.10.a.4.4) VERNE Road (O.21.c.92.95) (Sheet TRENCH map WYTSCHAETE 28 S W 2) Visited ADS & relay posts	S.V.K.
"	5th		Admitts 1 Officer + 3 O.R. transferred 1 Officer + 10 O.R 64 F.A. Evacuats 2 G 64 C.C.S. Lt. Gladden U.S.N.C. reports from leave Admitts 11 transferred 10 6 64 FA evacuated 16 71 C.C.S. Admitts 11 transferred 23rd Fd Amb & Capt Scott (F.G.) from 22nd F.A. Capt C.H. BISCHEL from 23rd Fd Amb taken on streng of unit. Visited ADS & relay posts	S.V.K.

(A7092). Wt. W12539/M1293. 75,000. 1/17. D. D. & L., Ltd. Forms/C.2118/14.

Army Form C. 2118.

WAR DIARY
or
INTELLIGENCE SUMMARY.
(Erase heading not required.)

Instructions regarding War Diaries and Intelligence Summaries are contained in F.S. Regs, Part II. and the Staff Manual respectively. Title pages will be prepared in manuscript.

Place	Date	Hour	Summary of Events and Information	Remarks and references to Appendices
YONCE STREET (near KENNEL)	April 6th		Visits ADS & relay posts. Admits 1 + 150 R. Evacuates 1 Offr + 140 R to 2 CCS. 1 to 3 Australian CCS & Transferred 1 Officer + 102 R to 64 Fd Amb.	E.J.K.
LOCRE	7th		Admits 8 OR. Evacuates 3 to 11 CCS & Transfers 5 to 64 FA. Handed over relay posts, ADS + Yonge St & 58th Irish Ambce and moved at 7.30 PM to BIRMINGHAM CAMP, LOCRE	EJK
"	8th		Remained in Billets	EJK
"	9th		Moved in billets. admits 3. Evacuates 1 & 10 CCS and ORs 2 & DRS. Evacuates 5 Officers 34 OR. Sent 3 Officers 10 ORs + ORs & 25 Emplts & etc. 3 Emergency Cal.	EJK
LA CLYTTE (N7c5.5) (Sheet 28)	10th		Took over at LA CLYTTE from 1/2 W Riding L. Ambce at 9.30 AM. Capt Grey, Capt Driscoll & Owens Owens went for duty with 64th Fd Ambce. 1 NCO and 6 OR went for duty with John Mainspector at DICKEBUSCH. All the personnel returned from 64th FA at 10 PM. Less Capt Grey & 40 OR & 28 FA at KEMMEL & also 62 Infy Ambce.	EJK
"	11th		Capt Grey & 40 OR proceeded to YONCE ST. Vients RAT13 and sent return Stretcher Bearer battalion to 62 Infy Ambce. Admits 2. OR 39. Evacuates 4 to DRS, remainder to CCS. La CLYTTE became heavily bombarded during station	EJK

Army Form C. 2118.

WAR DIARY
or
INTELLIGENCE SUMMARY.
(Erase heading not required.)

Instructions regarding War Diaries and Intelligence Summaries are contained in F. S. Regs., Part II. and the Staff Manual respectively. Title pages will be prepared in manuscript.

Place	Date	Hour	Summary of Events and Information	Remarks and references to Appendices
LACLYTTE	April 12th		admits 218 and evacuates <u>Field</u> St. Barns USRC reports for duty 16 OR to RAP Sig C4 th Dy Dev at GRAND BOIS ok D13 (Sheet 28)	P.K
"	13th		St. Barns returns to RE HQ Dr Col Stevens St. S. Bardal q 133 FA reports from temporary duty admits 260. Returns 14 to duty. Casualty evacuees	7K
"	14th		admits 140 Sent 9 to evt. Evacuates 131.	8K PK
Sheet 27 L 23 C 5.8 (near POPERINGHE)	15th		St. Shaw reports for duty to replace St. Nardel who returns to his unit. admits 294. Sent 6 to duty Evacuates 288. Moved from LACLYTTE to L23 c 5.8 sheet 27 to open Corps for Centre. Left 2 Officers + 140 OR to remain till 4 AM	
"	16th		St. Law returns to his unit Remains of personnel joined from LACLYTTE We act to open on walking wounded for corps and ret as for Centre admits 94 and evacuates them	2PK
"	17th		admits 432 and evacuates them. Sent 12 OR to reinforce Bearers at GRAND BOIS	7K
"	18th		admits 326 r evacuates them. Capt. Sinclair went for duty at parts Capt. Greif	8PK

WAR DIARY
or
INTELLIGENCE SUMMARY.

(Erase heading not required.)

Army Form C. 2118.

Place	Date	Hour	Summary of Events and Information	Remarks and references to Appendices
L 23 c 5.8 Shr 27	April 19th		Admitted 143 and evacuated them.	J.O.K
"	20th		Capt Greif & Field unit 40 OR rejoined HQrs & unit. Admitted 48 & evacuated them	E.O.K
"	21st		Admitted 73 and evacuated them	J.O.K
"	22nd		Admitted 31 & evacuated them. DDMS corps inspected dressing station	E.O.K
"	23		Evacuated 41.	J.O.K
"	24th		Proceeded 47 casualties	J.O.K
"	25		2 ORs & 40 OR proceeded to 64 FA. Evacuated 112 & casualties	J.O.K
"	26th		Admitted 1058 & evacuated them.	J.O.K
"	27		Admitted 347 and evacuated them. Capt Moore admitted Military Cross	J.O.K
"	28th		Personnel from 65th FA rejoined. 1 Officer & 1 Officer & 1907 from 65th FA rejoined unit. Admitted 269 & evacuated them	J.O.K
"	29th		1 Officer & 32 OR proceeded to 64 FA for duty Admitted 600 & evacuated them	J.O.K
"	30th		Evacuated casualties.	J.O.K

E.O.Kavanagh
Major RAMC
OC 63rd Field Ambce.

140/2983.

COMMITTEE FOR
MEDICAL HISTORY
Date 9 JUL 1918

M.63 ╤ a.

May 9/18.

Army Form C. 2118.

WAR DIARY
or
INTELLIGENCE SUMMARY.
(Erase heading not required.)

MEDICAL

Vol 33

Place	Date	Hour	Summary of Events and Information	Remarks and references to Appendices
Sheet 27 K11 c74	MAY 1st		Left Reny Siding at 3:0 PM leaving turned over to 133rd F.A. 64 F.A. arrived back to unit.	BM
LEDERZEELE	2nd		Marched out at 8:0 AM and arrived at LEDERZEELE at 4:40 PM	BM
"	3rd		Remained in billets. Capt Inchil transferred to 8th Leicesters for duty. Capt F.W.G.GIBSON reports from du from 64 F.A and in (taken in temp)	BM
"	4th		Left billets at 8:0 AM and entrained at ARQUES. Motor ambulances proceeded by road with remainder of ambulance	BM
In train	5th		En route by train. Motor ambulances arrived at L'HERY	BM
"	6th		Entrained at BOULOUSE at 12:35 AM and marches to L'HERY Capt Scott reports for duty.	BM
L'HERY	7th		Remained in billets admitted 10 Sick/Acct wounds 1 was invalids & Sent	BM
"	8th		Hospital at 9g rg L'ABBAYE.	BM
"	9th		admitts 5. Wounds 1 evac invalid to 9 CMY L'ABBAYE	BM
"	10th		admitts 4. admitts 1 Misc + 5 DR. Evacuated 1 Misc to MONT NOIRE DAME (FRENCH HOSPITAL)	BM

Army Form C. 2118.

WAR DIARY
or
INTELLIGENCE SUMMARY.
(Erase heading not required.)

Instructions regarding War Diaries and Intelligence Summaries are contained in F. S. Regs., Part II. and the Staff Manual respectively. Title pages will be prepared in manuscript.

Place	Date May	Hour	Summary of Events and Information	Remarks and references to Appendices
CHERY	11th		admitted 1 discharged 1 blunt brazets 3 to Montnotre Dame (Fuck Hosps) admitted 14 brazets 1 to 37 CCS	Appx
"	12th		admitted 14 brazets 1 to 37 CCS	Appx
JONCHERY	13th		had orders 7 AD and reached JONCHERY abt 5:30pm. OC's cupr met unit on road and ordered us to JONCHERY (entry of VAUX VARENNE) We took over from 171 French Ambulance (Lt BENNETT USNC detached for duty) admitted 2 officers + 20 R brazets 2 officers + 37 CCS. transfund 32 + 65 FA	Appx
"	14th		admitted 2 officers + 14 OR brazets 46 to 37 CCS Opened an officers Rep station. Gave grey and does ward to military Cross.	Appx
"	15th		admitted 5	Appx
"	16th		Their grey opened 6 yds on 110 ft Inf/be to serve sick and wounded for sanitation in their area. admitted 1 officer + 10 R brazets 16 to 37 CCS	Appx
"	17th		admitted 1 officer + 27 OR and 5 Fund 1 Italian. Swac to the latter French Hosps. TRANSFER. Discharges 1 OR	Appx
"	18th		DON. (confer infected Rest station) admitted 3 officers + 3 OR wounded, 1 officer + 20 R to 37 CCS. transfund 1 to 64 FA Discharged 1 but	Appx
"	19th		admitted 18 OR + 1 Fund. brazets 1 officer + Fund Hosps. 15 OR + 37 CCS discharged 1 brazet.	Appx

Army Form C. 2118.

WAR DIARY
or
INTELLIGENCE SUMMARY.
(Erase heading not required.)

Instructions regarding War Diaries and Intelligence Summaries are contained in F. S. Regs., Part II. and the Staff Manual respectively. Title pages will be prepared in manuscript.

Place	Date	Hour	Summary of Events and Information	Remarks and references to Appendices
JONCHERY	MAY 20th		admits 2. Evacuats 3 to 37 CCS, 1, 15 Genl Infectious Hosp. Igny l'Abbaye. Wounded 2 to duty	7pk
	21st		admits 2 Officers + 24 OR wounded 1 to 37 CCS, 15 Gen Hosp. Igny l'Abbaye	8pk
	22nd		Wounded 17 to duty admits 2. Evacuates 3 to 37 CCS. En[?]	9pk
	23rd		18 OR proceed to 65th GH. to be sent as sanitary men (temporarily) to huts in the line, admits	8pk
	24th		admits 1. Evacuates 48 SCCS	8pk
	25th		admits 1 officer + 3 OR. Gnld[?] 1 to 37 CCS 1 to 65 CCS r Lanr[?] + Lanr[?] 76 twy 9 OR + 19 proceed to 87 CCS for Company duty.	7pk
	26th		admits 3 Officer + 10 R. Sent 78 OR to CCS when unfit men[?] 2 OR	7pk
	27th		Sent 5 OR to duty. German officer men. Sent Capt Sebron + 2 men r section to 65th field Ambce admits 2 officer sick + wounded. 54 OR sick + 91 OR wounded.	7pk
			1 Genl sick + 19 wounded 2 wounded all Copr gabon + 2 men wounded Ladn[?] army myll	
VILLE-EN TARDENOIS	28th		18 OR wounded when with unit in line. Left Jonchery at 8 AM and moved to TARRENELLES and under orders to FÈRE-EN-TARDENOIS admits evacuates + wounded etc	8pk

Army Form C. 2118.

WAR DIARY
or
INTELLIGENCE SUMMARY.
(Erase heading not required.)

Instructions regarding War Diaries and Intelligence Summaries are contained in F. S. Regs., Part II. and the Staff Manual respectively. Title pages will be prepared in manuscript.

Place	Date	Hour	Summary of Events and Information	Remarks and references to Appendices
FESTIGNY	MAY 29th		Moved to FESTIGNY. Major Grey rejoined unit.	SDK
BOURSALT	30th		Moved to BOURSALT. Awaits 2 sick and wounded then	SDK
SOULIÈRES	31st		Moved to SOULIÈRES. Awaits 10 officers & 90 OR + wounded then.	SDK
			G.D. Forsyth Major RAMC OC 63 = Field Amb	

160/3076.

No. 637.0.

June 1918

COMMITTEE FOR THE
MEDICAL HISTORY OF THE WAR
Date 7 AUG 1918

Army Form C. 2118.

MEDICAL

WAR DIARY
or
INTELLIGENCE SUMMARY. 62/3 Field Ambulance
(Erase heading not required.)

O.C.

Place	Date	Hour	Summary of Events and Information	Remarks and references to Appendices
CONDÉLIZY	June 1st		Received orders to accompany the 21st Inf in our advance over the Seine. Personnel entrained at SOUILLY at 8AM and detrained by VARDY and marched to CONDÉLIZY. On orders transport marched by road – the remainder with 20 Amb personnel went to 85th Dec'd. Ambulance to open tent wards we are on the line of march & join H.Q.E. Casualties 6 sick, 1 wounded + 1 gad wounded.	S/K
"	2nd		Major Grey & Lt Bennett + 20 OR proceeded to form A.D.S. in wood just North of M in CHAN PAILLET. Reconnoitred our front & visited the 3 batts. Four men were actually to be A.D.S. presence of M.O.'s Two cars were sent & picked up wounded. Formed the M.D.S. and one evacuated. Casualties 11 sick and 1 wounded.	SM SD
"	3rd		Arrangements for C.C.V. beginning retirement. Major Grey Main dressing Station at ECOLE COMELIZY formed. 6 OR Det & form relay post at VASSY for R.A. Post TR Y. Sent 1 car + 60R & T rand Ambe 1½ kilometres south of TROISSY. to evacuate Cases from R.A.P. at TROISSY. One car blown up by shell fire near VASSY. Results 12 sick + 3 wounded. Sick & wounded RAPs prevents thin. Various reinforcements from RAPs. Casualties 7, Sick, troops 6 Evacuated ____	SM
"	4th		Died 1 6 Eng'y	S.M.

Army Form C. 2118.

WAR DIARY
or
INTELLIGENCE SUMMARY.
(Erase heading not required.)

Instructions regarding War Diaries and Intelligence Summaries are contained in F. S. Regs., Part II. and the Staff Manual respectively. Title pages will be prepared in manuscript.

Place	Date	Hour	Summary of Events and Information	Remarks and references to Appendices
CONBLIZY	June 5th		Admits 15 sick & 3 wounded. Evac 2 sick & 3 wounded. Reinforcements 16. Lt. Gluckin sent to reinforcement camp 21st Infantry. See for temporary duty. Visits to posts	FM
"	6th		Admits 1 officer sick, 13 OR sick, 3 OR sick & 1 wounded. Evac 7 wounded. Visits to posts	PM
"	7th		Major Irvine & Capt Jebson relieved by Capt T. St. Arnauld & Lt. Mr Cush 1 OR sick 2 sick 76 wounded. Admits 1 Officer sick, 11 OR sick, Evac 2 sick 7 wounded. Evacuated sick. Visits posts	SM
"	8th		Admits 1 Officer 1 sick & 1 wounded. O.R. 16 sick & 7 wounded. Evacuated sick. Visits to posts. 6	PM
"	9th		Admits 1 Officer sick & 1 O.R. sick & 1 wounded. O.R. 2 sick & 1 wounded. Evac 1 Officer sick & 1 sick and wounded. Casualties	PM
"	10th		Admits 8 sick & 1 wounded Evac and 5 sick and 1 wounded Jent. Discharged 3 to duty 1 out to evac to hosp. 7 to hosp & 5 sent to CCS.	PM
"	11th		Admits 6 sick & 1 wounded. On duty 2 escort 1 wounded 14 OCCS. Admits 2 sick 10 sick & 8 wounded. Evacuated 14 CCS Visits HQ & relay posts	PM

WAR DIARY
or
INTELLIGENCE SUMMARY.
(Erase heading not required.)

Army Form C. 2118.

Place	Date	Hour	Summary of Events and Information	Remarks and references to Appendices
CONBLIZY	June 12th		Admitted British 10 sick & 1 wounded. Evacuated 10 sick. Admitted French 10 Officer wounded OR 6 sick & 7 wounded. Evacuated all to CCS. Visits ADS & relay post. Capt Scott reports from leave.	J.M.
"	13th		Admitted total 5 sick & 1 OR & 2 French sick. Evacuated all to CCS. Visits ADS & posts.	J.M.
"	14th		Admitted 1 Officer wounded OR 12 sick & 1 wounded. Evacuated to CCS. Capt. Scott relieved Major Jarvie at ADS.	J.M.
"	15th		Admitted 4 sick & 7 wounded total 2 sick & 7 wounded French. Evacuated all to CCS. Visits ADS & relay post	J.M.
"	16th		Transfer with 9th Bn Loyal 10 AD and march with transport to TOURON-LA-MONTAGNE. 91st Independent Noe to CCS Admitted 1 sick & evacuated to CCS	J.M.
"	17th		Officers & OR at ADS and relay huts returned by the French on Infantry were relieved at 5.15 AM and marched to 1 mile south of unit marched MB at 5.15 AM and marched to VASSIMONT. Transport travel as at 12 noon JGMY & ambulances to take & wounded & evacuate them to CCS Admitted 1 British sick & transferred to CCS	J.M.
VASSIMONT	17th			J.M.

Army Form C. 2118.

WAR DIARY
or
INTELLIGENCE SUMMARY.
(Erase heading not required.)

Instructions regarding War Diaries and Intelligence Summaries are contained in F. S. Regs., Part II. and the Staff Manual respectively. Title pages will be prepared in manuscript.

Place	Date	Hour	Summary of Events and Information	Remarks and references to Appendices
VASSIMONT	June 18th	3:30 PM	Left VASSIMONT at 1 PM and marched to SOMMESOUS and entrained at 3:30 PM. Motor Ambulance proceeded by road. Admtts 2 sick & 1 wounded then	SPA
(ENROUTE)	19th		24 hours en route to INVAL-BOURIN.	APA
INVAL-BOURIN	20th		Detrained at 12:30 AM and marched to INVAL-BOURIN. Incorporated with 65th F.A. as 2nd wound unit. Capt Gibson attached for temporary duty with 15th Durham L.I. St. Gladden returned for duty with 14th Northumberland Fusiliers (Pioneers). Admtts 1 sick & 1 wounded, him & C.I.	SPA
LE CORNET	21st		Marched Vb at 3 PM and billets at LE CORNET. Admtts 1 Officer & 10 OR. Sounds thin & C.I.	FA
DEVILLE	22nd		Marched Vb at 10 AM to DEVILLE. Admtts 14 sick. Evacuates 4 F.C.S.	FA
GRANDCOURT	23rd		Marched Vb at 2 PM to GRANDCOURT. Admtts 13 sick. Discharges 26 duty. Transfers 23 to 65 F.A.	SPA
"	24th		Admts 1 sick to 65 F.A. Unit is undergoing course of training in drill & duties.	FA
"	25th		Admts 1 OR to 65 F.A. Unit moves to be ready to transfer by rail. Awaits orders in 2 & in use	SPA

(A7093). Wt. W12859/M1293. 75,000. 1/17. D. D. & L., Ltd. Forms/C.2118/14.

Army Form C. 2118.

WAR DIARY
or
INTELLIGENCE SUMMARY.
(Erase heading not required.)

Instructions regarding War Diaries and Intelligence Summaries are contained in F. S. Regs., Part II. and the Staff Manual respectively. Title pages will be prepared in manuscript.

Place	Date	Hour	Summary of Events and Information	Remarks and references to Appendices
GRANDCOURT	June 26th		Remained in billets. During the week contrary to instructions received orders to be prepared to move at 24 hrs notice and orders for move in 2 pts was cancelled.	S.M.
"	27th		Admits 1 sick and transfer transits to 6 C.C.S.	S.M.
"	28th		Admits 1 and evacuates to 6 C.C.S. 22 O.R. joined as reinforcements	S.M. M.
"	29th		Admits 1 Officer & 69 O.R. evacuates 1 C.C.S.	S.M.
"	30th		Admits 1 Officer & 29 O.R. evacuates to C.C.S. Received order to move to another area transferred less one limber left by road under orders of Major Irvine	

E. J Kavanagh
Major R.A.M.C.
OC 63rd Field Ambulance

140/3134

63rd F.A.

18/6/18

WAR DIARY or INTELLIGENCE SUMMARY

Army Form C. 2118.

No. 63
63rd Cas[ualty]
MEDICAL

Place	Date	Hour	Summary of Events and Information	Remarks and references to Appendices
GRANDCOURT	July 1st		Marched out at 7AM to BLANGY and entrained at 4.30 PM	JJK
BEAUQUESNE	2nd		Detrained at CANDAS at 2.30 AM and marched to BEAUQUESNE. Admitted 190 O.R. Evacuated to C.C.S.	JJK
"	3rd		Transport arrived. Admitted 240 O.R. Evacuated 156 C.C.S., admitted 6 to D.R.S.	JJK
"	4th		Admitted 238 O.R. Evacuated 10 to C.C.S. and sent 8 to D.R.S.	JJK
"	5th		Admitted 101 O.R. and evacuated him to C.C.S. Lts. KNOX E.S. & JOHNSON J.L. U.S.M.C. reports for duty and are taken on strength.	JJK
"	6th		Admitted 120 O.R. Evacuated 28 C.C.S. and 28 to D.R.S. Capt. Scott details for duty with 2nd Lincoln Regt.	JJK
"	7th		Capt. Fischel (C.H.) found for duty and is taken in strength. Beauch. Admitted 108 O.R. Evacuated him to C.C.S. and 18 to D.R.S.	JJK
"	8th		Major Irvine and Prof. attended lecture on Diarrhoea & Dysentery by Lieut. Colonel in Pathology, 3rd Army. A figure lodge at officers mess from No. 62 & staff & divisional officers on "Liaison between field ambulances and R.M.O.'s"	JJK
"	9th		Admitted 1. Evacuated him to C.C.S.	JJK

WAR DIARY
or
INTELLIGENCE SUMMARY.

Army Form C. 2118.

Place	Date	Hour	Summary of Events and Information	Remarks and references to Appendices
BEAUQUESNE	July 10th		Unit was inspected by Corps Commander with 62, 2nd Bde & R.E. Group. Admitted 2. Evacuated 18 to C.C.S.	F.D.R.
"	11th		Admitted 9. Evacuated 10 to C.C.S.	F.D.R.
"	12th		Admitted 8 Officers & men to Unit & C.C.S.	F.D.R.
"	13th		Admitted 1 Officer, S.O.R. Discharged 1 & 2 of Evacuated 1 Officer & 7 O.R. to C.C.S. Capt. Fischel proceed on leave.	F.D.R.
"	14th		Admitted 1 Officer & 3 O.R. and evacuated the CCS Capt. Gibson rejoined unit for duty	F.D.R.
"	15th		Admitted 1 Officer & 2 O.R. Evacuated to & to C.S. 129th Field Ambulance arrived bad delayed early as we take over from them with them grief move 10 & 17 th. Lival hospital move	S.D.R.
"	16th		Orders received at 10 P.M. to lival hospital move 1 Officer & 2 O.R. to C.C.S. Admitted 1 Officer & 8 O.R. Evacuated 1 Officer & 2 O.R. to C.C.S.	F.D.R.
"	17th		Admitted 1 Officer & 2 O.R. Evacuated to & C.C.S.	F.D.R.
"	18th		Admitted 6. Evacuated 2 to C.C.S.	F.D.R.

WAR DIARY
or
INTELLIGENCE SUMMARY.

Army Form C. 2118.

Place	Date	Hour	Summary of Events and Information	Remarks and references to Appendices
BEAUQUESNE	July 19th		admits 4. Evacuats 8 C.C.S.	SM
"	20th		admitted 1	SM
"	21st		admits 1. Evacuats 2 C.C.S	SM
"	22nd		admits 1.	SJK
"	23rd		Evacuats 1 & 2 C.C.S 1 & 2 & 3 Casuals C.C.S	
"	24th		Major Freis, Sts Bennett, Johnson & Powell with 2 men ambulance & 2 tent subdivisions proceeded as advance party to take over the line from 148th Field Ambulance (63rd RN Division) the Line Brown 148th Field Amb at 7.15 A.M. Reached outpost Took over ambulances from 64th & 65th Field Ambulances 1 officer, 1 Bearer subdivision & ACHEUX - where advanced party reports for duty until the unit arrives.	SM
ACHEUX	25th		admits 4. Discharged 14 sub-units Evacuats 4 C.C.S. Unit marched out at 10 A.M and reached ACHEUX at 1.15 P.M took over the D.S at ACHEUX from 148 Fd Amb. HQ at ENGLEBELMER. MAILLY-MAILLET and ADS at ENGLEBELMER. Early in the afternoon. Have men at Line 62nd Bde in the line. Have men at Line Bde Brigade in the line. O 2 central, reserve R.A.P O 7 b 76. R.A.P O 3 c 95. Support R.A.P O 2 central There are also 1 NCO + 2 squads at Relay Post O 8 b 6 0.	SM

WAR DIARY or **INTELLIGENCE SUMMARY.**

Army Form C. 2118.

Place	Date	Hour	Summary of Events and Information	Remarks and references to Appendices
ACHEUX	July 25		64th Bde in Centre outposts. Line RAP Q16 C.8.2. Support RAP Q8 C.5.3. Reserve RAP Q7C 7.2. Each RAP except reserve RAP Leave RAMC personnel (Varying in numbers according to circumstances) Relay Posts at Q14 C.1.8 & Q 15- C 3.3. 110th Suff. Doc on right subsector. Line RAP at Q 28 C 6.7 with Support RAP RAMC 1NCO & 2 Spinds (reinforced when necessary) Reserve RAP Q 26. L 6.6. with 1 Spinal R.H.L. & reserved R.A.P. Q.19. C.g. 9.6. Q26 L 6.6 with 1 Spind R.H.L & reserved R at BEAUSSART. P.11.b.4.5. Relay Post between Q 21 S.3.3. Placed at Coy & men at nearby points to 8 Parties collecting points for wounded from RAPs been out to 8 posted such Posts and Jame RAP Admitted sick 2 Officer 20R, Wounded 1 Offr & 4 OR Evacuates 2 Officer & 5 OR & C.C.S.	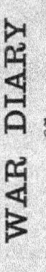
	26th		Visited the two ADS and RAPs & relay posts of Centre Brigade. Admitted 5 sick, 7 wounded. Evacuated 7 & C.C.S.	
	27th		Visited the two ADS and RAPS & relay posts of Left Brigade. Admitted sick 1 Offr & 10 OR, Wounded 2 OR Evacuated 13 to C.C.S.	
	28th		Visited the two ADS & relay posts RAP. right 1 Sgt admitted Sick 1 Offr & 6 OR. Wounded 1 Officer & 6 OR Evacuated 2 Offrs & 2 ORs CCS	

WAR DIARY or INTELLIGENCE SUMMARY.

Army Form C. 2118.

Place	Date	Hour	Summary of Events and Information	Remarks and references to Appendices
ACHEUX	July 29		Admitted Sick 1 Officer & 19 OR. Wounded 8 OR. Sick up 1 Ortz. Evacuated 29 det CCS. Visited 2 ADS & RAP's Centre Infusse. D.M.S. their Army inspected the Unit. Heavy fire shelling during the night around ADS.	E.J.K.
	30th		Proceeded to ADS NAILLY MAILLE T. Sham attack on Corps Front. Passed thro' a great number of gassed cases. Admitted sick 3 Officers +100R. Wounded 98 OR. Evacuated 21 to CCS.	E.J.K.
	31st		Admitted sick 4 Officers + 100R. Wounded OR 6. Evacuated 19 to CCS. Capt Fischel reports from leave. He was actually with 7 Leicesters Regt in relief of Capt Stephens for duty with sick Evacuated A.H.T. Davis reported for attached duty for instruction in front line work	E.J.K.

E. J. Kavanagh
Major R.A.M.C.
O.C. 63rd Field Ambulance

140/3200

COMMITTEE FOR THE
MEDICAL HISTORY OF THE W.
Date 5 OCT. 1918

63rd F.A.

Aug. 1918.

WAR DIARY or INTELLIGENCE SUMMARY

Army Form C. 2118.

MEDICAL

WL 36

Place	Date	Hour	Summary of Events and Information	Remarks and references to Appendices
ACHEUX	1st		Admits 12 sick & 7 wounded. One car sent forward to 2nd Field Amb: ADS at ENGLEBELMER and RAPs and relay posts 8 AM & 6 PM. 25 J cases passed to ADMS Corps.	
"	2nd		Admits 8 sick & 10 wounded. Evacuated 152 C.C.S. Visits ADS MAILLY BAILLY & RAPs & relay posts of Cake Row HOY MAILLY	
"	3rd		Admits sick 1 officer 30 OR wounded B.O.R. Visits MAILLY, HOY MAILLY. Evacuated 35 J cases 1 officer & OR	
"	4th		MAILLY & relay posts RAPs & left side admits sick 1 officer & 70 OR wounded 20 OR. Evacuated for J cases Centre. Evacuated 1 officer & OR. Visits 2 J.D.S. admits sick 1 officer & 70 OR wounded 12 cases & sick cases	
"	5th		Evacuates 1 off & 17 O.R. Passed 12 cases & sick dere. Evacuates to RAMC MDS & left dere. Visits MDS ADS relay posts RAMC MDS & left dere. Exchanged 3 grout serments 3 F.C.S. admits 8 sick and 1 wounded.	
"	6th		Admits Officers 2 sick & 3 OR sick & 10 wounded. Evacuates 2 officers & 2 H.D.S. 13 OR F.C.S. Visits 2 H.D.S. RMS 1 went BADS & visits RAP which was near Road by 62nd Inf Ate.	
"	7th		Visits relay post OR & RAP 6.8.6.0. We evacuate cases quiet from the by Capt F.H. Dix. Capt F.W. CHAMBERLAIN reported for duty with the unit from 65th Field Ambulance in relief of Capt JOHNSTON who went to 65th F.A.	

WAR DIARY
or
INTELLIGENCE SUMMARY

Army Form C. 2118.

Place	Date	Hour	Summary of Events and Information	Remarks and references to Appendices
ACHEUX	August 7th		Admitted sick 1 Officer 10 OR & wounded 7 OR. Evacuated 1 Officer 15 OR to CCS.	EJK
"	8th		Admitted sick 6 OR wounded 2 Officers & 2 OR. Evacuated 2 Officers & 29 OR to CCS. On duty. One Dressing ADS Section evacuated to ADS MAILLY MAILLET. Capt Gibson returned from 38 CCS.	EJK
"	9th		Capt Cameron at ADS on leave going on. Capt Davis relieved Capt Cameron at ADS on relief party of Ry. Hospital. 14 days leave. Visits RAP. 1st 3 wounded Officers 1 OR 10. Admitted Officers sick 1, OR 3 wounded Officers 1, OR 13 OR to CCS. Visits RAP 3rd relay post. Discharged 1 A.Surg? 1 wounded 2 Officers & CCS entre mise. Admitted sick 14 wounded evacuated 11 CCS.	5 OR 8 EJK
"	10th		Admitted 3 sick & 6 wounded evacuated 8 & CCS	8 OR
"	11th		Visits ADS 1st Ing 2 & L. mCR + RAP 1 + relay posts 1 Officer wounded ADMS?	8 OR
"	12th		DDMS Corps inspects ADS at Mar 224. Mailly T. MDS. Admits sick 3 Officers 14 OR & wounded 4 OR. Evacuates 2 Officers 17 OR to CCS. Capt Gibson relieves Major Grey at ADS. Overnight Carpentier? & freak Sunshower? removal of RAP B28 c6 75 and orderly post B21 c3.9 plus RAP was shown up by own Division.	EJK

WAR DIARY or INTELLIGENCE SUMMARY

Army Form C. 2118

Place	Date	Hour	Summary of Events and Information	Remarks and references to Appendices
ACHEUX 	August 13th		admitted 9 wounded. Cement. DCCS Visits 2 ADS and RA73 Offr. scolds	SJK
"	14th		Major Graham Capt Strode and 40 OR from 64th Field Ambulance reports for duty. Enemy returns on our front. 2 a.m. Heir released Capt Patterson and Bennetts sick officer. 2 OR. 3 wounded. 6 sick. Lieut: F (with DTO Col. Capt H.N. MATTHEWS (F.S.) taken on Strength. 2nd Lieut. T. E. Syft. C.E. in 3 Movements # Officer & 93 OR. 2 wounded 2 sick.	SJK
"	15th		Scotch Med. Movements 4 on 4 Moments 4 Officers & RAP.3 of 64th ADE moved to Surrey Keep in Each with enemy wheeled station. On car Q 12 Q 26. Sent 4 Officers Bearers with wheeled station. Came to STATION HOUSE sent to Q 11 at 8.9 in BEAUMONT HAMEL. 4 West took Cases to Q. D.S. wounded were cleared twenty Q.8 Q 6.0 and are cleared by Car Q. R. Ditch. 1 RSO & 2 Brown & 75 Patients. 1 RSO & 2 Brown Sent RAP & HESSIAN Q 28 C 6.75. Patients 1 RSO & 2 Brown Sent 7th Leics on moved RAP & HESIAN Q Q 12 Q 26. 15th Durham L.I. moved to Q 10 A 8.8	SJK
"	16th		RAP of Yorks remained at Q 12 Q 26. and 9th Q 20 Q 41 to MAILLY-MAILLET. admitted sick 2 Officers 16 OR. wounded 2 Officers & 32 OR. discharged 1 Lieut. Canrades 5 officers & 36 OR & CCS 1 Officer & 10 OR. died. 64th ADE RAP & relay post & 40 OR from 64 OR. Visitor 62nd & 64th ADE. RHQ & relay post Strained.	SJK
"	17th		62nd ADE relieved 64th ADS in line. RAP from line D.10.d.7.7 Relay post Q 16 Q 14. Car post at Q.9. c.8.9 & another car post at Q 8 Q 6.0 Sub Car RAP at Q 7 a.7.6. Cases carried by wheeled stretcher bearers to ADS. RAP Q 16 C 8.2 & these cases for & relay post at Q 16 D. 14 & HQ BDE three bears	

WAR DIARY or INTELLIGENCE SUMMARY

Army Form C. 2118.

Place	Date	Hour	Summary of Events and Information	Remarks and references to Appendices
ACHEUX	August 17th		RAP at Q.26.a.8.9. & covers three by wheeled stretcher RAPs. Reserve RAP at Q.19.c.2.5. Cars carried direct to ADS. Bright night. RAPs relayed into Divisional reserve. One M.O. transferred. Capt Stroud & remaining personnel from 64th DA. Major Graham, Capt Stroud, Capt Stone. rejoins their unit. 2Lt N.J. Cork visits MDS. Capt Gibson relieves 2Lt Johnson at ADS ENGLEBELMER. 2Lt Knott proceeds to ADS HAILLY-MAILLET. Acquitte rich & Maur. 18 OR wounded, 1 Officer & 8 OR evacuated & wagon. wounded 3 Officer & 90R to CCS	E.K.
"	18th		Visits RAPs & relay posts & left ADS. Evacuate between 2nd Lieuts. outposts & enemy lentern clearer to 2nd Lieut & HP Casualties. Evacuates directly they got to RAP. Evacuates rich Officer 1, OR 2 wounded 100R wounded 1 Officer & 120 OR CCS	E.K.
"	19th		Visits RAPs & relay posts. Acquitte 1 Officer sick, wounded Officer 1 & OR 10 TOX evacuate 1 Officer wounded Officer 3 & OR 10 BCCS	E.K.
"	20th		Hinder san ADS ENGLEBELMER & 38th Division Personnel from the reported for duty at ADS HAILLY-MAILLET. Troops settling and remained to Divisional reserve. 65th DA reported for duty in rear of Divisional Operation. 3 Divisional Spins & each battalion	E.K.

Army Form C. 2118.

WAR DIARY
or
INTELLIGENCE SUMMARY.
(Erase heading not required.)

Instructions regarding War Diaries and Intelligence Summaries are contained in F. S. Regs., Part II. and the Staff Manual respectively. Title pages will be prepared in manuscript.

Place	Date August	Hour	Summary of Events and Information	Remarks and references to Appendices
ACHEUX	21st		Division attacked. I ran cars in morning to station AUCHONVILLERS - later to BEAUMONT HAMEL and made AUCHONVILLERS collecting post. 3 Lis relay post in front of BEAUMONT HAMEL as troops have forward to carry cases from SPEARS R.A.P. Casualties evacuated Major Graham and Lieut Emerson of 64th F.A. reported for duty	EDT
	22nd		Division still in action. 3 Lis motor cars at BEAUMONT-HAMEL. Cases evacuated satisfactorily	SM
	23rd		However annoying I detailed Lt Johnson G.P. to BEAUMONT-HAMEL with many cts to see patients were fit for journey before being put in car opened there an advanced H.Q.S. Cases were evacuated hourly. Sent to relay to BEAUMONT before cars were placed as accents cases. Cars were sent to BEAUCOURT & relieve Junior Shipten collecting Post at AUCHONVILLERS Cases sent direct to ADS by Cpl Hawkes on ACHEUX & 65th F.A. Later ambulance moved up	SM
MAILLY-MAILLET	24th		Moved ADS to BEAUMONT-HAMEL & later to BEAUCOURT. All casualties evacuated. 190 B severance wounded. Forty reports for any a stretcher bearers	PPT
MIRAUMONT	25th		Ambulance moved up to MIRAUMONT and opened ADS. Cars collecting cases from stations at LESARS and at COURCELETTE. Handed over MAILLY-MAILLET to 65th F.A	
	26th		Opened ADS at QUARRY LESARS MIRAUMONT became M.D.S. Capt Chamberlain, Lt Knot and 18 OR reported for duty with 17 F.D.S. 17th Div at POZIERES. 65th F.A. took over from me evacuation of the line	

(A7092). Wt. W12639/M1293. 75,000. 1/17. D. D. & L., Ltd. Forms/C.2118/14.

Army Form C. 2118.

WAR DIARY
or
INTELLIGENCE SUMMARY.
(Erase heading not required.)

Instructions regarding War Diaries and Intelligence Summaries are contained in F. S. Regs., Part II. and the Staff Manual respectively. Title pages will be prepared in manuscript.

Place	Date	Hour	Summary of Events and Information	Remarks and references to Appendices
MIRAUMONT	August 27th		Remained at MIRAUMONT admitted 21 sick & 39 wounded. Evacuated to C.C.S.	SM
"	28th		Nothing to note. admitted 26 sick & 17 wounded. Evacuated to C.C.S.	SM
"	29th		admitted 13 sick & 8 wounded. Evacuated to C.C.S. 98 OR 64 OR. Nf. No details returned to this unit.	SM
"	30th		admitted 21 sick & 24 wounded. Evacuated 26 Out. Evacuated 42 C.C.S. Major Grey went on leave	SM
"	31st		Remained. 96 Infantry planned regained unit. admitted 1 officer + 16 OR sick. Evacuated to C.C.S.	SM

E. G. Konrad
Major R.A.M.C.
OC 63rd Field Amb.

140/3259.

63rd F. Amb.

Feb. 1918

COMMITTEE FOR THE
MEDICAL HISTORY OF
Date

WAR DIARY or INTELLIGENCE SUMMARY

Army Form C. 2118.

63rd Fd Amb

V8 37 MEDICAL

Place	Date	Hour	Summary of Events and Information	Remarks and references to Appendices
MIRAUMONT	September 1st		Admitted Sick 1 wounded Evac to C.C.S.	J.M.
"		2nd	Admitted 9 sick Evac to C.C.S	J.M.
"		3rd	Admitted 9 sick Evac to C.C.S.	J.M.
"		4th	Admitted 5 sick 1 wounded Evac to C.C.S	J.M.
GINCHY		5th	Moved to GINCHY at 8 A.M. Major Irvine, Lt Johnson and 1 O.R. returned from SAILLY-SAILLESEL and took over Bearing Station from 130th & 131st Field Ambces	
SAILLY-SAILLESEL		6th	Remainder of unit moved to SAILLY-SAILLESEL	
"		7th	Admitted Officers Sick 3 Wounded 4 O.R. Sick 39 Wounded 128. Evacuated to C.C.S. Officers Sick 3 Wounded 4 O.R. Sick 39 Wounded 176. Died O.R. 2 (I wounds)	D.H.
"		8th	Admitted O.R. Sick 10 Wounded 2. Evacuated to C.C.S. O.R. Sick 10 Wounded 2. O.C. proceed on 10 days leave in U.K. France.	
"		9th	One N.C.O. & O.R. 8 proceeded on a Holding party at M.D.S. V.23. Central Sheet 57.C. Admitted Officers Sick 1 O.R. Sick 9. Evacuated to C.C.S. Officers Sick 1 O.R. Sick 9. Wounded 5. Evacuated to C.C.S. Officers Sick 1 O.R. Sick 9 transferred 5. Lieut Jorrisson M.C.R.C. attached to M.D.S. V.23 Central Sheet 57.C	J.M.

WAR DIARY or INTELLIGENCE SUMMARY

Army Form C. 2118.

Place	Date	Hour	Summary of Events and Information	Remarks and references to Appendices
Suzanne South	10th		Capt W.J. Gibson R.A.M.C. (T.C.) detailed for Duty at 38 C.C.S. Barbarin on Front. Admitted Officer 1 sick O.R sick 2.	DDH
	11		Evacuated Officer sick 1 to O.R sick 2 to C.C.S.	DDH
			Admitted O.R sick 7. O.R wounded 1. Evacuated O.R sick 6 ? wounded	DDH
	12		O.R 1 to C.C.S. Two G.S. Waggons under orders of A.D.M.S proceeded to Meaulte Mallet to collect stretchers left there by a Divisional Ambulance. Admitted O.R sick 14. O.R wounded 4. Evacuated O.R sick 14 to C.C.S. O.R wounded 2 to C.C.S. 4 discharged to duty. O.R wounded 2	DDH
	13		Admitted O.R wounded 1, Discharged O.R 1 to duty, Two G.S Waggons returned from Meaulte-Mallet with 112 stretchers	DDH
	14		No admissions. Sick & local Units attended to.	RAH
	15		No admissions & sick & local Units attended to.	DDH
ETRICOURT	16th		H.Q & Unit with Transport moved to V.2.d.5.8 sheet 57.C. 8th R.A.M.C. O.R reported for duty	DDH

Army Form C. 2118.

WAR DIARY
or
INTELLIGENCE SUMMARY.
(Erase heading not required.)

Instructions regarding War Diaries and Intelligence Summaries are contained in F.S. Regs., Part II. and the Staff Manual respectively. Title pages will be prepared in manuscript.

Place	Date	Hour	Summary of Events and Information	Remarks and references to Appendices
ETRICOURT	17		Lieut Johnson M.R.C. detailed for Temp duty at 17th Div MDS (53rd Field Amb) in relief of Capt Chamberlain R.A.M.C. Capt Chamberlain & 7 O.R. detailed for temporary duty with No 3 C.C.S. BEAULNCOURT. 13. O.R. R.A.M.C. detailed for dressing duties – 1 each as under. H.B. 62, 64, 110, 5th Inf Brigade, H.B. 94 & 95th Battns R.F.A. 9/94 15/94 C/94 D/94 Batt. R.F.A. 9/95 15/95 C/95 D/95 13th R.F.A. One Ford Car detailed for duty with 65th Field Amb & two stage cars to Combined A.D.S. (38th Division)	AH J
"	18th		Returned from leave 17th Major Frey & Pte Brown leave arrived in camp. One O.R. A.C.N.T. uniform & establishment transferred to 64th D.A	JM
"	19th		Remained in camp	JM
"	20th		Nurses attached to 65th D.A reported for duty at NDn	LD R
"	21st		Nothing to note	LR
"	22nd		Nothing to note	to SM
"	23rd		Personnel attached to the 9th Bn reported	L M
"	24th		8 O.R attached to 94th & 95th AU RFA returned	

Army Form C. 2118.

WAR DIARY
or
INTELLIGENCE SUMMARY.
(Erase heading not required.)

Instructions regarding War Diaries and Intelligence Summaries are contained in F. S. Regs., Part II. and the Staff Manual respectively. Title pages will be prepared in manuscript.

Place	Date	Hour	Summary of Events and Information	Remarks and references to Appendices
FINS	SEPTEMBER 25th		Unit moved and took over A.D.S. at FINS (V.11 & 6.0) and the line from 52nd Field Ambulance (attached) (wounded) 1 runner and 2 squads to each half of 62nd Infy. Bde. 180R reports from C.M.D.S. between runner 3. 65th J.A. reports on duty Capt. Cannon and runner runner 3. 64th J.A. reports on duty Capt. Stroud and runner runner 2 squads from 6.5th J.H. to each half of attached (runner and 2 squads the same from 6.4th J.H. to each Batt. 64th & 65th J.H. to each Batt. 64th & 65th J.H.)	SK
			Bttys R.H.A. Bearer posts at W.16.a. central where I could M.O. and 2 Bearer posts at W.12.c. W.4. a.D.4. The Bearer squads also Bearer posts on accoutred on the line.	
			Each hut one reinforced connecting from the line. We evacuate by R.A.P. and walking from to posts and motor the R.A.P.s. Bearer reports on duty Several to post and 100 Infantry Bearer reports on duty.	SK
	26th		R.A.P.s. evacuate casualties	
	27th		12/13 Northumberland Fusiliers attacked. Casualties evacuated. 1 Visits their R.A.P.s & all evacuation. Heavy casualties	SK
"	28th		Evacuate casualties	Tot

WAR DIARY
or
INTELLIGENCE SUMMARY.
(Erase heading not required.)

Army Form C. 2118.

Places	Date	Hour	Summary of Events and Information	Remarks and references to Appendices
COURCELLCOURT	September 29th		I moved all Nurses from old headquarters @ R 31.6.4 and established H.Qrs. Dr Collecting Cars practically direct from R.A.Ps. with Boss Cars in D/G 17 & Divn. Major Irwin & Capt Bremner handed over site at M D/G & F1.N.S - COURCELCOURT road. and moved to W.2.C.8.2 on F1.N.S - COURCELCOURT road. I visited all R.A.Ps. Capt Williams reported in relief of Capt Stroude who returned to his unit.	2/K
"	30th		Evacuate casualties. Visited R.A.Ps. which are situated in CONNELIEN & VILLERS-PLOUISLANS. Collecting cases from them directly by Ford Cars.	T/K

G. J. Kavanagh
Lieut Col. R.A.M.C.
O.C. 63rd Field Ambulance

Oct 1918

No. 63. Fd Amb

160/3324

COMMITTEE FOR THE
MEDICAL HISTORY OF THE WAR
Date 4 DEC 30

Army Form C. 2118.

WAR DIARY
or
INTELLIGENCE SUMMARY.
(Erase heading not required.)

MEDICAL

Instructions regarding War Diaries and Intelligence Summaries are contained in F.S. Regs., Part II. and the Staff Manual respectively. Title pages will be prepared in manuscript.

Place	Date	Hour	Summary of Events and Information	Remarks and references to Appendices
GOUZEAUCOURT	October 1st		Moved A.D.S. and transport to GOUZEAUCOURT. Visits R.A.P.s and relay posts. Casualties evacuated.	P.M.
"	2nd		Evacuated Casualties. Visits R.A.P.s	8 P.M.
"	3rd		Evacuated Casualties. Visits R.A.P.s	8 P.M.
"	4th		Evacuated Casualties. Visits R.A.P.s	3 P.M.
"	5th		Evacuated Casualties. Visits R.A.P.s	5 P.M.
BANTOUZELLE	5th		Moved my H.Qrs to BANTOUZELLE. A.D. and transport moved to BANTEUX.	5 P.M.
"	6th		Moved H.Qrs to M.33.b.2.8.	
"	7th		Took up my H.Q. Dr at CRATTE TRANCHE FARM M.35.a.2.4. (Shelters & D.O.)	5 P.M.
"	"		Visits R.A.P.s & relay posts.	
"	8th		Enemy attacked. Casualties rapidly evacuated. Visits R.A.P.s & relay.	7 P.M.
"	"		Moved my H.Q. Dr to M.36.a.7.7	9 P.M.
"	9th		Evacuated Casualties. Visits R.A.P.s	
WALINCOURT	10th		Entire unit moved to WALINCOURT. Surgeons relieved. Personnel & officers from 64th & 65th Field Ambces. reported their unit.	5 P.M.
"	11th		Infantry stretcher bearers attached reported unit. Bearers attached to battns. rejoined units.	

WAR DIARY or INTELLIGENCE SUMMARY

Army Form C. 2118.

Place	Date	Hour	Summary of Events and Information	Remarks and references to Appendices
WALINCOURT	Oct 12th		Remained in billets.	FJK
"	13th		Remained in billets. Lt. Kent invented to CCS and struck off strength	FJK
"	14th		Remained in billets	FJK
"	15th		Remained in billets	FJK
"	15th		Remained billet	FJK
"	16th		Remained billet 7OR (reinforcement) reported	FJK
"	17th		Remained in billet.	FJK
"	18th		Remained in billet	FJK
"	19th		Remained in billet	FJK
"	20th		Remained in billet	FJK
"	21st		Remained in billet	FJK
NURLU	22nd		Marched out at 1000 hours and moved to AUDENCOURT left knapsack, moving section the journey to NEUVILLY with Major Jack and leaves division Capt Cameron to beaver division to 65th DIV reports true per Mjr Spokesman and receiver division 76b 2nd DIV reports burnt receiver + renews attached to Jack. Capt Mr. P Livenson Brigades B62 2nd Div reports Jones Dir	FJK

WAR DIARY or INTELLIGENCE SUMMARY

Army Form C. 2118.

Place	Date	Hour	Summary of Events and Information	Remarks and references to Appendices
OMILLERS	October 23		Division attacked and as they progressed we formed our posts & relay posts to close up. Finally joined up on new posts at OMILLERS. Major Graham's mounted bringade. Major Irvine went on duty to 65th S.A. Sub advanced Corps to VENDEGIES-au-BOIS. Invited all posts relay posts. Casualties - Nil.	 J.M.
VENDEGIES au BOIS	24th		Moved to VENDEGIES-au-BOIS. Sub advanced Corps to POIX-du-NORD and had relay posts there. Invited all posts. Casualties - Nil.	J.M.
"	25th		Jumped / moved to OMILLERS. Casualties - Nil.	
"	26th		Things quiet. Casualties - Nil. Inv'td all posts. Unit moved to NEUVILLY. Removed with bullion reported with line to O/C 53rd S.A. Reserved B 64 & 65 SA reported their unit. Hants Rene attacks. None returned.	D.L.
NEUVILLY	27th		Remained in billets. Major Irvine and Greig attended D.C.M. Invest'th 45 C.C.S. Staff Sergt (Brooks advanced)	J.M.
"	28th		Remained in billets. Capt J.G. SLADE RAMC (T.O.) reported for duty & Lieut J.G. GREIG (Eng) returned from C.E.F.	J.M.
"	29th		3 Army S/Bears attached to each bath B 62 & 2 Infy Bde Major Greig and Brown Irvine proceeded to 65th SA for duty. Capt Slade went for duty to 65th SA.	J.M.

WAR DIARY
or
INTELLIGENCE SUMMARY.

Army Form C. 2118.

Place	Date	Hour	Summary of Events and Information	Remarks and references to Appendices
NEUVILLY	October 30th		One tent subdivision proceeded per ant to F Corps M.D.S. Interpreter Jonquin left unit and struck off sough	S.O.K.
"	31st		Remained in billets.	SM.

J Margan Rees
Lieut R.A.M.C.
O.C. 63rd 2nd Field Ambulance

16/3401

Nov 1918.

63rd F.A.

COMMITTEE FOR THE
MEDICAL HISTORY OF THE WAR
Date 10 JAN. 1919

Army Form C. 2118.

WAR DIARY
or
INTELLIGENCE SUMMARY.
(Erase heading not required)

MEDICAL Not 39pm

Place	Date	Hour	Summary of Events and Information	Remarks and references to Appendices
NEUVILLY	November	1st	Remained in billets	
"		2nd	Major Irvine evacuated to C.C.S. Capt Slade returned from 65th FA	fox
"		3rd	Remained in billets	fox
"		4th	Capt Slade proceeded to I Corps R.O. W'ex'c	fox
			16 OR sent to 65th FA	fox
			16 OR sent to I Corps M.D.S. all cars proceeded to 64 FA	
"		5th	Remained in billets	fox
VENDELIES AU BOIS		6th	moved to VENDELIES-au-BOIS	
LOCQUIGNOL		7th	moved to LOCQUIGNOL	fox
LA TETE NOIR		8th	moved to LA TETE NOIR	fox
"		9th	Remained in billets	fox
AYMERIES		10th	moved to AYMERIES. Major Grey & Lecuyer rejoined from 64th FA. Had wire from 10 BR.C. hospital that Major Irvine was dead	fox

Army Form C. 2118.

WAR DIARY
or
INTELLIGENCE SUMMARY.
(Erase heading not required.)

Instructions regarding War Diaries and Intelligence Summaries are contained in F. S. Regs., Part II and the Staff Manual respectively. Title pages will be prepared in manuscript.

Place	Date	Hour	Summary of Events and Information	Remarks and references to Appendices
	NOVEMBER			
AYNERIES	11th		Remained in billets	S/M
	12th		Move to BACHANT. Personnel at Coke 22 OR 20 myself	S/M
BACHANT	13th		Remained in billets. Capt Williams reported for instruction 64th FA.	S/M
	14th		Remained in billet. Capt Heade returned	S/M
	15th		Remained in billet. W/Col Kavanagh gusten leave to Paris 14 days.	M
	16th		Remained in billets	
	17th		Remained in billets. Capt Williams DRMC Rand appointed temp? Major whilst in command of a section 64 FO and remained in billets. Major in reserve appointed Director	rung rung
	18		Remained in billets. Officer quart.	
	19		Unit inspected by ADMS. Remained in Billets	rung rung
	20		Unit remained in billets	
	21		Remained in billets	
	22		Remained in billets. Reported 21st Divs HQ at Sover 3-0. At AULNOYE.	

2353 Wt. W2544/1454 700,000 5/15 D. D. & L. A.D.S.S./Forms/C. 2118.

WAR DIARY or INTELLIGENCE SUMMARY

Army Form C. 2118.

Place	Date	Hour	Summary of Events and Information	Remarks and references to Appendices
BACHANT V18 d cent	Nov 23		Remained in billets	nil
	24		Remained in billets	nil
	25		Receive Seven motor Ambulances from workshops M.T. captured by A Coy 1/3 NP proceeds to unit	nil
	26		Remained in billets	nil
	27		Remained in billets. 2 O.R. 1 Sgt & 1 Lcpl proceeds on advanced billeting party for unit, entrain at CANDRY 9.30 am	nil
	28		Remained in billets	nil
	29		Remained in billets	nil
	30		Personnel remained in billets. Staff sports arranged for St Andrews day. Capt Hadé detailed with medical orderly to proceed with 1 large Coy transport to CRÉ AULNOYE for proper journey as M-O to the Cos RE who precedes to new area.	nil

Am Sees
Major NP
for OC 63rd FA Amb.

14079421

Dec 1918

No 65 7. A.

COMMITTEE FOR THE
MEDICAL HISTORY OF THE WAR
6 MAR 1919
Date

WAR DIARY
or
INTELLIGENCE SUMMARY

Army Form C.

DECEMBER 1916

MEDICAL

Vol 40

Place	Date	Hour	Summary of Events and Information	Remarks and references to Appendices
BACHY	1		Remained in billets	?
"	2		Remained in billets	?
"	3		Unit marched to PONT sur SAMBRE on occasion of H.M. The King's visit to the area	?
"	4th		Returned from leave. Lt Knott reported for duty. Remained in billets	?
"	5th		Remained in billets	?
"	6th		Remained in billets — M. SALAÜN returned to interpreter	?
"	7		Remained in billets interpreter	?
"	8th		Remained in billets	?
"	9th		Remained in billets	?
"	10th		Remained in billets	?
"	11th		Remained in billets	?
"	12th		Remained in billets	?

Army Form C. 2118.

WAR DIARY
or
INTELLIGENCE SUMMARY.
(Erase heading not required.)

Instructions regarding War Diaries and Intelligence Summaries are contained in F.S. Regs., Part II. and the Staff Manual respectively. Title pages will be prepared in manuscript.

Place	Date	Hour	Summary of Events and Information	Remarks and references to Appendices
	DECEMBER			
BACHANT	13th		Remained in billets	M
"	14th		Remained in billets	SDK
"	15th		Remained in billets	FDK
"	16th		Remained in billets	FDK / SDK / FDK
ENCLEFONTAINE	17th		Unit marched to ENCLEFONTAINE and arrived at 2 15PD	
INCHY	18th		Unit marched to INCHY arrived at 1 P.M.	
ST. PIERRE à COUY	19th		Dismounted personnel proceeded by bus and detrained at PICQUIGNY marched to ST. PIERRE à COUY. Horse transport proceeded by road with 62nd Divs B of Coys under Major Williams	8DK
"	20th		Remained in billets. Capt Slater reported for duty Sent 7 OR & 46 C.C.S.	SDK
"	21st		Remained in billets	fox
"	22nd		Lt Knot proceeded for temporary duty at 41 Stationary Hospl	FDK
"	23rd		Remained in billets	SDK
"	24th		Remained in billets	SDK
"	25th		Remained in billets	FDK

Army Form C. 2118.

WAR DIARY
or
INTELLIGENCE SUMMARY.
(Erase heading not required.)

Instructions regarding War Diaries and Intelligence Summaries are contained in F.S. Regs., Part II. and the Staff Manual respectively. Title pages will be prepared in manuscript.

Place	Date	Hour	Summary of Events and Information	Remarks and references to Appendices
ST PIERRE à GUY	DECEMBER 26th		Remained in billet	F.y.s.
"	27th		Remained in billet.	F.y.s.
"	28th		Remained in billet	F.y.s.
"	29th		Remained in billet	F.y.s.
"	30th		Remained in billet	F.y.s.
"	31st		Remained in billet. Brigadier General Gater Comd 62nd Div. bid farewell General address to unit	F.y.s.

31-12-1918.

E. J. Kavanagh
Major R.A.M.C.
OC 63rd Field Amb.

2353 Wt. W2544/1454 700,000 5/15 D. D. & L. A.D.S.S./Forms/C. 2118.

40/3496

21 DIV

Bot 1876

No. 63 7. a

Jan 1919

Army Form C. 2118.

WAR DIARY
or
INTELLIGENCE SUMMARY.
(Erase heading not required.)

63 Field Ambulance

January 1918

Place	Date	Hour	Summary of Events and Information	Remarks and references to Appendices
ST PIERRE A GOUY	January 1st 1918		Remained in billets	GOR
"	2nd		Remained in billet	SLt
"	3rd		Remained in billets. Huts arrived which are now ready for issue & storm	7tr
"	4th		Remained in billets	pt
"	5th		Remained in billets	pr
"	6th		Remained in billets	8Rt
"	7th		Remained in billets	7tr
"	8th		Remained in billets	7tr
"	9th		Remained in billets	8tr
"	10th		Remained in billet	7tr
"	11th		Remained in billet. A Small progress in times.	7tr
"	12th		Remained in billet. Opened Red Station	SLt
"	13th		2 Remained in billet	
"	14th		Admitts 1 Officer + 17 OR Evacuats 1 Officer + 3 OR to 46 CCS, discharges to duty	8Rt
"	15th		Admitts 11, Evacuats 8 to 46 CCS.	8Rr
"			Admitts 1 Officer + 18 OR Evacuats 1 Officer + 9 OR to 46 CCS	7tr
"			Admitts 9, Evacuats 5 to 46 CCS	7tr

2353 Wt. W2544/1454 700,000 5/15 D. D. & L. A.D.S.S./Forms/C. 2118.

Army Form C. 2118.

WAR DIARY
or
INTELLIGENCE SUMMARY.
(Erase heading not required.)

Instructions regarding War Diaries and Intelligence Summaries are contained in F.S. Regs., Part II. and the Staff Manual respectively. Title pages will be prepared in manuscript.

63RD
W. DIVSR. (T.F.)
FIELD AMBULANCE

Place	Date 1919	Hour	Summary of Events and Information	Remarks and references to Appendices
ST PIERRE A GOUY	JANUARY 16th		Evacuate 10 to 46 C.C.S.	SJJ
	17th		Admitts 1 Offier & 50 OR. Evacuats 1 Offier & 49 OR to 46 CCS. Discharges 16 OR duty	JR
"	18th		Admitts 9. Evacuats 5 to 46 CCS. Discharges 18 duty	JR
	19th		Admitts 5. Discharged 18 duty	JR
	20th		Admitted 9. Evacuats 13 to 46 CCS. Discharges 16 duty. Prayer Service	JR
	21st		Proceeded on leave	
	22nd		Admitts 1 Officer & 10 OR. Evacuate 1 Officer & 7 OR to 46 CCS. Discharges 18 duty	JR
	23rd		Admitts 11. Evacuats 5 to 46 CCS.	JR
	24th		Admitts 1 Officer & 12 OR. Evacuate 1 Officer & 11 OR to 46 CCS. Discharges 2 duty	JR
	25th		Admitts 1 Officer & 12 OR. Evacuats 1 Officer & 10 OR to 46 CCS. Discharges 2 duty	JR
	26th		Admitts 1 Officer & 7 OR. Evacuats 2 Officer & 6 OR to 46 CCS. Discharges 2 duty	JR
	27th		Admitts 10 Officer & 14 OR. Evacuats 1 Officer & 11 OR to 46 CCS. Discharges 2 & OR.	JR
	28th		Admitts 11. Evacuats 4 to 46 CCS. Discharges 3 duty	JR
	29th		Admitts 5 OR. Evacuats 5 to CCS. Discharged 1 duty	JR
	30th		Admitts 4 OR. Evacuats 2 to 46 CCS. Discharged 5 to duty	SJR

Army Form C. 2118.

58TH
W. LANCS. (T.F.)
FIELD AMBULANCE

WAR DIARY
or
INTELLIGENCE SUMMARY.
(Erase heading not required.)

Instructions regarding War Diaries and Intelligence Summaries are contained in F. S. Regs., Part II. and the Staff Manual respectively. Title pages will be prepared in manuscript.

Place	Date	Hour	Summary of Events and Information	Remarks and references to Appendices
St PIERRE a Gouy	March 1917 30th		admits 6. evacuates 6 to 5 CCS. discharges 18 duty	
	31st		admits 7. evacuates 6 to 5 CCS. discharges 2 to duty	
			E J Kavanagh Lt Col RAMC O.C. 63rd Field Ambulance	

140/3524

No. 63 Field Ambulance.

Feb. 1917

COMMITTEE FOR THE
...ICAL HISTORY OF THE WAR
Date

Army Form C. 2118.

63 3rd Army
MEDICAL
Vol 42

WAR DIARY
or
INTELLIGENCE SUMMARY.
(Erase heading not required.)

Place	Date	Hour	Summary of Events and Information	Remarks and references to Appendices
ST PIERRE a GOUY	February 1st		admits 60R. Evacuates 20R & 46 CCS. Discharges 2 Bouts	JM
	2nd		admits 20R. Evacuates 4&46 CCS. Discharges 2 Bouts	MM
	3rd		admits 60R. Evacuates 2 ta 6 CCS	JM
	4th		admits 80R. Evacuates 5 & 40 CCS. Discharges 1 Bout	JM
	5th		admits 4 OR. Evacuates 6 &46 CCS. Discharges 2 Bouts. 2 yr feet	MM
			returned from Leave.	MM
	6th		admits 40R. Evacuates 16 44 CCS. Discharges 2 Bouts	JM
	7th		admits 10R. Evacuates 36, 46 CCS Discharges 2 Bouts	JM
	8th		admits 2OR. Discharges 1 Bout	JM
	9th		admits J. Simmonds 16 43 CCS. 66.40 CCS Discharges 2 Bouts	SM
	10th		admitted J. Simmonds. Evacuates 12. Evacuates 6 & 41 StH Hope	MM
	11th		Lt Hand departs from leave.	
	12th		admits 1 offr 76 OR. Evacuates 1 offr 10 OR & 41 StH Hope	JM
			& 1 to S.I. Camp	
	13th		admits 4. Evacuates 22 to StH Angl. Dis chgd 18 cont	JM

Army Form C. 2118.

WAR DIARY
or
INTELLIGENCE SUMMARY.
(Erase heading not required.)

Place	Date	Hour	Summary of Events and Information	Remarks and references to Appendices
ST PIERRE A GOUY	FEBRUARY 14th		Admits 5 O.R. Evacuates 3 to 41 Stat'y Hosp. discharges 1 to duty	SDK
	15th		Admits 2 Officers & 10 O.R. Evacuates 2 Officers & 6 O.R. to 41 Stat'y Hosp. discharges 1 to duty	SDK
	16th		Admits 1 Officer & 8 O.R. Evacuates 1 Officer & 8 O.R. to 41 Stat'y Hosp. discharges 1 to duty	SDK
	17th		Admits 1 Officer & 7 O.R. Evacuates 1 Officer & 5 O.R. to 41 Stat'y Hosp. discharges 3 to duty	SDK
	18th		Admits 1 Officer & 5 O.R. Evacuates 1 Officer & 7 O.R. to 41 Stat'y Hosp. Evacuates 1 to 18 C.C.S.	SDK
	19th		Admits 3 O.R. Evacuates 2 to 18 C.C.S. discharges 5 to duty	SDK
	20th		Admits 8 O.R. Evacuates 5 to 41 Stat'y Hosp.	SDK
	21st		Admitted 2 O.R.	SDK
"	22nd		C.O./moved to Divisions to attend conference admitted 8 O.R. Evacuated to 41 Stat'y Hosp 5. 6. O.R. Discharged to duty 2. O.R.	
	23rd		Admitted 10 O.R. Evacuated 2 O.R to 41 Stat'y Hosp. Discharged to duty 30 R.	
	24th		Admitted 6 O.R. Evacuated to 41 Stat'y Hosp. 4 O.R. Returned to duty of Infantry 3 R.	

Army Form C. 2118.

WAR DIARY
or
INTELLIGENCE SUMMARY.
(Erase heading not required.)

Instructions regarding War Diaries and Intelligence Summaries are contained in F. S. Regs., Part II. and the Staff Manual respectively. Title pages will be prepared in manuscript.

Place	Date	Hour	Summary of Events and Information	Remarks and references to Appendices
ST MARIE A GUVY	25th		Admitted 4 OR. Discharged to Duty 20 OR, 1 NYD. SA Bennett USMC reported for duty - Instructions received for arms for Capt Christiansen & Personnel at 19 CCS to be taken up tonight if the wind is in Capt Knot's mind at 4. Duty Hosp. Transferred at 46 CCS from the 19th.	King King
	26th		Admitted 50 R, Transferred to 18 CCS 4 OR, to 46 CCS 4 OR & OR Discharged to Duty 3 OR	King
	27		Admitted 50 R, Transferred to 46 CCS 7 OR, to Duty 3 OR	King
	28		Admitted OR 4, Transferred to 18 CCS 1 OR	King

Nurses
Major in charge

160/3551.

27 JUL 1919

63 M39

Mar. 1919

Army Form C. 2118.

WAR DIARY
or
INTELLIGENCE SUMMARY.

83rd (W. LANCS. T.F.) FIELD AMBULANCE

(Erase heading not required.)

Instructions regarding War Diaries and Intelligence Summaries are contained in F.S. Regs., Part II. and the Staff Manual respectively. Title pages will be prepared in manuscript.

Vol 43

Place	Date	Hour	Summary of Events and Information	Remarks and references to Appendices
ST PIERRE AGNY	MARCH			
	1		admitted 6 O.R. Evacuated to 46 CCS 7 O.R.	nmg
	2		admitted 1 O.R. Evacuated to 41 Stationary 3 O.R. To duty 1 O.R.	nmg
	3		admitted 2 O.R. Evacuated 541 Stationary 9 O.R. Commenced to run transport to LONGPRÉ Cavié Park	nmg
	4		R/Col Kavanagh returned from Conference at DOULLENS. admitted 1 O & 3 O.R. Evacuated to CCS 1 Off & 5 O.R.	nmg
	5		admitted 2 offrs & 5 O.R. and evacuated them to 46 CCS	nmg
PICQUIGNY	6		moved to Picquigny 4 O.R. evacuated the CCS.	fx
	7		2 O.R. admitted Evacuated 1 to 46 CCS	fx
	8		Capt Bennett R.A.M.C. transferred to 53 Labour Corps Group and is struck off strength	fx
	9		Remained in billets	fx
	10		Capt Starling reported on duty from 65th Field Ambulance	fx
	11		Remained in billets	fx
	12		Remained in billets	fx

Army Form C. 2118.

WAR DIARY
or
INTELLIGENCE SUMMARY.

(Erase heading not required.)

55th (W. LANCS. T.F.)
FIELD AMBULANCE

Instructions regarding War Diaries and Intelligence Summaries are contained in F. S. Regs., Part II. and the Staff Manual respectively. Title pages will be prepared in manuscript.

Place	Date	Hour	Summary of Events and Information	Remarks and references to Appendices
MEQUIGNY	March 13th		Major Goulf M.C. departs for demobilisation	Appx
"	14th		Remained in billet	Appx
"	15th		Remained in billet	Appx
"	16th		Remained in billet	Appx
"	17th		Remained in billet	Appx
"	18th		Remained in billet	Appx
"	19th		Remained in billet	Appx
"	20th		Remained in billet	Appx
"	21st		Remained in billet	Appx
"	22nd		Remained in billet	Appx
"	23rd		Remained in billet	Appx
"	24th		Remained in billet	Appx
"	25th		Remained in billet	Appx
"	26th		Remained in billet	Appx
"	27th		Remained in billet	Appx
"	28th		Remained in billet	Appx

2353 Wt. W2544/1454 700,000 5/15 D. D. & L. A.D.S.S./Forms/C. 2118.

Army Form C. 2118.

WAR DIARY
or
INTELLIGENCE SUMMARY.

(Erase heading not required.)

Instructions regarding War Diaries and Intelligence Summaries are contained in F. S. Regs., Part II. and the Staff Manual respectively. Title pages will be prepared in manuscript.

3rd (W. Lanc) 1.5.1
FIELD AMBULANCE

Place	Date	Hour	Summary of Events and Information	Remarks and references to Appendices
Picquigny	March 29th		Remained billet	mx
"	30th		Remained billet	mx
"	31st		Remained billet	mx

G.J. Kavanagh
Lt Col
Commanding
3rd (W. Lanc) Field Ambulance

CONFIDENTIAL

WAR DIARY
OF THE
63rd Field Ambulance.
(West Lancs. T.F.)

From April 1st 1919
To April 30th 1919.

Army Form C. 2118.

WAR DIARY
or
INTELLIGENCE SUMMARY.
(Erase heading not required.)

Instructions regarding War Diaries and Intelligence Summaries are contained in F.S. Regs., Part II and the Staff Manual respectively. Title pages will be prepared in manuscript.

Place	Date	Hour	Summary of Events and Information	Remarks and references to Appendices
PECQUENCY	April 1st		Remained in billets	8xx
"	2nd		Remained in billets	8xx
"	3rd		Remained in billets	8xx
LONGUET	4th		Moved to LONGUET	8xx
"	5th		Remained in billets	8xx
"	6th		Capt Stanley transferred to I Corps Concentration Camp	8xx
"			Capt Little attached for temporary duty	8xx
"	7th		Remained in billets	8xx
"	8th		Remained in billets	8xx
"	9th		Remained in billets	8xx
"	10th		Capt Little detailed for entrainment 3D & Labour group	8xx
"	11th		Remained in billets	8xx
"	12th		Remained in billets	8xx
"	13th		Remained in billets for temporary duty with 41st Stationary Hosp	8xx
"	14th		Lt Leavett from temp leave to Brussels	8xx

2353 Wt. W2541/1454 700,000 5/15 D. D. & L. A.D.S.S./Forms/C. 2118.

Army Form C. 2118.

WAR DIARY
or
INTELLIGENCE SUMMARY.
(Erase heading not required.)

Instructions regarding War Diaries and Intelligence Summaries are contained in F. S. Regs., Part II. and the Staff Manual respectively. Title pages will be prepared in manuscript.

Place	Date	Hour	Summary of Events and Information	Remarks and references to Appendices
LONGUET	April 15th		Remained in billet	App
"	16th		Remained in billet	App
"	17th		Remained in billet	App
"	18th		Remained in billet	App
"	19th		Remained in billet	App
"	20th		Remained in billet. 1st Class Staff S/M Beverey of Lt transferred	App
"	21st		Remained in billet	App
			to D.I. the River Drain	
			Co. S/M Mas or Willmott appointed for out	
"	22nd		Remained in billet	App
"	23rd		Remained in billet. Le Havre report down. Even	App
"	24th		Remained in billet. Received order than mentioned for	App
"	25th		Remained in billet. United Kingdom on 30th inst	App
"	26th		Remained in billet	App
"	27th		Remained in billet	App
"	28th		Remained in billet	App
"	29th		Remained in billet	App
"	30th		Marched to LONGPRE and entrained for LE HAVRE en route to United Kingdom	App

G. J. Kavanagh
Lt. Col. R.A.M.C.
2 Field Ambulance
O.C. 63

"M.S." Confidential WO45
 Cleared

WAR DIARY
OF THE
63rd Field Ambulance

From 1/5/19
To 7/5/19

* This Unit embarked for U.K. on 7/5/19 28 JUL 1919

Army Form C. 2118.

WAR DIARY
or
INTELLIGENCE SUMMARY.
(Erase heading not required.)

Instructions regarding War Diaries and Intelligence Summaries are contained in F.S. Regs. Part II. and the Staff Manual respectively. Title pages will be prepared in manuscript.

Place	Date	Hour	Summary of Events and Information	Remarks and references to Appendices
LE HAVRE	May 1st		Arrived at LE HAVRE Station about 4 AM. Marched to No 2 Wing reception Camp (about 9 AM) HARFLEUR after delousing and were re inspected marched to No 2 Wing Despatch Camp	PMK
(HARFLEUR)	2nd		Remained in camp	PMK
"	3rd		Remained in camp	PMK
"	4th		Remained in camp	PMK
"	5th		Remained in camp. Transport half horses in SS Donna	PMK
"	6th		Embarked on SS TURBINIA - Marepon SS Jonna.	PMK
EN ROUTE	7th		Landed at SOUTHAMPTON and proceeded to CATTERICK CAMP	PMK

G.J. Kavanagh
OC 63rd Field Ambulance

www.ingramcontent.com/pod-product-compliance
Lightning Source LLC
Chambersburg PA
CBHW080859230426
43663CB00013B/2579